PRIVATE LAW AND PROPERTY CLAIMS

Private Law and Property Claims sets out a distinctive analysis of some
general issues in private law, including the nature of categories such
as contract, tort and property, duties and liabilities as the basis of
claims in private law, and the relationship between primary rights and
remedies. In the light of this analysis, it offers a new approach to
property in private law, including claims that arise to protect and
recover property. It goes on to discuss the law of trusts, fiduciary relationships and tracing; the remedial role of the trust; the nature of
equity as a legal category; and the relationship between property and
claims in tort to protect property. It also exposes the misconceptions
underlying the modern approach to restitution and unjust enrichment and the problems this is causing in private law.

PRIVATE LAW AND PROPERTY CLAIMS

PETER JAFFEY

·HART·
PUBLISHING

OXFORD AND PORTLAND, OREGON

2007

Published in North America (US and Canada) by
Hart Publishing
c/o International Specialized Book Services
920 NE 58th Avenue, Suite 300
Portland, OR 97213-3786
USA
Tel: +1 503 287 3093 or toll-free: (1) 800 944 6190
Fax: +1 503 280 8832
E-mail: orders@isbs.com
Website: www.isbs.com

Hart Publishing, 16C Worcester Place, OX1 2JW
Telephone: +44 (0)1865 517530 Fax: +44 (0)1865 510710
E-mail: mail@hartpub.co.uk
Website: http://www.hartpub.co.uk

British Library Cataloguing in Publication Data
Data Available
ISBN-13: 978-1-84113-633-2 (hardback)

Typeset by Hope Services, Abingdon
Printed and bound in Great Britain by
TJI Digital, Padstow, Cornwall

Preface

This book developed out of work on aspects of the law of property and trusts, and the law of contract, that are now usually regarded as part of the law of restitution or unjust enrichment. It seemed to me that the persistent problems in this area could only be resolved by approaching them through a broader study of private law and private law theory, and this is reflected in the first three chapters in particular. I do not aim to provide a detailed, black letter account of the law, or comprehensive coverage of the case law. My aim is to illuminate the structure of private law, and some general principles and important doctrines of private law, to clarify some areas of confusion and expose some misconceptions, and to suggest the right framework for dealing with some controversial questions.

The first chapter deals with classification and the nature of categories such as contract, tort and property in private law, and duties and liabilities as the basis of claims in private law. The second chapter deals with the relationship between primary and remedial rights or 'rights and remedies'. These chapters identify what I argue are certain common fallacies in legal reasoning, arising from the conflation of different types of classification, or from a preoccupation with a remedial perspective at the expense of primary rights. The third chapter, drawing on the analysis in the first two chapters, offers a new approach to the concept of private property (including money in tangible and intangible forms), and in the light of it an analysis of property claims or property-based claims, and the relationship between property-based claims and claims in tort. These three chapters lay the foundations for the remaining chapters, which are concerned with various overlapping property-related topics in private law.

Chapter 4 deals with equity as a legal category and its relationship with the common law. The argument is strongly in favour of the 'substantive fusion' of equity and the common law. Chapter 5 sets out an analysis of the trust and fiduciary relationships in terms of property law and contract law. Chapter 6 takes up the discussion begun in chapter 3 of claims to recover property invalidly transferred.

This includes the important practical matter of proprietary claims and priority in bankruptcy; and it includes the law of tracing, which is generally thought of as an arcane and technical area of law, but actually raises issues that are fundamental to the nature of property. Chapter 7 takes up from chapter 3 the discussion of tort claims to protect property and the relationship between property and tort. It also deals with certain problems concerning duties and liabilities in tort law that arise in this context. Chapter 8 considers the influential 'theory of unjust enrichment' behind the recognition of a category of restitution or unjust enrichment in the common law. Drawing on arguments from earlier chapters, it shows that the theory is misconceived and identifies some of the problems it is causing. Chapter 9 brings together some points and discussion from earlier chapters to address another perennially controversial topic, the constructive trust.

Most of the book was written during research leave from Brunel University in the calendar year 2005, partly funded by a Research Leave award from the AHRB (now AHRC). I spent two months in the spring of 2005 at the University of Queensland, for which I am grateful to Professor Charles Rickett, Head of the TC Beirne School of Law.

I am grateful to the organisers and participants at the following seminars and conferences where aspects of this work were presented: 'Obligations II', at the University of Melbourne, in July 2004; the SLS Conference, Jurisprudence Section, in September 2004; a staff seminar at the University of Central Lancashire, in January 2005; a research seminar, University of Queensland, in April 2005; the British Association for Canadian Studies Conference on Perspectives on Unjust Enrichment/Restitution, in June 2006; the UCL Law and Philosophy Colloquium, in July 2006; the UKNCCL Conference in September 2006; and the SLS Conference, Tort Section, in September 2006.

I am also grateful to my colleagues and ex-colleagues Emmanuel Voyiakis, George Letsas, Steve Allen, Paul Dougan, and Mahmood Bagheri for discussion and assistance on various points.

Lastly, I would like to thank Seeromanie for her love and support.

Contents

1

Classification in Private Law

INTRODUCTION

The idea of classification in law sometimes carries connotations of crudeness and artificiality.[1] This may be associated with the idea that it involves constructing a table or matrix that can be used to read off a legal solution for a set of facts in the way that one might use a railway timetable to find a train. This in turn may come from the association of legal classification with the discredited notion of 'mechanical jurisprudence', according to which all legal questions can in principle be resolved by applying a settled rule of precise scope to the facts in question. Certainly tables or trees setting out schemes of legal classification were more common in the legal literature in the era of mechanical jurisprudence than they are nowadays.[2]

But classification is not intrinsically related to mechanical jurisprudence and it plays a crucial role in a sound understanding of the law, as in other areas of rational inquiry. Legal rules or principles or claims or causes of action or other such elements of the law may be described as contractual, tortious, proprietary, restitutionary, compensatory, fiduciary, or be said to be part of the law of obligations or private law or the law of wrongs or unjust enrichment, etc. Abstract concepts like these are often used without explanation or elaboration in legal reasoning, and sometimes this is the cause of persistent confusion or controversy. One might say that the answer is simply to investigate the meaning, or to develop a theory, of the concept in question. But at least part of the solution to such problems can be found in considering the *kind* of concept in issue, and how it relates to other concepts or kinds of concept; in other words, in characterising the concept as a category in a scheme of classification that associates it with other equivalent concepts and

---

[1] See eg SM Waddams, *Dimensions of Private Law* (Cambridge, CUP, 2003) ch 1. This is a sceptical response to the revival of interest in classification sparked off by the work of Birks on unjust enrichment and restitution, as discussed further in ch 8.

[2] For a discussion of some of these see R Pound, 'Classification of Law' (1923–24) 37 *Harvard Law Review* 933.

then differentiates between them. For example, is contract the same type of category as tort, and if so what is the nature of the classification? What about property or restitution? This is a question of legal taxonomy or classification.[3] The significance of the classification depends on the role of that type of concept in legal reasoning.

Another source of hostility to the idea of classification comes from the misplaced idea that there must be a single, authoritative, one-dimensional classification, applicable for all purposes. In fact it is always possible to classify in different ways for different purposes, in the law as elsewhere. Animals can be classified by diet or habitat or by genetic or evolutionary proximity, for example, and the context determines which is appropriate. Sometimes there may be a dominant classification by an essential or defining characteristic—for example, genetic proximity for living things—but this is not necessarily the case and it does not preclude the use of other types of classification where appropriate. The misconception that in law all useful concepts must be forced into a single one-dimensional scheme is another reason why legal classification has sometimes seemed crude and artificial. The purpose of this chapter is to identify various different types of legal classification, and some of the errors that can result from conflating them. The main types of classification that will be considered in this and subsequent chapters are classification by justification, by remedy, and by normative type or 'modality'.

A classification has a subject matter, and often one speaks simply of 'the law' as the subject matter and a classification of the law into areas or departments or categories. Sometimes the subject matter of the classification is taken to be particular elements of the law, such as rules or principles or claims or causes of action as mentioned above, or rights, relations, concepts, 'causative events'[4] and so on, and sometimes it may be more apt to speak of categories of these elements. I will generally refer to categories of claims, though I may sometimes refer simply to legal categories. This seems to me largely a matter of presentation, though sometimes it may be necessary to distinguish between different possible elements. By 'claim' I mean a right of action or remedial right.[5]

---

[3] For the usage of 'classification' in law to mean construing a legal concept to place a certain case within or outside it, see N MacCormick, *Rhetoric and the Rule of Law* (Oxford, OUP, 2005) 70–72.

[4] This is the element used by Birks, below, p 236.

[5] Thus 'claim' should not be equated with 'assertion', nor with Hohfeldian 'claim-right'; see below p 20.

Justificatory Classification

A good example to begin with is contract law. What sort of category is this? It would be widely agreed that contract law is about agreements and claims arising from agreements. But, if this is so, why is it that claims arising from agreements are treated as part of a single category? Why is it that there is a recognised category of claims arising from agreements but not, say, a category of claims arising on a Tuesday? The answer must be that agreement is a significant concept because of the significance of the moral principle that agreements should be kept. Contract law is, I will say, a justificatory category,[6] meaning a category of claims arising by virtue of a body of rules based on a certain general moral principle.[7] This suggests that the traditional division in private law between contract law and tort law is part of a classification by justification. One might formulate the general principle underlying tort law as a principle of responsibility, or of reasonable care to avoid foreseeable harm to others. The underlying principle provides the basis for a body of rules by virtue of which a claim arises, and it is reflected in the characteristic concepts of the category and the framework of standard issues that arise in connection with claims under the category: for example in contract, what sorts of agreement should be legally binding, how an agreement should be interpreted, what remedies should arise in the event that the agreement is not performed as agreed, etc, and in tort whether there is a duty of care, what the required standard of care is, etc. I will attempt to deal with some objections to this approach in the course of the discussion.

---

[6] Justification refers to the moral basis of a body of law, not the source or authority of the rules. I will not discus whether the underlying general moral principles that I refer to should also be understood as legal principles, or if they are reflected in distinct legal principles. This is at the heart of the debate on positivism.

[7] Cf M Moore, 'Theories of Areas of Law' (2000) 37 *San Diego Law Review* 731; M Moore, *Placing Blame* (Oxford, Clarendon Press, OUP, 1997) ch 1. See also MacCormick, above n 3, at 113. Penner refers to categories based on interests: JE Penner, *The Idea of Property in Law* (Oxford, Clarendon Press, OUP, 1997) ch 3. The interests he has in mind seem to be interests in the application of an underlying principle. Penner understands his classification as an application of Raz's theory of individuation: J Raz, *The Concept of a Legal System* (Oxford, OUP, 2nd edn, 1980). But the theory of individuation is concerned with identifying individual elements rather than the categories into which they might be classified. In particular Raz is concerned with defining a rule principally by reference to its source, as part of a system of authority, rather than by reference to its justification in the sense of underlying principle.

One important role of justificatory categories is to indicate the nature of the moral basis for a claim, free of technical detail. This role has no bearing on legal reasoning, but classification by justificatory category also has a practical role in legal reasoning. I will come back to this after a brief discussion of aspects of legal reasoning.

Deductive and Analogical Legal Reasoning

Often it is adequate to understand the law as of a body of rules and legal reasoning as the process of identifying the applicable legal rule and applying it to the facts in issue. On this view, legal reasoning is purely deductive or syllogistic—it involves showing that the facts in question fall within the scope of the rule and inferring that the rule applies. This is not to say that it is always straightforward. Technical skill and knowledge may be involved in identifying the relevant rules, for example where they have to be ascertained from various statutory provisions or cases. Sometimes it has been thought that this is all there is to legal reasoning: the rules are certain in scope and exhaustive of possible issues. This is the approach referred to above as mechanical jurisprudence.

Often of course the problem is that the law is unsettled: there is a conflict between two rules that appear to apply; or there is no recognised rule; or the applicable rule is ambiguous or vague; or it seems to have unfair or anomalous consequences in the circumstances. These problems cannot be solved by deductive reasoning and are concealed in the simple approach of mechanical jurisprudence.[8] I think it is reasonably uncontentious to say that, broadly speaking, the court deals with this problem by drawing on the rationale or justification of recognised rules to devise a new rule or modify an existing one, and this is usually referred to as analogical reasoning.[9]

For example, where a court 'distinguishes' an earlier case that purports to govern the case at hand, the court qualifies the rule established by the earlier case on the ground that, according to the rationale for the rule, its formulation in the earlier case is too broad

---

[8] This is the standard criticism of 'formalism': see eg F Schauer, 'Formalism' (1989) 97 *Yale Law Journal* 509, 511–13.

[9] See eg N MacCormick, *Legal Reasoning and Legal Theory* (Oxford, OUP, rev edn, 1994) ch 7; J Raz, 'Law and Value in Adjudication' in *The Authority of Law* (Oxford, Clarendon Press, OUP, 1979). The classic example of analogical reasoning is drawing an analogy between particular cases, which is narrower than analogical reasoning as stated. Some writers think of analogical reasoning as the application of a special sort of judgment or a faculty of moral intuition: see eg LL Weinreb, *Legal Reason* (Cambridge, CUP, 2005). This is not necessary for analogical reasoning as described.

and should not apply to the present facts. Conversely, it may be that according to its current formulation a rule does not apply to the facts in issue, but its rationale suggests that it ought to. Then the court can extend the rule to cover the new situation. This may lead to the unification of analogous rules, or the subsumption of a rule into a more general rule.

Analogical reasoning presupposes that, even if an existing rule is not applicable to the facts in issue, its rationale should be accepted as a relevant consideration in formulating a rule to apply. Thus it presupposes the value of coherence. The principle of formal justice (as it is sometimes called) requires that like cases should be decided alike. Arguably, the principle is fully satisfied if the law is formulated in terms of rules, because this means that a particular case is not decided in isolation but by reference to a generalisation that applies to other equivalent cases as defined by the rule. But analogical reasoning can be said to promote coherence in the sense of consistency at the deeper level of underlying rationales. Furthermore, coherence increases transparency and clarity by directing attention to the justification for rules rather than their mechanical application.

On one view, analogical reasoning as described above can be extended beyond the immediate rationales for particular rules to higher and higher levels of abstraction, drawing on theories about justificatory categories and about the law itself, reaching up to theories concerning the role of judges in the legal and political system and general theories of morality such as utilitarianism or moral rights. This is of course the approach associated with Ronald Dworkin,[10] and he refers to the process as justificatory or theoretical ascent.[11] This departs from the conventional idea of analogical reasoning, though it seems to be a natural extension of it.

Some commentators are sceptical about the role of such general and abstract theorising, and about the assumption that the law is or ought to be pervasively coherent in some way, and regard analogical reasoning as a limited and localised technique for solving the problem of a gap or a conflict in the law.[12] For example, Sunstein extols the virtues of 'incompletely theorised' agreement, meaning

---

[10] R Dworkin, *Law's Empire* (London, Fontana, 1986).

[11] R Dworkin, *Justice in Robes* (Cambridge, Mass, Harvard UP, 2006) 25, 53. Dworkin's approach incorporates arguments 'on the merits' as a dimension of what I am referring to as analogical reasoning, whereas on a conventional view of analogical reasoning the issue arises whether analogical reasoning excludes such arguments. It is unnecessary for present purposes to pursue this.

[12] eg, Raz, above n 9.

that through localised analogies judges can give grounds for their decisions that do not risk disagreement on controversial general theories.[13] Another objection is that a judge dealing with a particular set of facts may not be well placed to consider all the issues relevant to a theory affecting a wide area of law or anticipate the ramifications of such a theory.[14]

It is difficult to see how unresolved issues are to be addressed if not by way of theoretical ascent, whatever difficulties this may sometimes involve. But, as Dworkin observes, even accepting his expansive view in principle, in the ordinary course judges will operate in a localised way, making limited modifications to specific rules, unless the resolution of the issue in front of them and the arguments presented to them compel them to consider more abstract theoretical issues.[15] I will use 'analogical reasoning' to include abstract theoretical arguments as well as 'low level' or incompletely theorised arguments.

Analogical reasoning can take place in the context of a justificatory category. In addressing an issue of unsettled law, the court might locate case law by reference to a justificatory category and it might identify the underlying principle and use it to guide the interpretation and development of the law. Classification itself here plays no real part in analogical reasoning; it serves only to identify the relevant body of law. But classification by justificatory category can sometimes play a direct role in analogical reasoning.

Justificatory Categories in Analogical Reasoning and Errors of Classification

In a case on unsettled law, in practice the first step is to allocate it to a justificatory category, which brings it under a framework that determines in general terms how it is addressed and resolved. This involves an assumption that the case is analogous to a standard case in the category, so that it should be governed by the same general principle. It does not necessarily involve any consideration of the underlying principle or rely on a theoretical understanding of the category. The court may simply judge in an impressionistic way that the case falls in the category and then try to develop and apply the law to it in a low-level, partly intuitive and 'incompletely theorised' way. In this way, classification by justificatory category has a direct role in analogical reasoning.

[13] See CR Sunstein, *Legal Reasoning and Political Conflict* (Oxford, OUP, 1996) esp ch 2.
[14] This is the problem of partial reform: see Raz, above n 9, at 200–01.
[15] Dworkin, above n 10, at 54.

This process depends on a distinction between what might be called 'true justificatory categories' and 'conventional-justificatory categories'. For example, to take the case of contract, in the conventional-justificatory sense, 'contract' refers to an established body of rules referred to in the case law and textbooks and in legal practice and teaching as the law of contract, which implements the underlying principle in a particular way. Referring to this body of law does not involve invoking or applying an underlying principle, and in the way suggested above, it can be applied without any examination of the principle.

One might instead wish to refer to a putative or hypothetical contractual claim, meaning a claim that is not available under the rules as they stand, but would be available if the contractual principle that agreements should be performed were given effect through a modified body of rules. Here the expression is used in the true justificatory sense. The conventional-justificatory sense is apt for the purpose of identifying the established rule or body of rules, whereas the true justificatory sense is apt for the purpose of invoking the underlying principle itself or some interpretation of it.

Similarly, one might argue that a certain claim actually recognised in the law, though not conventionally described as contractual, is *really* contractual and ought to be so treated, because its true basis is the contractual principle that agreements should be fulfilled. It is certainly arguable that there are claims based on this principle that are conventionally treated not as part of the law of contract, but as part of the law of equity,[16] or the law of restitution or unjust enrichment,[17] or even the law of tort.[18] If this is the case, these claims are in the true justificatory category of contract, though not the conventional-justificatory category. I will describe as 'false differentiation' the application of the same principle in different guises through different conventional-justificatory categories. The effect of this may be to apply different rules to equivalent cases. It may be that there are material differences that justify the different treatment, but the effect of the false differentiation is to conceal this question. False differentiation is a form of incoherence arising from an error of analogical reasoning, and in particular from a classificatory error, arising from the divergence of the conventional-justificatory category from the true justificatory category.

[16] Below p 119.
[17] Below p 228.
[18] Possible examples are *Hedley Byrne v Heller* [1964] AC 465 and *Junior Books v Veichi* [1982] 3 WLR 477. See AJE Jaffey, 'Contract in Tort's Clothing' (1985) 5 *Legal Studies* 77.

Sometimes, where a claim is denied in, say, contract because of a restrictive rule, allowing a claim under a different category is thought of as a skilful common law technique to develop the law while respecting the existing law of contract. An example might be a case where a court denies a claim because of the rules of privity or consideration, which it insists cannot be modified, but then allows a claim in another category, though the only underlying basis for a claim is the agreement and the principle that agreements should be kept.[19] Here the false differentiation amounts to subversion of the existing law. Although the conventional-justificatory category of contract may be unaltered, the law based on the true justificatory category has been developed. This is not of course to say that the law should not be developed; the point is that, if it is open to the courts to develop it, they should be able do so without creating incoherence in this way.

Another type of incoherence is 'false assimilation', where issues that are different in material respects and should be governed by different principles are treated as if they were the same in relevant respects. Some legal fictions are cases of false assimilation. The notorious 'implied contract' fiction involved treating a claim as contractual, or 'quasi-contractual', even though it was not based in any way on the principle that agreements should be enforced. For example, a claim to recover a mistaken payment was said to be based on an implied agreement to repay the money, though clearly the recipient of a mistaken payment has not agreed to repay it, and the underlying justification for such a claim does not lie in the contractual principle that agreements should be enforced. There is a fiction, because the claim is supposed to be based on an agreement and yet there was no agreement, and this attributes a false justification to the claim and obscures its true basis. The fallacy is particularly clear where a claim is denied for a reason that is really applicable only if the claim is genuinely based on agreement, for example the defendant's lack of contractual capacity.[20]

In other cases, it may not be as easy to say whether there is really a fiction. The problem is how to distinguish a fiction from a sound analogy. In the case of the mistaken payment as an implied contract,

[19] Below p 224, 228.

[20] As in the House of Lords decision in *Sinclair v Brougham* [1914] AC 398. The basis of the claim to recover a mistaken payment is often now said to be the principle of unjust enrichment, though in my view it falls in the justificatory category of property as considered in ch 3.

there is no sound analogy and the fiction is obvious. But consider the claim for payment for mistakenly-provided services, which is sometimes equated with the claim to recover a mistaken payment on the ground that both are claims to recover an invalid or vitiated transfer.[21] This is an apt description of the latter, but ostensibly, one would think, not the former. As a matter of ordinary English usage, one would think that providing a service or doing work is not a transfer, and being paid for it is not the recovery of a transfer. But the literal meaning is not the issue (though it may reflect a relevant moral distinction). Is it a fiction to treat the claim in respect of mistaken services as a claim to recover a transfer? Or is it a case of extending the legal meaning of a term as part of the development of the law through sound analogical reasoning? It depends whether the analogy between the two claims is indeed sound, which here means whether the two claims fall in the same justificatory category. Sometimes this may not be easy to say. In my view, they fall in different justificatory categories, though many commentators treat both cases as falling in a justificatory category of unjust enrichment.[22]

False differentiation and false assimilation are liable to occur or go unnoticed where analogical reasoning is conducted with inadequate theoretical ascent. They can be corrected by analogical reasoning at a higher level of theoretical ascent, spanning different conventional-justificatory categories. Of course, these issues are liable to be controversial, and the examples suggested above are intended as merely illustrative.

What are the Justificatory Categories of Private Law?

It is in principle easy to identify conventional-justificatory categories of private law by reference to ordinary usage, as the recognised categories used to provide a framework for presenting and arguing claims and expounding them in the standard works. However, conventional-justificatory categories can change; analogical reasoning can create them and it can mould them and eliminate them. Such changes reflect the practical success of arguments, in the academic literature and in the courts, over particular cases or categories of claim. But it remains open to argument which conventional-justificatory categories are genuine justificatory categories, based on a genuine justifying principle, and whether some other genuine justificatory category has not been recognised.

---

[21] As to invalid and vitiated transfers, see below p 97.
[22] Below p 234.

   Contract is a clearly established conventional-justificatory category
and I will assume that it is a true justificatory category based on the
principle referred to above. The traditional view is that there is a
series of distinct conventional-justificatory categories of torts, such as
trespass, nuisance, defamation and conversion, as well as the law of
negligence, whereas the modern tendency is towards recognising a
single conventional-justificatory category in the form of the law of
negligence, which has subsumed or is capable of subsuming the other
categories. On this approach, the statement in *Donoghue v Stevenson*
that 'there must be, and is, some general conception of relations giving rise to a duty of care, of which the particular cases found in the
books are but instances',[23] marked the beginning of a process that
should encompass other recognised torts. This is how I interpret the
debate over whether there is or should be a law of torts or a law of
tort.[24] The question is whether there is a single fundamental principle of tort law, along the lines of the neighbour principle, that can
generate ostensibly different types of tort in different types of standard situation,[25] or a number of distinct and irreducible principles
accounting for the separate torts. I do not have to address this issue,
but I will generally assume that there is a single justificatory category
of tort. In chapter 3, I will argue that there is a justificatory category
of property in private law, which will involve distinguishing this
concept of property from others.[26] It is doubtful whether there is a
conventional-justificatory category of property in the common law,
though possibly equity has recognised one.
   In general, it seems to me helpful to associate a justificatory
category of private law with a particular type of practical problem
involving a conflict of interests.[27] For example, the making and performance of agreements, which contract law facilitates, helps to overcome co-ordination problems. Two parties might refrain from
carrying out a mutually beneficial exchange of goods or services for
payment because neither is willing take the risk of acting first and
finding that the other does not reciprocate. The moral principle that
parties should keep their agreements came to be recognised and
developed as a means of overcoming this problem. Thus, one might

---

[23] [1932] AC 562, 580, per Lord Atkin.

[24] See eg B Rudden, 'Torticles' 6/7 *Tulane Civil Law Forum* 105 (1991–92). This ancient
debate appears to have been revived recently: see NJ McBride and R Bagshaw, *Tort Law*
(Harlow, Longman, 2nd edn, 2005) 21.

[25] See also below p 194.

[26] I suggest a fourth category, below p 215–6.

[27] See further, below p 67.

say that the justificatory category reflects a functional category, meaning a type of practical problem that arises from features of human
nature and social circumstances. Similarly, as a functional category,
tort law is concerned with the problem of the conflict between the
interest of one person in being free to carry out an activity and the
interest of another in not being harmed by it. The principle of reasonable care is a distinctive type of justification for a claim, which
provides a possible solution to the problem.[28]

Some Objections to Justificatory Categories

One objection to justificatory categories might be that a category
such as contract or tort cannot be based on a general moral principle
because the law should not simply enforce moral principles; and furthermore it is apparent that the law does not do so—for example,
some agreements and promises are not legally enforceable though
they are morally binding.[29] It is true that the law does not simply
enforce moral principles as such. Various considerations can influence
the way in which and the extent to which a general moral principle
is given effect in the law, and there are controversial questions concerning the status of such principles, and whether they should be
understood as part of the law or distinct from it though relevant to
legal reasoning.[30] But, whatever the problems these issues raise, there
seems no reason to think that they undermine the possibility of bodies of law based on general moral principles and forming justificatory
categories as suggested above.

Another objection might be that underlying principles of the sort
mentioned above are too vague and too controversial to be of any
practical relevance.[31] It is inevitable that there will be vagueness in
the principle and disagreement about how to interpret and imple-
ment it, but this does not undermine the role of justificatory categories. The underlying principle is not applied directly to a set of facts
to determine the legal position; indeed, as the discussion above
shows, for a justificatory category to function in the way described it
is not even necessary for it to be explicitly considered or interpreted.
It is necessary only that there be an assumption that the category is

---

[28] 'Functionalism' is sometimes understood to refer to an approach that avoids theoretical and conceptual questions by concentrating on the practical problems faced by the law.
Although functionalism in this sense helpfully emphasises the need for a proper understanding of the facts in issue, it cannot escape the traditional problems of legal reasoning.

[29] H Collins, *Regulating Contracts* (Oxford, OUP, 1999) 34.

[30] Referred to by Dworkin as the concept of law in the taxonomic sense: above n 11, at 4.

[31] I take this to be one of the arguments in Waddams, above n 1, esp in chs 1, 11.

based on some such principle, and the character of the category as a justificatory category, and its concomitant role in legal reasoning, reflects this assumption.

A rather different objection is that to characterise an established body of law in terms of a general principle, or a certain interpretation of a general principle, is necessarily selective, because it involves endorsing some recognised rules and discarding others as mistaken because they cannot be understood in terms of the general principle. Thus, the law as it stands is inevitably misrepresented, and at the same time distorted by any form of classification.[32] But, to the contrary, the existence of an underlying principle is necessary to explain the character and function of categories like contract and tort. This does not mean that the established rules of the category are fluid or open to the extent that the underlying principle is controversial. This is the difference between the established rules, which constitute the conventional-justificatory category, and the underlying principle itself. The underlying principle may be invoked to solve problems where the law is unsettled or incomplete. Where this is the case, the law can certainly evolve through analogical reasoning, but whether this distorts the law, or straightens it out and develops it, depends on whether the analogical reasoning is sound, which is itself of course liable to be controversial.

It might also be suggested that recognising a category based on a general principle is liable to engender excessive uniformity, concealing important differences between different types of case.[33] For example, in contract there are important differences between an ordinary sale of goods contract, a contract of employment, and an agency contract. But there is nothing in the idea of a justificatory category to preclude differentiation between different types of case within the category. In different types of situation a general principle can have different implications, or be faced with different countervailing considerations. Consistent application of the principle is consistent with the different treatment of different types of case. By the same token, it is possible that parts of the law that differ considerably in matters of detail may prove to be derived from a common principle: this is one view of tort law, as mentioned above. It is also liable to happen where as a result of false differentiation analogous issues are dealt with in different conventional-justificatory categories.

---

[32] Waddams, above n 1, at 222.
[33] eg, Collins, above n 29, at 47.

Some discussions of classification in the law seem to be based on a quite different picture of the law from that assumed above. On this alternative view, the law does not consist of discrete bodies of law supported by distinct moral principles, but is instead something in the nature of an undifferentiated or homogenous mass, so that claims differ from each other in many different ways, to a greater or lesser degree, and are collected into categories only for convenience in teaching and administration.[34] The content of the categories is just an historical accident and is arbitrary. These categories are 'purely conventional' categories;[35] their names are simply convenient labels for a body of law and the claims that arise under it, for the purposes of identification and exposition. They can have no role in legal reasoning. This sort of understanding is suggested by the statement that 'tort is what is in the tort books, and the only thing holding it together is the binding'.[36]

This seems to me a quite implausible view of the law, and of categories such as contract and tort. If contract and tort were correctly understood as purely conventional categories, it would be difficult to understand the way they operate in the law or why there are sometimes hard-fought arguments over the characterisation of a claim as a contract or tort claim or some other type of claim; and it would also be puzzling that these categories or closely analogous categories are recognised in quite different legal systems.

Spurious Justificatory Categories

It is in practice possible for there to be a recognised conventional-justificatory category that is not founded on a genuine justifying principle at all—a spurious justificatory category. This is possible because of the way a conventional-justificatory category arises and functions in analogical reasoning. As suggested above, cases on unsettled law are liable to be allocated to a conventional-justificatory category, bringing them under a framework that determines in general terms how they are addressed and resolved, without any consideration

---

[34] Some of the following seem to contain suggestions along these lines: S Hedley, 'Unjust Enrichment as the Basis of Restitution—an Overworked Concept' [1985] *Legal Studies* 56–58; PS Atiyah, *Essays on Contract* (Oxford, Clarendon Press, OUP, 1986) 48; P Cane, *The Anatomy of Tort Law* (Oxford, Hart Publishing, 1997) 198, rejecting a 'dispositive' role for classification in favour of an 'expository' role; T Weir, *Introduction to Tort Law* (Oxford, Clarendon Law Series, OUP, 2nd edn, 2006) ix. Sceptics about issues of justification are naturally prone to understand categories as conventional. Cf Collins, above n 29, at 43.

[35] Or 'nominal' categories: see Moore, *Placing Blame*, above n 7.

[36] Weir, above n 34, at ix.

of the underlying principle or any theoretical understanding of the category.

It is easy to see that some possible categories cannot possibly be genuine justificatory categories. For example, the category of 'claims arising on a Tuesday' clearly cannot constitute a justificatory category, because the nature of the category is unrelated to the reason why the claim arises. It is impossible to imagine such a category becoming established as a conventional-justificatory category. In other cases, it may not be easy to say whether a category is a genuine justificatory category.

It was at one time argued that contract claims, properly understood—ie, in the light of their true justification—are not based on the principle that agreements should be performed, but are either tort claims based on a duty of reasonable care or restitutionary or unjust enrichment claims based on a principle of unjust enrichment. This was the 'death of contract' theory.[37] The argument can be understood to be that there is no true justificatory category of contract—presumably not because there is no principle at all along the lines of the contract principle, but because it is taken to be irrelevant to the law—and accordingly sound analogical reasoning should lead the rules of contract law to be absorbed into what are implicitly the true justificatory categories of tort and unjust enrichment. More recently, this argument has fallen out of fashion, and contract and tort (rightly in my view) remain distinct conventional-justificatory categories.[38]

The law of equity sometimes seems to be understood and to function as a conventional-justificatory category, so that a judge might say 'this claim arises in equity, not in contract', as if to imply that equity is an equivalent sort of category. The effect of the substantive fusion of equity and the common law (if it comes about) will then be to eliminate a conventional-justificatory category, and some of the opposition to substantive fusion seems to be based on the idea that

---

[37] Or the 'contract as tort' theory: see PS Atiyah, *The Rise and Fall of Freedom of Contract* (Oxford, Clarendon Press, OUP, 1979) and G Gilmore, *The Death of Contract* (Ohio, Ohio State University Press, 1974).

[38] Some scepticism is still expressed about whether contract and tort are distinct categories: see eg A Robertson, 'On the Distinction between Contract and Tort' in A Robertson (ed), *The Law of Obligations* (London, UCL Press, 2004). It is sometimes said that the distinction is illusory because although contract is in principle concerned with 'voluntary obligations' and tort with 'involuntary obligations', often a party's legal position in contract does not depend on what he actually agreed to do. It is true that many issues that arise under a contract are not provided for by any actually agreed provision—it is impossible to make provision for every contingency. But when this problem arises it is addressed under a framework based on the principle that agreements should be enforced.

equity is a genuine justificatory category. It seems to me clear that, insofar as equity operates in this way, it is a spurious justificatory category. This issue is discussed in chapter 4.

In modern times, many commentators have argued strenuously for the recognition of a category of restitution or unjust enrichment law. The argument has been that historically there were various isolated bits of the law all concerned with claims arising from the receipt of a benefit by the defendant D, which are all, properly understood, based on the same general principle, namely the principle of unjust enrichment. Consequently these fragments should be united, for the sake of coherence, into a single category of law. I will refer to this argument as the 'theory of unjust enrichment'. It seems clear that this proposed category is intended as what I have called a justificatory category, and that it has developed by analogical reasoning along the lines suggested above. It now seems to have attained the status of a conventional-justificatory category,[39] and its arrival has displaced the law of 'quasi-contract', which was at one time a conventional-justificatory category but has now almost completely disappeared from the case law and textbooks.

But is unjust enrichment a true justificatory category? It depends on whether there is indeed a justifying principle of unjust enrichment. It is not obvious whether this is the case or not. This is certainly not like the case of 'claims arising on a Tuesday' because the fact that D received a benefit is clearly relevant to the justification for the claim. But in the large and expanding literature on unjust enrichment, and in the case law, though the principle is often invoked, there is curiously little consideration of what exactly the principle is. To give a name to a supposed principle is not to formulate it. And as pointed out above, a category can be recognised and operate as a justificatory category without the need for the principle to be formulated and applied. In my view the recognition of the law of unjust enrichment as a justificatory category is a mistake. This will be discussed in chapter 8.

It seems to me that enrichment is an event or state of affairs that can be relevant to different types of claim, arising by virtue of different principles. It may be a relevant fact in a claim in contract law or in property law, as considered in later chapters, and the significance of the enrichment and the way it is analysed is liable to differ in these different categories because of the different bases for the claims. In

---

[39] See ch 8.

this respect enrichment is like the concepts of reliance and loss. These are also relevant in different ways in different justificatory categories by virtue of different underlying principles. If this is right, and there is indeed no genuine principle of unjust enrichment, this confirms the point made above that a category can function in practice as a justificatory category in analogical reasoning without any deep examination of the underlying justifying principle, that is to say, without any theoretical ascent.

A spurious justificatory category is a source of incoherence, including false differentiation and false assimilation and legal fictions. The effect of recognising a spurious justificatory category is to subject to uniform treatment under a common framework claims that, properly understood, come from different justificatory categories and should be treated quite differently. At the same time it may have the effect of treating some claims differently from analogous claims in other genuine justificatory categories. The signs of a spurious justificatory category are a lack of evident rationale for the rules, and a tension between what seems important or relevant to a claim and the issues that the law actually raises; in short, opacity, and artificiality or unnecessary complexity. One would expect spurious categories to be exposed and eliminated over time through analogical reasoning. But it is understandable that a spurious justificatory category should arise and persist. As discussed above, fundamental issues concerning the nature of a category are not necessarily addressed at all. Also, there may be good reason to be slow and cautious in recognising or eliminating categories. Even if it is clear what the position ought to be, any dramatic change of this sort is liable to involve an enormous amount of reinterpretation of established terminology and concepts.

SOME OTHER TYPES OF CLASSIFICATION

There are other types of classification that are quite independent of classification by justificatory category.

Classification by Remedy

A remedy is a measure ordered by a court in satisfaction of a claim. There are several different types of remedy, for example compensation, injunction and specific performance, restitution of goods or money, satisfaction of debt, reasonable payment for goods or services (quantum meruit or quantum valebat), etc.[40] Claims can be classified according to the type of remedy that is sought through the claim. This is clearly different from a classification according to justification. It may be that claims having a certain type of justificatory basis will always lead to a certain type of remedy, or that a certain type of remedy always arises out of a certain justificatory category, but the two are not the same and there is no reason to equate them.

However, there seem to be cases where the two are conflated, where a remedy is taken to define a justificatory category: this will be referred to as the 'remedy-as-justification' fallacy, and is discussed further in the next chapter. The fact that two claims are both claims for a certain type of remedy provides no reason for treating them as analogous in the sense that they should be subject to a common framework for determining when a claim should arise, which depends not on the remedy but on the justification of the claim. The old implied contract fiction mentioned above reflects this type of fallacy. The remedy for a claim for the payment of a contractual debt is an order to repay a sum of money. Similarly, if C has made a mistaken payment to D, C's claim is for the repayment of a sum of money. The remedy is the same or similar, though the justificatory category is different. In the former case the justificatory category is contract, whereas in the latter case it is clearly not contract, though it remains controversial what it is: as mentioned above, it is now commonly said to be unjust enrichment. It seems that it was because the remedy sought was the same in the latter case that the claim came to be treated as analogous with respect to its justification. Thus false assimilation, in the form of a legal fiction, resulted from the remedy-as-justification fallacy.

In my view, the modern law of restitution or unjust enrichment is based on the same type of error. The law developed as the law of restitution, which appears to be a type of remedy, namely the recovery of transfers of property or money, though it has come to be used to include the remedy of reasonable payment for services or for the use of property.[41] Thus one can identify a remedial category of restitution claims. More recently it has become common to refer to the law of unjust enrichment, which appears to be intended as a justificatory category based on a principle of unjust enrichment, in

---

[40] There are other measures that are loosely though not correctly described as remedies, including punitive damages, as discussed below p 57.

[41] Below p 216.

accordance with the theory of unjust enrichment as explained above. But if, as suggested above, this is a spurious justificatory category, it appears that one factor behind its recognition is the conflation of the remedial category with a justificatory category, and if so it is an example of the remedy-as-justification fallacy.

Procedural Classification

The ostensible difference between criminal law and civil law is that they are enforced through different court systems, and so they can be said to be procedural categories.[42] It must presumably be appropriate for civil and criminal law to be administered separately because of some more fundamental distinction that calls for different procedures. Thus one would expect a procedural classification to be parasitic on some other type of classification that justifies it. Criminal law is sometimes explained as a separate justificatory category, though this in itself does not explain the need for a different procedure. This issue will be touched on in the next chapter.

Before the Judicature Acts 1873–75, the most obvious distinction between the common law and the law of equity was that they were procedural categories in the same sense. Equity was enforced in the Chancery courts and the common law in the common law courts. Again one would think that there must be some other type of distinction between equity and the common law that justified or was thought to justify the procedural distinction. Since the procedural fusion effected by the Judicature Acts, it would seem that this underlying distinction must be the basis for the continued recognition of a division between common law and equity. Sometimes, as mentioned above, equity is treated as a distinct justificatory category. The nature of equity and its relationship to the common law remain controversial. This is discussed in chapter 4.

The Old 'Forms of Action'

At one time, proceedings could be taken only by following one of the forms of action.[43] The forms of action were an awkward mixture of justificatory, remedial, and procedural classification. A form of action was characterised by a standard pleading formula specifying a certain set of events and circumstances, which might reflect a certain

---

[42] This is not a classification of claims, since there are claims only in civil law. It might be thought of as a classification of wrongs.

[43] See generally Maitland, *Forms of Action* (1936). The forms of action were largely abolished by the Common Law Procedure Act 1852.

type of justification for a claim, and also a certain procedure or court system, and a certain type of remedy.

The forms of action are long gone, but possibly their influence persists. First, the forms of action promoted fictions. In order to bring a case within the form of action on a novel set of facts, these facts were equated with or deemed to constitute the facts required by the standard formula. This was a means of developing the law but sometimes it involved a fiction. A standard example is the case of the implied contract fiction mentioned above, where a claim arising from a mistaken payment was deemed to be based on an implied agreement in order to bring it within the relevant form of action. There may still sometimes be an undue respect for the use of fictions as a tool for developing the law, or, it might be better to say, a tendency to confuse fictions and analogies (ie sound analogies). In making an analogy, the court equates two sets of facts on the ground that they are materially the same in the light of underlying principle, for example by bringing them under the same justificatory category. In practice, it may not be clear, at least in the short term, whether a decision is based on a fiction or a sound analogy, because it may remain obscure or controversial what the real justification for a decision is. By legitimating fictions the forms of action obscured this question and so inhibited sound analogical reasoning.

More particularly, in employing a fiction under the forms of action the court equated a new set of facts with a standard formula as a means of awarding the standard remedy. If the analogy was not justifiable, and there was a fiction rather than sound analogical reasoning, this would also be a case of the remedy-as-justification fallacy. In the modern law there may still be a tendency to emphasise remedial categories at the expense of justificatory categories, and to conflate the two, leading to the remedy-as-justification fallacy.

Source-based Classification

One can also classify by source or type of authority, ie into statute, common law and custom.[44] This is of course a crucial distinction for some purposes, because of the power of Parliament to override the common law. But it does not raise any general problems for present purposes or loom large in private law.

---

[44] Again this is not a classification of claims; it is usually understood as a classification of rules. Cf above n 6.

Modalities of Legal Relation

Many rules impose a duty on D for the benefit of C, for example a duty of reasonable care or a contractual duty of performance. In such cases, one can say that there is a right-duty relation between the parties, C's right being correlated with a duty of D's. (Some would take issue with the idea of legal relations or correlated rights and duties—this issue will be considered briefly in the next chapter.) Rules can involve other types of legal relation. For example, a rule may create a power-liability relation. If A has a power vis-à-vis B, A can alter B's legal position by acting in the prescribed way. B has a correlative liability, ie, a susceptibility to the alteration of his legal position. There are, for example, powers to make a contract, to waive a claim, and to dispose of property or license the use of property. Another type of legal relation is where A has a liberty vis-à-vis B. A has a liberty to do X vis-à-vis B if A does not have a duty to B not to do X. For example, A might have a liberty to enter into competition with B, or, by virtue of a licence from B, a liberty to cross B's land.[45] Hohfeld's famous work set out a classification of these types of legal relation.[46] I will refer to them as normative types or 'modalities'.

Distinguishing between different types of modality is crucial to understanding and formulating rules with clarity and precision. This is illustrated by an example of Hohfeld's.[47] Hohfeld pointed out that the term 'right' is not used in a uniform sense. In a strict sense, A has a right against B when B has a correlative duty. Hohfeld used the expression 'claim-right' to refer to this. Sometimes instead A is said to have a right against B when he has a liberty vis-à-vis B. Say that A sets up in business and then subsequently B sets up in competition and his competition damages A's business. A argues that he has a right to carry on business, and therefore that B owes him a correlative duty not to damage his business by competing with him. The argument equivocates between two senses of 'right'. A has a right to carry on

---

[45] B can be said to have a 'no-right', so the relation is 'liberty-no-right': WN Hohfeld, *Fundamental Legal Conceptions as Applied in Judicial Reasoning* (D Campbell and P Thomas (eds), Aldershot, Ashgate, 2001), originally published (1913) 23 *Yale Law Journal* 16 and (1917) 26 *Yale Law Journal* 710.

[46] Ibid. Hohfeld referred to the elements of legal relations—right, duty, liability, power etc—as 'fundamental conceptions'.

[47] Ibid, 34–35; NE Simmonds, 'Introduction' in Hohfeld, ibid, xix.

business only in the sense that he has a liberty to do so. This means that he does not act wrongfully by carrying on business—he does not breach a duty to B (or anyone else), and B does not have a right that A should not carry on business. But it is quite a different thing to say that A has a right to carry on a business in the sense that he has a right that B not interfere with his business by carrying on a competing business. Generally this is not the case, because B also has a liberty to carry on a business. The example shows that formulating a rule clearly and precisely involves identifying its modality, which in this case means distinguishing between different usages of 'right'.

Modalities are not the same as justificatory categories. The principle behind a justificatory category is implemented through a body of rules of various modalities. For example, in tort law there are duties of care, and there can be a power to waive a duty of care. In contract law, there is a power to make an offer, and a power to accept an offer; and there can be a contractual duty of performance. Modalities are concepts employed in formulating a rule, but they are not tied to a particular type of principle or justification.[48]

Modalities and justificatory categories play different roles in legal reasoning. Classification by justificatory category contributes to analogical reasoning where the law is unsettled, as discussed earlier. Hohfeldian analysis in terms of modalities contributes to clarifying the meaning of legal rules, but it does not give any guidance on how to resolve unsettled law through analogical reasoning, except by way of clarifying the meaning of existing and proposed formulations of a rule.

It is helpful here to refer to the distinction employed in ethical theory between 'thick' and 'thin' normative concepts.[49] Thin normative concepts are formal or abstract concepts for expressing normative propositions. They are not tied to particular types of situation or moral principle, and can be employed in expressing normative propositions that vary widely in terms of their content and justification. Concepts that are Hohfeldian modalities such as right, duty, liability, power are thin normative concepts.

Thick normative concepts are used to express normative propositions concerned with particular types of situation and behaviour. Typical examples are courage, treachery, cruelty and selfishness. Their characteristic feature is a 'union of fact and value':[50] the

---

[48] Cf the discussion of the 'bundle of rights' concept of property in ch 3.
[49] See B Williams, *Ethics and the Limits of Philosophy* (London, Fontana Press, 1985) 129.
[50] Ibid.

concept is a certain type of character, conduct, state of affairs, etc, but it also carries a moral significance and its use conveys a moral judgment. There must be a moral principle that lies behind the concept, by virtue of which certain facts have this moral significance, though normally the moral principle remains tacit and people who use and understand the concept may not find it easy to formulate a principle to go with the concept. Indeed there is liable to be controversy over exactly what the principle is.

Concepts such as contract and tort that form justificatory categories are tied to particular principles. Insofar as the justificatory category has been reduced to and operates simply as a body of rules applied to the facts, only thin concepts are involved, and the same is true where an underlying principle is subjected to interpretation and analysis. But where a judge is presented with a claim on unsettled law and assimilates it to a justificatory category as a matter of impression, it appears that he is applying the underlying principle without explicitly referring to it or formulating it, by virtue of an understanding of the fact situations that instantiate it, and this implies that there is a thick concept of contract or tort at the heart of the justificatory category.[51]

Two Types of Claim

The usual understanding is that claims in private law are based on primary right-duty relations. A primary right or relation is to be contrasted with a remedial right or relation. The primary relation between C and D is the relation by virtue of which a claim arises for C against D. For example, D may owe C a primary duty of care in tort, or a primary duty of contractual performance. If D commits a breach of the duty, a remedial relation arises, typically consisting of a right of C's to compensation and a duty of D to pay compensation. C's claim is his remedial right to compensation.[52] (The distinction between primary and remedial relations and the relationship between them is considered in more depth in the next chapter.)

---

[51] Generally ordinary thick normative concepts like the ones mentioned above carry an implication of either praise or condemnation, because the underlying principle is a principle concerned with how one ought to behave. But it is not necessarily true of these legal concepts that the implication is of breach of legal duty or legal wrongdoing. (It may be true of tort.) There is no legal equivalent to praise. For example, in the case of contract, the significance of the set of facts described—the contract or agreement—is that it involves the exercise of a normative power to create a duty or other normative relation.

[52] In fact a claim or remedial right to compensation is better understood as a power correlated with a liability, not a right correlated with a duty: see P Jaffey, 'Hohfeld's Power-Liability/Right-Duty Distinction in the Law of Restitution' (2004) 17 *Canadian Journal of Law & Jurisprudence* 295; below p 94.

In this type of case, the claim arises from a wrong, a wrong being a breach of duty. It is often thought that all claims in private law are wrong-based, or, in other words, that all primary relations in private law are right-duty relations. But take, for example, the well-known rule in *Rylands v Fletcher*.[53] Under the rule, if a dangerous thing kept by the defendant D on his land—for example a dangerous animal, or water in a reservoir—escapes and causes harm to a neighbour, the claimant C, C has a claim for compensation, and the claim does not depend on D's having failed to act in some way to prevent the escape, which he may have been incapable of doing. If D has a duty, it is a 'strict liability' duty, meaning a duty that D can breach without fault because the performance of the duty is not under his control. D simply has a duty that harm not be caused in this way, whether or not there is anything he can do to prevent it. Strict liability duties have long been controversial. The objection is that a rule that imposes a duty should act as a genuine prescription or requirement of action for the people it regulates, and a strict liability duty does not do this because it may not be possible for D to perform it, and when a claim arises against D it cannot be because he failed to act as required. Nevertheless some commentators insist that strict liability duties are quite justifiable, and regard the rule in *Rylands v Fletcher* as an example of a rule creating a strict liability duty.

I will not address the arguments over strict liability duties directly, but I will adopt an alternative approach that does not rely on them. On this approach, I will understand 'duty' in the 'subjective' sense to mean a genuine prescription or requirement for action (or inaction), so that a wrong or breach of duty involves fault, and where D is subject to a claim arising from a wrong it is because he has failed to act as he was required to act by law.[54] This is not to deny that there are claims that do not arise from wrongs understood in this way; I will say that, properly understood, some claims, including the claim arising under the rule in *Rylands v Fletcher*, do not arise from a primary right-duty relation at all, but instead from what I will call a primary 'right-liability' or primary liability relation.[55] A primary liability relation specifies a contingency, an act or event whose occurrence generates a claim, though the act or event is not a breach of duty or wrong, for example the infliction of harm by the escaping thing under the rule in *Rylands v Fletcher*. A primary liability is not a strict

---

[53] (1868) LR 3 HL 330.

[54] Subjective and objective duties are considered again in ch 7.

[55] See also P Jaffey, 'Duties and Liabilities in Private Law' (2006) 12 *Legal Theory* 137.

liability duty, though the expression 'strict liability' is ambiguous as between a primary liability and a primary strict liability duty. The primary liability claim is not based on a breach of duty at all: D was at liberty to act as he did.[56] It is not that D acted wrongly though without fault.[57]

Consider another example, from contract law. In contract, there is normally said to be a duty to perform in accordance with the agreement, and a correlative right to performance, ie a right-duty relation. But many aspects of contract suggest that this may not be the case. Often if there is a contractual duty it must be a strict liability duty requiring of D something that he may not be capable of doing; also, often a contracting party is not compelled to perform his contract by order of specific performance, even though there is no hardship involved in doing so; and in other respects a contracting party is not treated as having acted wrongfully by not performing the contract. This suggests, as has often been pointed out, that there is, in the ordinary case, no primary duty to perform the contract. One might object that if there is no duty there can be no breach of duty and therefore no contractual claim at all; but a contract claim can be understood as a claim arising from a right-liability relation. This case will be considered again in the next chapter in connection with the relationship between primary and remedial rights.

Another case will be important in later chapters[58]: this is the case of the claim to recover an invalid transfer. Say C owns money or property that comes into D's possession or control without a valid transfer by or on behalf of C, because of a mistake by C or his agent, say, or because the property was taken and passed on by an unauthorised third party. The transfer is invalid because there was no valid exercise of the owner's power of transfer by or on behalf of C, and as a result of the invalid transfer C has a claim against D to recover the money or property or its value. But it can hardly be said that the

---

[56] Or at least, if D was not at liberty to act in this way, this is not relevant to the claim.

[57] It goes without saying that in the expression 'right-liability', 'right' is not used in the strict sense of Hohfeld's 'claim-right', in which it correlates with a duty; and 'liability' is not used to mean susceptibility to a power, as in the case of a liability correlated with a power. But this is just a matter of terminology. It does not involve any departure from Hohfeld's 'correlativity thesis': on the correlativity thesis, see MH Kramer, 'Rights Without Trimmings' in MH Kramer, NE Simmonds and H Steiner, *A Debate Over Rights* (Oxford, OUP, 1998) 24–29. However, it does contradict what one might call the 'completeness thesis', that Hohfeld's scheme can 'be employed to classify and clarify all empirical phenomena that might be found': Kramer, ibid, 30.

[58] Esp chs 3 and 6 below.

transfer to D, which was not effected by D or even within his control, and may have been completely outside his knowledge, was a breach of duty by him. C's claim to recover his property or its value arises from a primary liability relation. More generally, the claims that are often described as unjust enrichment or restitution claims arise from the receipt of a benefit, including the transfer of money or property, and they are based on primary right-liability relations.

A primary right–liability relation can be understood as a direct allocation of risk, in the sense that it imposes on D rather than C the responsibility for a certain risk, but without imposing a duty on D to prevent the risk materialising. If the risk materialises D is subject to a claim, but not by virtue of having committed a wrong. On this understanding a contract allocates risk concerning the activities specified by the agreement rather than imposing duties to perform the agreement; and a right of ownership, insofar as the type of claim mentioned above is concerned, subjects potential recipients of the property to the risk of a claim to recover the property or its value, and in both cases it is this allocation of risk that constitutes the primary right–liability relation.

I will take the view that in private law there are two modalities of primary relation, and two corresponding types of claim. Where the primary relation is a right–duty relation, the claim arises from a breach of duty or wrong by D, meaning that D has failed to comply with a requirement of action imposed by the law. Where the primary relation is a right–liability relation, the claim arises from an event that is not a wrong in this sense, but is specified as a contingency, the risk of which is borne by D rather than C. This may be an act by D, but if so the claim does not depend on characterising the act as a wrong and, so far as the primary relation is concerned, D was at liberty to commit it.

Negligence in tort law is an interesting case that will arise later.[59] There is normally said to be a duty of reasonable care, requiring D to reach a certain 'standard of care'. This is a right–duty relation, and if D fails to reach the required standard of care he commits a breach of duty. But the traditional position (though often criticised) is that the duty is 'objective', meaning that the standard of care required of D depends not on D's own particular characteristics but on the characteristics of a 'reasonable person' in D's position. This means that for some people the required standard may be very burdensome or even

---

[59] Below p 196.

beyond reach, and the duty is a strict liability duty in the sense above. This suggests that the primary relation may not be a right-duty relation at all, but a right-liability relation.[60] On this basis, if D fails to reach the specified standard of care he incurs the risk of liability for any loss caused, but he has not (by virtue of this legal relation) committed a breach of duty. The standard of care allocates risk rather than imposing a duty. This is consistent with the approach of some tort scholars who regard the duty of care in tort not as a genuine duty but merely as a condition of liability.[61] Possibly the two modalities of primary relation, right-duty and right-liability relations, are both capable of arising in the justificatory category of tort law based on a general principle of reasonable care or responsibility. This is the view taken with respect to contract law in the next chapter.

Some Objections to Primary Right-liability Relations

There are some possible misinterpretations of primary right-liability relations and objections to them. As mentioned above, primary liability relations are sometimes presented, or, on my view, misrepresented, as strict liability duties.[62] Alternatively, to avoid the notion of a strict liability duty, or in recognition of the fact that D is free to do the act that generates the claim, it is sometimes said that D's only duty is the duty to provide a remedy, arising from the harm or other event that generates the claim, or, along the same lines, that D has a conditional duty to provide a remedy, the condition being the event

---

[60] Cf N MacCormick, 'The Obligation of Reparation' in *Legal Right and Social Democracy* (Oxford, Clarendon Press, 1982).

[61] See the comments in McBride and Bagshaw, above n 24, at 20, criticising 'duty-sceptics'.

[62] See eg A Ripstein, 'Philosophy of Tort Law' in J Coleman and S Shapiro (eds), *The Oxford Handbook of Jurisprudence & Philosophy of Law* (Oxford, OUP, 2002); J Gardner, 'Obligations and Outcomes in the Law of Torts' in J Gardner and P Cane (eds), *Relating to Responsibility: Essays for Tony Honoré on His Eightieth Birthday* (Oxford, Hart Publishing, 2001). According to Tony Honoré, *Responsibility and Fault* (Oxford, Hart Publishing, 1999), strict liability in tort should be understood in terms of 'outcome responsibility', which is a form of allocation of risk. This approach differs from the position in the text in that (1) it is said to generate a strict liability duty, so that a claim arises from a wrong, and (2) the discussion is confined to tort, and the implication is that outcome responsibility is a type of justificatory principle lying behind liability in tort, rather than a modality of relation in the sense suggested in the text. Cane appears to regard strict liability in tort as not being based on a duty: P Cane, 'Fault and Strict Liability for Harm in Tort Law' in W Swadling and G Jones (eds), *The Search for Principle: Essays in Honour of Lord Goff of Chieveley* (Oxford, OUP, 1999); P Birks, 'Rights, Wrongs and Remedies' (2000) 20 *Oxford Journal of Legal Studies* 1, 25 refers to a 'not-wrong' as an event generating a claim.

that generates the claim.[63] But these formulations refer only to a remedial duty, corresponding to C's claim, and do not help to identify or characterise the primary relation by virtue of which the claim arises. If such a formulation adequately describes what I have called a primary liability claim, it would also adequately describe any claim at all, including claims that clearly arise from a breach of duty.[64]

A remedially-oriented approach along these lines is encouraged by the traditional preoccupation with remedies, arising in part from the old forms of action. It leads to a tendency to use 'duty' in an artificial or fictional way, as a verbal formula to denote that a claim will arise from a certain act or event, which disguises the difference between right-duty and right-liability primary relations.[65] It is true that the practical concern of the claimant C is whether a remedy is available on the facts, and the law can often be adequately expressed in the form 'in the event of X, C has a claim against D' without specifying whether X constitutes a breach of duty, or some other act or event that triggers a claim under a primary liability relation. But sometimes it is important to say whether the claim arose from a breach of duty or not. In particular, as discussed in the next chapter, it may be important in connection with remedies and the relationship between primary and remedial relations.

Another reason why the primary right-liability relation is usually hidden or ignored in legal analysis may be the assumption that it is unjust for D to be subject to a claim if he has not committed a wrong.[66] Sometimes what is intended here is the different proposition that it is unjust to hold D to have acted wrongfully if he has not been at fault. This amounts to denying the legitimacy of strict liability duties, not primary liability relations.

---

[63] One might say that D has a duty either to refrain from committing an act or to provide a remedy: see eg H Sheinman, 'Tort Law and Corrective Justice' (2003) 22 *Law and Philosophy* 21, 41. But it is not clear that this really identifies a primary relation either. Also, in some cases the claim does not arise from an act that D chose to perform.

[64] A further objection is that, as noted above, n 52, C's claim for compensation is better understood as a power correlated with D's liability, not a right correlated with a duty.

[65] It is sometimes said that the availability of compensation as a remedy is the hallmark of a duty, or the 'test' of whether there is a duty. But compensation is often the appropriate remedy for a primary liability claim. The availability of 'specific enforcement' by way of an injunction or specific performance indicates that there is a duty, but sometimes specific enforcement will be impossible or impracticable. Punishment also implies that there was a breach of duty, but again is not always appropriate.

[66] See eg SA Smith, 'Justifying the Law of Unjust Enrichment' (2001) 79 *Texas Law Review* 2177, 2182–83.

Some writers assume that if a claim does not arise from the breach of a duty owed by D to C, there is no reason why the particular defendant D, rather than someone else, or the state, should have to provide a remedy to C. This is often expressed in terms of corrective justice. It is said that any such claim is unjust to D, because it is not based on any right of C's against D. In the context of tort law, it might be thought that if the claim does not arise from a duty owed to C its object must be 'loss-spreading', meaning reallocating losses as part of the allocation of benefits and burdens across the society as a whole, as a matter of distributive justice, so that it has the same sort of function as the system of taxation and social security benefits.[67] But this is not the implication of formulating the law in terms of a primary right-liability relation. Where there is a right-liability relation between C and D, C has a right against D. The relation represents an allocation of risk as between D and C, in accordance with the principle behind the justificatory category in issue. The harm or other triggering event may not be a wrong by D, but so long as it remains unremedied it constitutes an injustice, as between C and D, by virtue of the allocation of risk. I will return to this point briefly in the next chapter in connection with the discussion of corrective justice.[68]

Another possible objection to primary liability relations is the assumption that if a claim does not arise from a wrong it must be based on a sceptical or reductionist approach to the law, meaning an approach that purports to eliminate the 'internal' or normative realm from the law. From the internal or normative point of view of someone subject to a rule imposing a duty on him, the duty is a requirement or prescription directed at him. The rule may be enforced by a sanction, which gives D an incentive to comply with the duty, but the effect of the sanction is distinct from the normative force of the duty itself.[69] On a reductionist approach, rules are understood as defining acts or omissions to which sanctions are attached as an incentive or disincentive, and the concept of a duty has no distinct role to play; if the expression is used, it is understood as simply describing the behaviour that will attract a sanction.[70]

---

[67] eg, Bagshaw and MacBride, above n 24, at 38.

[68] Below p 65.

[69] One might say that there are 'primary rules of conduct', but I do not take this to mean that the rules necessarily operate in practice as a guide that is consulted by the people subject to them.

[70] This is the 'sanction theory of duty': see PMS Hacker, 'Sanction Theories of Duty' in AWB Simpson (ed), *Oxford Essays in Jurisprudence: 2nd Series* (Oxford, Clarendon Press, 1973); J Gardner, 'Backwards and Forwards with Tort Law' in J Keim-Campbell,

Some schools of thought tend to deny the existence of duties for reductionist reasons. It is well known that in the Legal Realism literature it is sometimes said that the law should be understood, from the standpoint of a subject of the law, purely in terms of the sanction he will suffer for doing something, not whether he has a duty not to do it.[71] Similarly the modern economic analysis of law sometimes appears to treat measures imposed by the court as sanctions, understood as incentives and disincentives directly influencing or manipulating behaviour without imposing any duties (except in the artificial sense mentioned above), and so appears to be reductionist in the same sense.[72]

The primary right–liability relation does not involve a duty, but it is not reductionist. The allocation of risk does not represent merely the risk of a sanction. It is a genuine legal relation or norm or 'reason for action' for D, though it is not mandatory and does not require certain conduct from D.[73] In this respect it is like some other legal relations, for example the power–liability relation.

In any case, it is worth pointing out that the distinction between right–duty relations and right–liability relations, or an analogous distinction, is also recognised from a reductionist point of view. From the reductionist point of view what is significant is the different characteristic types of legal response or sanction that are appropriate in the two types of case, in respect of a wrong or breach of duty as compared to a causative event that is not a wrong.[74] I will return to some of these issues in the next chapter.

M O'Rourke and D Shier (eds), *Law and Social Justice* (Cambridge Mass, MIT Press, 2005). The point can be expressed in terms of reasons for action. A sanction for the breach of a duty is a self-interested or prudential reason for action: it provides an incentive to comply with the duty. On a reductionist approach, this is the only reason for action. But from the internal point of view the duty itself constitutes a reason for action, though a normative rather than a prudential one, in particular a mandatory reason for action. Thus whether the duty exists depends not on whether there is a sanction but whether there is a valid rule imposing the duty. The sanction provides an additional prudential reason to comply with the duty.

[71] This 'externalist' approach is associated with OW Holmes, *The Path of the Law* (1897) 10 *Harvard Law Review* 457, 458–61. Modern duty-sceptics in tort law are criticised by NJ McBride, 'Duties of Care—Do they Really Exist?' (2004) 24 *Oxford Journal of Legal Studies* 417, and JP Goldberg and BC Zipursky, 'The Restatement (Third) and the Place of Duty in Negligence Law' (2001) 54 *Vanderbilt Law Review* 657.

[72] As discussed by J Coleman, *The Practice of Principle* (Oxford, OUP, 2001) 35.

[73] For rejection of the idea of a claim not based on a breach of duty as being reductionist, cf Gardner, above n 62.

[74] The distinction corresponds, it appears to me, with the distinction in the economic analysis of law between 'property rules' and 'liability rules' see G Calebresi and AD Melamed, 'Property Rules, Liability Rules and Inalienability: One View of the

Opposition to the Idea of Classification

As mentioned above, some commentators express a general hostility to classification in the law.[75] Such hostility should always be understood as hostility to a particular classification or to the misuse of a classification. Classification itself is part of the rational investigation of any subject matter. In general terms, classification involves identifying appropriate criteria for differentiating or assimilating among the elements of the subject matter, and without this it is impossible to formulate the concepts necessary to describe and understand it. In law, rejecting classification means refusing even to investigate the nature and the role of concepts such as contract, tort, property, restitution, compensation, wrongs, liabilities, and so on, and their relation to each other.

As mentioned at the start of the chapter, one source of hostility to classification may come from an association of classification with 'mechanical jurisprudence', which might suggest that a classification should operate to provide a legal solution in a mechanical or algorithmic way. It may be the misconception that a legal classification should operate in this way that is behind the feeling that it is futile if it does not do so. In the reaction against mechanical jurisprudence it has sometimes been implied that the law should be able to protect individual interests and promote the general welfare without the traditional baggage of legal concepts and classification.[76] This is another illusion. It will always be necessary to employ concepts whose meaning and significance and inter-relation need to be investigated and explained through an exercise of classification.

Cathedral' (1972) 85 *Harvard Law Review* 1089. A 'property rule' is a rule that protects a right by way of an injunction or by threat of punishment to compel D to act, and a 'liability rule' is a rule that protects a right only by way of compensation for loss. This is not how this distinction is usually translated into Hohfeldian relations: see eg S Munzer, *A Theory of Property* (Cambridge, CUP, 1990) 27. On the suggested approach, 'property rule' is an inappropriate usage because there is no necessary link between duty and property.

[75] For a wide-ranging discussion of arguments sceptical of legal classification, see Waddams, above n 1, especially chs 1, 11. See also G Samuel, 'Can the Common Law Be Mapped?' (2005) 55 *University of Toronto Law Journal* 271; S Hedley, 'The Taxonomic Approach to Restitution' in A Hudson (ed), *New Perspectives on Property Law, Obligations and Restitution* (London, Cavendish, 2004).

[76] This idea is associated with Legal Realism, exemplified by Felix Cohen, 'Transcendental Nonsense and the Functional Approach' (1935) 35 *Columbia Law Review* 809. On the need for technical terms in the law because of its 'systematicity', see J Waldron, 'Transcendental Nonsense and System in the Law' (2003) 100 *Columbia Law Review* 16.

Mutual Exclusivity and Justificatory Categories

A particular concern in connection with classification has been the issue of mutual exclusivity.[77] It is sometimes suggested that to classify claims by reference to mutually exclusive legal categories is artificial and liable to distort and oversimplify the law. Such comments tend to reflect the implausible understanding of the law mentioned earlier,[78] as being something like a homogenous mass that has been divided up into conventional categories, purely for convenience of exposition, and not because there are actually discrete categories based on distinct principles. It would indeed make no sense to assign a new case on unsettled law exclusively to such a category for the purposes of deciding it by analogical reasoning. A judge might reasonably think that the claim at hand has something in common with various such categories and draw on considerations from all of them. But this does not apply to justificatory categories consisting of bodies of rules that give effect to a certain general principle or type of justification. In analogical reasoning in terms of justificatory categories, the issue is whether the claim should be brought under the reach of the underlying principle, by the development of the rules that give effect to it. It would make no sense to say that a claim is partly justified under one category and partly justified under another and that these can be added together to justify a claim overall, because the underlying principles themselves cannot be combined in this way. Thus one cannot make a half-analogy with one category and a half-analogy with another category and find a whole claim in a hybrid category. Claims fall in a single justificatory category in a classification of mutually exclusive justificatory categories.

However, the general proposition that justificatory categories are mutually exclusive is potentially misleading without elaboration. First, there is no suggestion that there cannot be concurrent claims, ie two distinct claims from different justificatory categories that arise on a particular set of facts. Also, it might be the case that the fundamental justification for a claim is, say, the principle that an agreement should be observed, so that (on the argument above) the claim is in the true justificatory category of contract, but it is actually recognised as a tort claim in order to avoid a restrictive rule of contract law. This

---

[77] Generally classification does mean classification into mutually exclusive categories, because only then can it serve the purpose of differentiating between the elements to be classified.

[78] Above p 13.

means that there is a mismatch of true justificatory and conventional-justificatory categories. As discussed above, it involves a form of incoherence, namely false differentiation.

Furthermore, a claim in one justificatory category can depend on the law of another justificatory category in the following sense. A contract may relate to property, as where there is a contract to transfer property. In such a case, a claim in contract may involve determining a disputed issue in property law. Conversely, a contractual right can be the object of ownership, as in the case of contractual rights to payment that function as money. Similarly, there can be a duty in tort law imposing a requirement to avoid causing damage to property, so that it may be necessary to determine the scope of a property right as part of the determination of a tort claim. In these types of cases, a claim in one category presupposes the position under another. One might say that the output of one provides the input for another. But the two categories and the issues arising in connection with them remain discrete. Some aspects of the relationships between property and contract and property and tort are discussed in chapter 3.[79]

Independent Dimensions of Classification

A claim can fall into categories from different schemes of classification, eg justificatory categories, categories of modality, and remedial categories. Although a claim cannot be both contractual and tortious (if these are understood as justificatory categories), it could be contractual (justification), based on a wrong or duty as opposed to a primary liability (modality), and compensatory (remedy).

Some expressions are used ambiguously or inconsistently to signify concepts from different types of classification. This is true of 'property', as discussed in chapter 3. Similarly with 'tort': I take this to be a justificatory category, which seems to correspond to its standard use, though as mentioned above some might say that tort law consists of several distinct justificatory categories; and some would say that it is the law concerning wrongs, whatever the basis for the duty, which characterises it as a type of modality;[80] and sometimes it seems to be defined in terms of a remedy or remedial principle.[81] Also it

[79] Below p 82, 103.

[80] This approach is associated with P Winfield, *The Province of the Law of Tort* (Cambridge, CUP, 1932); see also McBride and Bagshaw, above n 24, ch 1. This approach appears to involve ad hoc exclusions of equity and contract. Samuel describes this as the 'formalist' approach, to be distinguished from the 'functionalist' approach, which as he defines it is a remedial category: G Samuel, *Cases & Materials on Torts* (Exeter, LawMatters, 2006) 9.

[81] ie, the principle that a wrong should be remedied, as discussed below, p 72.

seems that 'wrongs' may be intended as a type of modality, or as the justificatory category of tort.

If different schemes of classification are not distinguished, classification into mutually exclusive categories appears to preclude for dogmatic reasons the range of considerations that a court can legitimately take into account. For example, Waddams points out that in the well-known case of *LAC Minerals v International Corona Resources*[82] reliance, restitution or unjust enrichment, property, contract, and wrongdoing were all considered relevant, and in fact the claim was explicitly concerned with breach of confidence and breach of fiduciary duty. According to Sopinka J in that case, the law of confidential information is 'sui generis' but relies on the 'jurisdictional bases for action' of contract, equity and property.[83] It seems that for Waddams the inference to be drawn from this is that a classification-based approach should be avoided, because it would for dogmatic reasons force the court to try to resolve the case by reference to only one of these various concepts, whereas instead the court should be free to employ any or all of them in a flexible, common sense, anti-classificatory approach.[84] In fact these various concepts may well come from different types of classification so that they are not mutually exclusive. The real problem is that it is often unclear what sorts of concept are in issue. Putting an emphasis on classification requires the various concepts to be located in a scheme of classification that reveals what type of concept each is and how it relates to other concepts. Far from hindering sound analysis, this is a prerequisite for it.

Of the concepts mentioned, contract is a justificatory category, as in my view is property, as discussed in chapter 3. Fiduciary law is sometimes treated as a distinct justificatory category, though in my view it is a part or sub-category of contract law, as considered briefly in chapter 5. Equity is not a justificatory category though it is sometimes referred to as such, and its nature is a matter of continuing controversy. The relationship between equity and the common law

---

[82] [1989] 2 SCR 574; Waddams, above n 1, at 78.

[83] At 615. Similarly Waddams says that the decision in *White v Jones* [1995] 2 AC 207 was justifiable on the basis of 'the breach of contract and the negligence when combined with considerations of unjust enrichment, public policy, and general considerations of justice': Waddams, ibid, 55. Waddams's understanding of *White v Jones* is criticised by A Beever and C Rickett, 'Interpretive Legal Theory and the Academic Lawyer' (2005) 68 *Modern Law Review* 320, 333.

[84] For a similar view, see J Dietrich, 'The "Other" Category in the Classification of Obligations' in A Robertson, *The Law of Obligations*, above n 38, at 125–26; Cane, above n 34.

is the subject of chapter 4. Wrongs or wrongdoing is most obviously
a modality of primary relation, though as mentioned above it might
be understood to refer to a justificatory category analogous to contract, ie tort law. Reliance is a feature of the situation that is sometimes relevant to whether a claim arises—a type of relevant fact. It
may be relevant to claims in contract, tort or property. But there is
no reason to think that there is a distinct justificatory category of
reliance, based on a 'principle of reliance'. Restitution is on the face
of it a type of remedy, though it is often equated with a supposed justificatory category of unjust enrichment, based on a principle of
unjust enrichment. In my view, as I have already said, enrichment is,
like reliance, a feature of the situation that can be relevant to certain
types of claim, including claims in the categories of contract and
property, but there is no 'principle of unjust enrichment' to support
a justificatory category of unjust enrichment.[85] Sopinka J represents
confidential information as a sort of hybrid or complex category.
Confidential information is touched on in chapter 3. In my view it is
right to say that it is not itself a genuine justificatory category (or a
part of one like fiduciary law), but is composed of parts from different justificatory categories,[86] though on this view it is doubtful
whether Sopinka J is right to include equity along with contract and
property.

---

[85] See ch 8.
[86] This point is considered below p 107.

2

Rights, Remedies and Remedialism

This chapter is about the relationship between 'rights and remedies', or primary and remedial rights, in private law. It is not about the nature of legal rights in general, but it is helpful to begin with a contrast between two concepts of a legal right, or possibly one might say two perspectives on the concept of a legal right.

On one view, a right simply represents the benefit conferred by a valid rule. A typical rule in private law will impose a duty on one class of people for the benefit of another class. The claimant C is in the class of those who benefit, or is treated as representative of them, and to say that C has a certain right amounts to stating the rule from C's standpoint. The defendant D is in the class of duty-bearers under the rule, or is representative of them. It follows that C's right and D's duty are correlated, since they are manifestations of the same rule from opposing standpoints, and one can say that there is a right-duty legal relation between C and D. A right or a relation in this sense is conclusive. It is not the basis or justification for a rule, capable of being outweighed by other considerations. It represents the legal position under a valid rule. As discussed in chapter 1, legal relations may have different forms or modalities, for example power-liability or right-liability as well as right-duty.[1]

On another understanding of a legal right, to say that C has a right is to say that he has an interest that the law has recognised to be worthy of legal protection, for example an interest in bodily security, or in making a contract, or in owning property. This is the 'protected interest' concept of a right.[2] On this understanding, the interest will

---

[1] I take this to be the concept of a legal right assumed by Hohfeld: WN Hohfeld, *Fundamental Legal Conceptions as Applied in Judicial Reasoning* (D Campbell and P Thomas (eds), Aldershot, Ashgate, 2001), originally published (1913) 23 *Yale Law Journal* 16 and (1917) 26 *Yale Law Journal* 710. Hohfeld did not recognise a 'right-liability' relation.

[2] J Raz, *The Morality of Freedom* (Oxford, Clarendon Press, 1988) 166; DN MacCormick, 'Rights in Legislation' in PMS Hacker and J Raz (eds), *Law, Morality and Society* (Oxford, Clarendon Press, 1977).

often justify a rule imposing a duty owed by other parties to C to protect the interest. However, there may be countervailing considerations that justify denying any protection for C's interest in some circumstances; and the issue of how the interest should be protected—what sort of rule is appropriate, and who should be subject to a duty—is not settled by the legal recognition of the right. One cannot infer from the fact that C has a right in the protected interest sense that any other party is subject to a duty, and in particular the right is not correlated with a duty.

The two concepts of a right have different roles. The conclusive right or relation is a way of stating the legal rule that applies to certain facts, or the position of a party under a rule in relation to certain facts. Thus it is apt for a pleading or for pronouncing judgment. I take it to be the traditional and standard practical legal usage. A right in the protected interest sense is the basis of a right in the conclusive sense, or, more broadly, the basis of a legal relation having any of the modalities considered in chapter 1. Its role is in analogical reasoning, in the broad sense discussed in chapter 1. Where the law is unsettled and the court seeks to devise a new rule or modify an existing rule by reference to the rationales for existing rules and general underlying principles, these may reflect rights in the protected interest sense. I will generally be concerned with rights or relations in the conclusive sense, as a way of expressing rules, rather than rights as grounds for developing rules by way of analogical reasoning.

In fact the distinction between the two approaches may not in practice be so clear-cut. A rule is liable to be refined or elaborated through analogical reasoning in the light of new considerations, so that no right arises in certain circumstances in which there would have been a right under the original form of the rule. Then the right arising under the original rule, though purporting to be conclusive, turns out to be really a protected interest right, subject to being overridden.[3] More generally, there is a continuum running from a simple legally-recognised interest to a fully conclusive right, according to the degree to which the law has been determined or specified by analogical reasoning in the light of relevant considerations. One might also express this as a matter of how abstract or concrete the right is.[4] Thus one might say, with respect to a particular justificatory category such as contract or tort or private property, that the general moral

---

[3] The way this is expressed implies that this is a matter of finding what the law is rather than changing it, as some would prefer, but nothing turns on this for present purposes.

[4] See R Dworkin, *Taking Rights Seriously* (London, Duckworth, rev edn, 1977) 294–331.

principle underlying the category generates an abstract legal relation, and the body of rules that develops to give effect to it, and takes account of considerations that may be relevant in particular types of situation, generates concrete legal relations.

Primary and Remedial Rights or Relations

In a typical case in private law, D has a primary duty to C, which he breaches and as a result becomes liable to pay compensation to C.[5] From the time of the breach of duty, C has a right to compensation. Compensation is a remedy and the right to compensation is a remedial right, which anticipates and is implemented by the court-ordered remedy of payment of compensation. Although a distinction is often loosely drawn between 'rights and remedies', strictly speaking one should distinguish between the primary right or relation and the remedial right or relation.

There is good reason to distinguish between primary and remedial relations. In connection with a primary right-duty relation, the issues are whether there is a duty and what it requires from D, and the primary relation determines when a claim arises. In connection with the remedial relation, the question is how D's position is affected by his failure to perform the primary duty—how D is required to act to remedy the position. It follows that the remedial duty is enforceable as such, in the sense that the court will order D to perform it. By contrast the primary duty is not itself enforceable as such, although of course it is 'actionable' in the normal sense that a breach of the duty will generate a claim. A 'claim' is the same thing as the remedial right corresponding to the remedial duty.

The distinction between the primary right and the remedial right is sometimes taken to be that the remedial right is substitutionary rather than specific. In the typical case, where D has breached a duty to C, and D is required to pay compensation for the loss, the remedy is substitutionary: the pecuniary compensation is a substitute for the performance of the duty. But sometimes D has breached a duty but he can still perform the original duty or a variant of it and the court

---

[5] I will generally refer to compensation rather than 'damages' because 'damages' is also used to refer to non-compensatory pecuniary remedies such as punitive or exemplary damages or so-called 'restitutionary damages'.

will (let us say) order him to do so by injunction. Here the remedial duty is sometimes described as specific rather than substitutionary (though this really seems apt only for the particular case of an order to transfer property). From the time of breach C has a remedial right and D a remedial duty, which may be in content the same as or similar to the primary right and duty. In this type of case, it is sometimes said that there is no remedial duty, and the court simply enforces the primary duty.[6] But this confuses the primary/remedial distinction with the specific/substitutionary distinction. The issue raised is remedial—whether and how D must respond to his failure to perform the primary duty. One may want to say that the remedial duty incorporates or varies the primary duty,[7] but it is best to maintain this distinction between primary and remedial relations in accordance with the rationale for the distinction given above.

Another misconception is that all claims arise from a breach of duty; but, as discussed in chapter 1, the primary relation can be a right-liability relation, which means that the claim arises from a triggering or causative event that is not a breach of duty by D. The primary relation specifies a contingency, and the claim arises if the contingency materialises, according to the content of the primary relation. As suggested in chapter 1, in contract there is often a primary liability relation, so that a claim for compensation—ie, a remedial right to compensation—can arise from non-performance of the contract even though non-performance is not a breach of duty. This example is discussed below. Also, where C owns property that by way of an invalid transfer comes into the hands of D, C has a claim—a remedial right—to recover the property or its value, arising from the invalid transfer to D, even though this is not a breach of duty by D. This type of case is the subject of chapters 3 and 6.[8] Sometimes in the latter type of case it is said that C's claim is a *primary* right because it does not arise from any pre-existing legal relation, the assumption being that if there was not a primary right-duty relation there was no legal relation at all.[9] But the very point of specifying a primary relation is to identify the legal relation out of which and by virtue of which the claim arises.

---

[6] See eg P Birks, 'Rights, Wrongs and Remedies' (2000) 20 *Oxford Journal of Legal Studies* 1.
[7] And the remedial duty might, as it were, revert to the primary duty once it has been fulfilled.
[8] See esp pp 93–99.
[9] Birks, above n 6.

'Monism' and 'Dualism' and the Dualist Fallacy

What is the relationship between primary and remedial rights? Two rival positions are sometimes distinguished in the literature under the labels of 'monism' and 'dualism'.[10] The monist position is that the appropriate remedy is implicit in the primary right and does not depend on any additional considerations of principle or policy. Once the court has fully determined the content of the primary relation, the determination of the remedy is just a matter of quantification, or of spelling out precisely what is required by the primary relation in particular cases. The dualist position is that the primary relation leaves open what the remedy should be, and a set of remedial rules, or a remedial discretion, drawing on distinct considerations of principle or policy, is necessary to determine what the remedy should be, even once the content of the primary relation has been fully ascertained.

The dualist position seems to be the conventional understanding. It is generally thought that when a claim arises from a wrong committed by D, it remains open what sort of remedy should be available, for example whether it should be an injunction or specific performance, or compensation, or punishment, or disgorgement, or restitution, or some combination.[11] Sometimes this is said to be a matter of discretion, but in any case it seems to depend on a separate body of rules reflecting a different set of considerations from those behind the primary relation. Dualism is sometimes expressed by saying that a justificatory category such as contract is concerned only with primary relations, and does not extend to remedies and remedial relations[12]; or, along the same lines, that certain justificatory categories are purely 'productive' or 'facilitative' (supposedly contract and property), meaning, it would appear, purely a matter of primary relations,[13] to be contrasted with other justificatory categories that are purely 'remedial' or 'protective' (supposedly tort and restitution or unjust enrichment). According to monism, by contrast, a justificatory category necessarily consists of both primary relations and the

---

[10] The terminology (as used in this context) comes from M Tilbury, 'Remedies and the Classification of Obligations' in A Robertson (ed), *The Law of Obligations* (London, UCL Press, 2004). Cf D Friedmann, 'Rights and Remedies' in N Cohen and E McKendrick (eds), *Comparative Remedies for Breach of Contract* (Oxford, Hart Publishing, 2005).

[11] See eg Birks, above n 6; R Craswell, 'Contract Law, Default Rules, and the Philosophy of Promising' (1989) 88 *Michigan Law Review* 489, 518.

[12] eg, SA Smith, *Contract Theory* (Oxford, OUP, 2004) ch 11.

[13] See P Cane, 'Corrective Justice and Correlativity in Private Law' (1996) 16 *Oxford Journal of Legal Studies* 47, at 475–76; D Friedmann, 'The Protection of Entitlements via the Law of Restitution—Expectancies and Privacy' (2005) 121 *Law Quarterly Review* 400.

remedial relations generated by the primary relation in particular circumstances.

In my view, the monist position is closer to the truth. The crucial
point is that the objective of the remedy should be, so far as possible,
to secure to the claimant C the benefit of the primary relation. This
follows simply from the function of the primary and remedial relations. The remedy serves to correct an injustice, and this injustice is
the injustice as defined by the primary relation. It is not open to the
court to seek to remedy an injustice in any broader or unrelated
sense. More particularly, the primary relation represents a resolution
of various conflicting considerations and, in identifying the injustice
to be remedied and the appropriate remedy, the court cannot implicitly contradict the primary relation or reopen an issue implicitly
resolved in the justification of the primary relation. I will describe this
as the monist principle, and I will say that an approach offends against
the principle and commits the 'dualist fallacy' if it seeks to achieve at
the remedial stage an objective other than the fulfilment of the
primary relation, or contradicts some aspect of the primary relation
or reopens a matter resolved in the determination of the primary
relation.[14]

Often the relationship between primary and remedial relations is
considered in connection with the remedy of compensation. But for
reasons that will be apparent there is a simpler case to consider first.
Say D has committed a breach of duty to C, but the circumstances
have changed only marginally, and D could now perform more or
less as before. It is difficult to see why the remedial duty should not
correspond to the primary duty, so that the court should actually
order D to perform. Any argument to the contrary must surely
involve the dualist fallacy. However, there do seem to be a couple of
such contrary arguments that should be considered.

Some Possible Objections to the Monist Principle

Enforcement

One might say, first, that D's primary duty is not the type of duty that
should be *enforced*—that is to say, enforced by compulsion to perform—by the use of the state's power of coercion. For example, it

---

[14] In fact although I have focused on the monist principle, the principle of consistency
which it represents also implies that an abstract primary relation must be consistent with a
concrete primary relation that arises out of it, as for example where an abstract duty of reasonable of care generates a duty to act in a particular way in particular circumstances: see eg
below p 196.

might be argued that, with respect to certain types of duty, although the law recognises a legal duty to perform, it is important that D perform the duty out of a sense that it is the right thing to do or that he ought to fulfil his legal duties, and not under coercion by way of a court order.[15] Or it might be argued that although D has a duty, it would amount to slavery, or would at least be an excessive intrusion on personal liberty, actually to force D to perform it.[16]

But whether it is justified to enforce a legal duty is an aspect of the question whether it should be recognised as a legal duty in the first place.[17] One might recognise that there is a moral duty to do something but then deny that there is any such legal duty, and the reason for such a conclusion would often be that it is not justified to compel performance of the moral duty. The remedy enforces the primary relation, but the primary relation, as a legal relation, is not, or not merely, an authoritative formulation of the moral position, but is designed to be enforced. The distinction between law and morality is not the same as the distinction between the primary legal relation and the remedial relation or remedy. Thus this type of argument cannot account for a failure of the court to compel D to comply with his legal duty.

Similarly, one might argue that a legal duty may be impossible or impracticable to enforce, for example because of problems of monitoring or oversight, and this is why the court does not compel performance. Certainly there appear to be such cases.[18] But, again, one would expect that issues of practicality would be incorporated into the question whether there is a duty in the first place. Generally the law does not recognise as a duty what it cannot enforce.

One might also object that sometimes the primary duty is simply incapable of being performed, generally or by D himself. This is the issue of strict liability duties mentioned in chapter 1. If there are strict liability duties, the monist principle cannot apply to them, unless a remedial duty is also something that the duty bearer cannot be

---

[15] SA Smith, 'Performance, Punishment and the Nature of Contractual Obligation' (1997) 60 *Modern Law Review* 360, and 'The Structure of Unjust Enrichment Law: Is Restitution a Right or a Remedy?' (2003) 36 *Loyola of Los Angeles Law Review* 1037, 1050–51.

[16] D Kimel, *From Promise to Contract* (Oxford, Hart Publishing, 2003) 96; SA Smith, ibid at 400–01.

[17] This might be described as 'remedial incorporation': see DJ Levinson, 'Rights Essentialism and Remedial Equilibration' (1999) 99 *Columbia Law Review* 857, 899.

[18] This is a ground for withholding specific performance in contract, as in *Ryan v Mutual Tontine Westminster Chambers Association* [1893] 1 Ch 116.

ordered to do, which makes no sense at all. The monist principle pre-supposes that D's duty is something that D is capable of doing and can if necessary be ordered to do. I argued in chapter 1 that supposed strict liability duties should be explained in terms of primary liability relations.

One might misunderstand this line of argument to say that D's primary duty is illusory and is really no more than the threat of punishment to coerce D into acting. This would be a version of the reductionist approach to duties mentioned in chapter 1.[19] But this is not the argument. Whether there is a legal duty should depend on whether it is justified to compel D to act in this way, and not just on whether D has a moral duty to do so. This seems quite justified, since the law is in the end concerned with what it is justified to coerce people to do, not just what they ought morally to do. The issue of enforcement should be taken account of in the determination of the primary duty. But when D is coerced to act the justification for doing so is that he has a legal duty to act in this way, and the legal duty exists independently of the legal response to it.[20]

Abstract and Concrete Rights and Relations

There is another argument that might be thought to contradict the monist principle. Sometimes a right is recognised in general terms, but then when it comes to a particular case in which C invokes the right the court weighs up the right against countervailing considerations to see whether in the particular circumstances C has a claim or not. For example, if C argues that by virtue of a general right of privacy he has a right that his employer D not monitor his email, the court may have to weigh up the right against the interests of the employer in monitoring his employees in order to determine whether D has broken his duty to C. Thus it is sometimes said that

---

[19] The 'sanction theory of duty': this theory is misconceived, because, although a legal system is unlikely to function adequately without effective sanctions, whether there is a duty depends on whether there is a valid rule imposing it, not on whether there is a sanction; and indeed, where a sanction is imposed, it is the existence of the primary duty and the fact of its breach that provides the justification for it. See PMS Hacker, 'Sanction Theories of Duty' in AWB Simpson (ed), *Oxford Essays in Jurisprudence: 2nd Series* (Oxford, Clarendon Press, 1973); J Gardner, 'Backwards and Forwards with Tort Law' in J Keim-Campbell, M O'Rourke and D Shier (eds), *Law and Social Justice* (Cambridge, Mass, MIT Press, 2005).

[20] A sanction, in the sense of the sanction theory of duty, is a measure designed to coerce or deter and this is not strictly speaking a remedy. In the strict sense, a remedy is a measure whose function is to protect or fulfil the primary relation in accordance with the monist principle, such as an order to perform the duty or compensation. The distinction between a remedy in the strict sense and a sanction or punishment is considered further below.

rights are abstract and remedies concrete, and the court has to fashion a remedy to suit the circumstances. Typically this arises in connection with a charter or constitutional bill of rights,[21] though the same sort of argument arises with respect to aspects of ordinary private law as well.[22] This appears to contradict the monist principle, but in fact the argument involves a confusion between the two different concepts of right discussed earlier. A 'general right of privacy', and other rights that might appear in a constitutional document have to be understood as protected interest or abstract rights, not conclusive or concrete rights. Thus what is involved here is the exercise, referred to above, of determining or specifying the content of the primary relation, as a conclusive or concrete right, derived from the protected interest or abstract right. It is not a matter of moving from the primary relation to the remedial relation, and so this argument also does not undermine the monist principle.

New Circumstances, the Hardship Argument, and Compensation

The discussion above began with the case where a breach of the primary duty changes the circumstances only marginally. Here the monist principle implies that the remedial duty should correspond to the primary duty. But generally the breach of duty will change the circumstances. Take the case of trespass by D on C's land. This may not alter the circumstances, and a court will generally order D to leave C's land and not to repeat the trespass. But say D has put up a building that intrudes into C's land. The monist principle may appear to require that D should be ordered to demolish the building in order to secure fully to C his right under the primary relation. But in fact the court might well allow the building to stand and require D only to pay compensation to C for the loss of part of his land, on the ground of the excessive burden to D involved in requiring him to remove the building. This is the oppression or hardship rule concerning mandatory injunctions.[23] It might appear that this contradicts the monist principle, on the basis that the failure to award the injunction simply

---

[21] See PH Schuck, *Suing Government* (New Haven, Yale UP, 1983) 26–28. Dualism in constitutional law is criticised as 'rights essentialism' in Levinson, above n 21. But Levinson seems to make the dualist mistake where, in criticising Dworkin's 'abstract theorising', at 927, he associates remedies with practical issues and rights with abstract principles. The contrast is between abstract and concrete rights (and this is not the same as the policy/principle distinction, pace Levinson, 871).

[22] See EL Sherwin, 'An Essay on Private Remedies' (1993) 6 *Canadian Journal of Law & Jurisprudence* 89.

[23] See eg *Shelfer v City of London Electric Lighting Co* [1895] 1 Ch 287.

contradicts the primary right of C to his land and the primary duty of D not to intrude on it. But the hardship rule for mandatory injunctions responds to circumstances that were not taken account of in the determination of the primary relation, by virtue of which the burden of securing the benefit of the primary relation is very much greater than it was originally. Thus in departing from simply protecting the primary relation, the court does not reopen or contradict any issue resolved in the primary relation. This is consistent with the monist principle and not does involve the dualist fallacy.

In the typical case where D's wrong has caused personal injury or damage to property, it is impossible to secure to C the actual benefit of the primary relation, which is to be free of the injury or damage caused by the breach of duty, and the only way to satisfy the interest protected by the duty, insofar as it can be satisfied, is by a payment of compensation. The general rule is of course that the measure of compensation is the amount necessary to put C in the position he would have been in if D had complied with his duty. This reflects the rationale of securing so far as possible the benefit of the primary relation, and is rightly the objective of compensation in accordance with the monist principle.

But the monist principle does not imply that the remedy for a breach of duty is necessarily the full measure of C's loss. The monist principle does not overcome the argument from hardship, which suggests that the full measure of compensation may be so large in some circumstances as to be unfairly burdensome to D.[24] The rule concerning mandatory injunctions provides some support for this, though the established rule is of course that compensation in the full measure is always due. The monist principle cannot be equated with an unqualified principle that a wrongdoer is responsible for remedying his wrong, which is the focus of attention in the corrective justice literature,[25] though the monist principle does appear to have something in common with the idea of corrective justice, as considered further towards the end of the chapter.

Consider by contrast the case of a primary liability relation by virtue of which D bears a responsibility for a loss caused to C by a specified activity. First, there would never be any ground for an injunction against D, because the primary relation does not impose a duty on D. Secondly, with respect to compensation, D would neces-

---

[24] This 'full compensation' issue has been the subject of some debate: see NJ McBride and R Bagshaw, *Tort Law* (London, Longman, 2nd edn, 2005) 41.

[25] Below p 65.

sarily be liable for the full measure of loss. There would be no room for the hardship argument, because the effect of the primary relation is simply to assign the risk of the loss to D rather than C, not to impose a primary duty on D to act in a certain way. Other types of primary liability relation will generate different types of remedy. As mentioned in chapter 1, where a claim arises from an invalid transfer of property, the primary relation is a right-liability relation, and here the remedy is the recovery of property invalidly transferred or its value. This type of claim is discussed in subsequent chapters.[26]

Because of the possibility of applying the hardship argument, the monist principle does not lead to the full monist position as stated above. The hardship argument raises considerations quite separate from anything in issue in the primary relation. However, the monist principle as stated above is an important constraint that captures what is really behind the monist position. It seems to me that, if the dualist fallacy is avoided and the monist principle applied, generally once a court has fully ascertained the content of the primary relation it will have no choice over the type of remedy to award. In any case, a number of examples of the dualist fallacy can be found in the standard analysis of various situations considered in this and subsequent chapters.

Contract Law and the Dualist Fallacy

The Remedial Issue in Contract

In tort law, there does not seem to be any obvious and systematic contradiction of the monist principle. There is generally taken to be a primary duty, but often an injunction to fulfil it is out of the question because the harm is irreversible; where it is feasible, although the award of an injunction is said to be discretionary, it seems that an injunction will generally be awarded except in the hardship case mentioned above.[27]

But ostensibly the law of contract presents a problem for the monist principle, and this is worth discussing at some length in order to illustrate the application and the implications of the monist principle. The usual understanding in contract is that the primary relation is a right-duty relation, viz, a right to performance correlated with a duty to perform. The standard remedy, however, is compensatory

---

[26] Below pp 93–99.
[27] See eg S Deakin, A Johnston and B Markesinis, *Tort Law* (Oxford, OUP, 5th edn, 2003) 847.

damages. A remedy of specific performance is available only exceptionally: the traditional rule is that specific performance is available only when 'damages are inadequate'.[28] Here it seems that the primary relation is a duty of performance, and yet the court refuses to order performance as a matter of course (even if there has been no significant change of circumstances that might raise the issue of hardship).[29]

More particularly, the usual understanding seems to be that D has a primary duty to perform because he promised to perform, and that the law has recognised the promise as generating a legal duty to perform. If the law gives effect to the promise, and the promise has not lapsed in the circumstances in question, the question whether there is a freedom not to perform in those circumstances has already been resolved in favour of C in the formulation of the primary relation. By treating the question whether D should be ordered to perform as a remedial matter left open by the primary relation, and then by generally withholding an order of specific performance, the standard remedial approach in contract effectively reopens this question and then contradicts the primary relation. Thus it commits the dualist fallacy.

One might argue that there is no real inconsistency between the primary and remedial relations because it cannot be of any consequence that specific performance is not ordered if damages are adequate. But this is not so. The question whether 'damages are adequate' is difficult and may involve a judgment of subjective factors. It involves a risk of under-compensation. If C had the right to specific performance he could use this to avoid the risk of under-compensation. Indeed, the right to actual performance entails a right to a premium above mere compensation for loss, since C can insist on such a premium in return for granting a release from the duty of performance.

Furthermore, as mentioned in chapter 1, although the 'damages are inadequate' rule is expressed as a purely remedial rule governing the appropriate remedy for breach of the primary duty (consistently with a dualist understanding), the usual arguments advanced in support of the general non-availability of specific performance do not appear to relate to remedial issues, but to the nature of the primary relation. Typically it is argued that, at the time when D chooses not to perform, if the circumstances are such that C can be adequately protected by compensation, D should be at liberty to take up an alter-

---

[28] See eg *Co-operative Insurance Society Ltd v Argyll Stores (Holdings) Ltd* [1998] AC 1.
[29] Generally the burden of specific performance is the same as the burden of the primary duty.

native more profitable opportunity subject to a liability to pay compensation, on the ground that this is in the public interest because it promotes contracting in general, or maximises the wealth created by contracting, or is otherwise efficient or wealth-maximising, according to the theory of 'efficient breach'; or on the ground that it is unfair to D to constrain him from taking up a more lucrative alternative if he can do so without prejudicing C, maybe because the parties would have agreed to this if they had considered it. These types of argument are directed at the primary relation, not at the issue of what remedial relation should arise from the breach of a primary duty of performance. Thus there is an explicit inconsistency with the primary relation.

Avoiding the Dualist Fallacy in Contract

There are two ways of avoiding the dualist fallacy in contract.[30] One approach is to say that the traditional remedial regime in contract is inadequate and that specific performance should be made generally available. One might suggest in support of this approach that the remedial position is an historical anomaly arising from the inability of the old common law courts to award specific performance, and the reluctance of the courts of equity to intervene to award specific performance except in extreme cases.[31] This approach would bring the remedial relation into line with the standard understanding of the primary relation as a right-duty relation. This has indeed been advocated by some commentators.[32] But this would involve a dramatic change in the practical effect of the law, and the possibility of such a change provokes a hostile response, not just from advocates of the law-and-economics theory of efficient breach, but from lawyers with knowledge of commercial practice who regard the current law as in practice commercially sound.[33]

---

[30] It is sometimes said that there is a conditional duty to perform or pay compensation but this does not disclose the nature of the primary relation at all, and it does not reflect the actual intention of the parties in the standard case: see above pp 26–27.

[31] Below p 122.

[32] See eg D Friedmann, 'The Performance Interest in Contract Damages' (1995) 111 *Law Quarterly Review* 628, where he argues that the law should protect the 'performance interest', which amounts to a right to actual performance, corresponding to a duty to perform; and C Fried, *Contract as Promise* (Cambridge, Mass, Harvard UP, 1981) 17.

[33] See *Attorney-General v Blake* [2001] 1 AC 268, 299, per Lord Hobhouse; *Surrey CC v Bredero Homes* [1993] 1 WLR 1361, 1370, per Steyn LJ; also D Campbell and D Harris, 'In Defence of Breach: a Critique of Restitution and the Performance Interest' (2002) 22 *Legal Studies* 208. Cf P Jaffey, 'Efficiency, Disgorgement, and Reliance in Contract: a Comment on Campbell and Harris' (2002) 22 *Legal Studies* 570.

The alternative solution is to say that the primary relation in contract has been misunderstood and misrepresented. Generally where specific performance is not available the reason is that there was no primary duty to perform, and where specific performance is available it is because there was a primary duty to perform. This means that the 'damages are inadequate' argument and other arguments about the availability of specific performance are really arguments about the content of the primary relation, not about what sort of remedy is appropriate for a breach of duty.

The problem with this is that it is generally assumed, in contract law as elsewhere, that the primary relation is a right–duty relation and that the claim arises from a wrong or breach of duty, and indeed that without a wrong there is no basis for any claim for compensation. However, as discussed in chapter 1, a claim can be based on a primary liability relation, so that it does not arise from the breach of a duty to perform. There may appear to be a problem in reconciling this with the fact that the basis of the primary relation is the agreement between the parties. As mentioned above, an agreement is generally understood to be an exchange of promises, and a promise to do something is the assumption of a duty to do it. If an agreement is given legal effect as a contract, it appears that this must involve recognising the duties generated by the promises as legal duties to perform as specified in the agreement.[34]

The Contractual Reliance Explanation

One way of explaining how the primary relation can be a right-liability relation is the idea that that contract law protects only contractual reliance on the agreement, that is to say it protects a contracting party in respect of his reliance on the assumption that the other party will perform as specified in the contract. This means that a contracting party does not necessarily have a duty to perform, or act wrongfully by not performing; in general he incurs only a liability to compensate the other party for reliance loss incurred as a result of non-performance, by virtue of a primary liability relation. However, if by virtue of the performance specified and the prevailing circumstances, it happens that C cannot be satisfactorily protected in respect of his reliance except by way of actual performance by D, then D incurs a primary duty to perform, which will be enforced by an order

---

[34] For other ways of explaining the apparent deficiency in contractual remedies, see eg SA Smith, 'Performance, Punishment and the Nature of Contractual Obligation' [1997] *Modern Law Review* 360; Kimel, above n 16, at 103.

of specific performance—ie, where 'damages are inadequate'. For example, whereas an ordinary supply contract will generate a primary liability relation, if D has agreed to supply a product to C and C has adapted his business accordingly, so that he cannot without adequate notice obtain alternative supplies elsewhere, D will have a duty to continue to supply C for a reasonable notice period. Or where D has purchased a business from C and accepted a term that he should pay a pension to a third party out of the profits of the business, D will have a duty to pay the pension, since this is the only practicable way to protect C's interest under the contract.[35] On this understanding, contrary to appearances, the 'damages are inadequate test' is indeed concerned with the content of the primary relation—whether it is a primary liability or a primary duty relation—not with what remedy or remedial relation arises from a breach of duty.

This contractual reliance analysis is not credible without some explanation of why the law should confine itself to protecting contractual reliance. If contract law enforces agreements, understood as an exchange of promises, why is it that the agreement is not given effect by the recognition of a duty to perform the promise?[36] There are a number of different versions of the reliance theory of contract.[37] One approach is based on a principle of political morality, the harm principle, which holds, on one version, that the law should be confined to protecting people against harm, and should not go further and enforce duties to confer benefits on others.[38] The implication is that, although contract claims are based on an agreement consisting of an exchange of promises of performance, and the parties incur moral duties to perform their promises, the law should not require them to confer the promised benefits on the other party, but only protect the other party in respect of harm resulting from reliance on the agreement.

Sometimes the reliance theory of contract is equated with the 'death of contract' or 'contract as tort' theory, which, as mentioned

---

[35] *Sky Petroleum v VIP Petroleum* [1974] 1 WLR 576; *Bewick v Beswick* [1968] AC 58. See further P Jaffey, 'Disgorgement and "Licence Fee Damages" in Contract' (2004) 20 *Journal of Contract Law* 57. The same principle is behind disgorgement, below pp 59–61.

[36] This has been described as the 'insuperable difficulty' with reliance theories: RE Barnett 'A Consent Theory of Contract' (1986) 86 *Columbia Law Review* 269, 274; Craswell, above n 11, at 498–501.

[37] LL Fuller and WR Perdue, 'The Reliance Interest in Contract Damages' (1936) 46 *Yale Law Journal* 52 and 373, emphasised the importance of contractual protection for reliance, but it was not an argument for a reliance theory because the argument was not that the protection of reliance was the function or essence or a general limitation of contract.

[38] J Raz, 'Promises in Morality and Law' (1982) 95 *Harvard Law Review* 916.

in chapter 1, holds that so-called contract claims are actually not based on an agreement at all.[39] They are actually either tort claims arising from the harm caused to C through reliance induced by D, or unjust enrichment or restitution claims arising from the receipt of a benefit.[40] The primary relation is not directly generated by the principle that agreements should be performed. One reason why this approach appeared attractive was the apparent inadequacy of the remedial regime if a contract was understood to be based on an agreement consisting of an exchange of promises of performance.[41]

Elsewhere I have suggested another version of the reliance theory, according to which an agreement should not be understood as an exchange of promises, at least in the usual sense, but as the mutual acceptance of responsibility for reliance. An agreement should be interpreted as meaning: 'We will proceed on the assumption that I will do X and you will do Y, and each of us assumes responsibility for the reliance of the other party on this assumption'.[42] Unlike the death of contract theory, this approach gives the agreement a genuine normative effect: the parties each exercise a normative power to generate the contractual primary relation, which allocates risk with respect to the failure of the parties to conform to the agreed performance. In this sense it is a type of promissory approach. However, neither party incurs a duty to perform, unless actual performance is necessary to avoid uncompensatable loss to the other; only where this is the case does the responsibility for reliance generate a primary right–duty relation. According to the 'efficient breach' theory, contracting parties should generally be free not to perform, and if this is consistent with the agreement actually made between the parties, as the economic approach surely requires, the implication must be that it is efficient for parties to make agreements in this reliance form, involving a primary right–liability relation, rather than by way of promises in the ordinary sense that necessarily generate duties of performance.[43]

---

[39] As mentioned in ch 1, above p 14, PS Atiyah, *The Rise and Fall of Freedom of Contract* (Oxford, Clarendon Press, OUP, 1979) and G Gilmore, *The Death of Contract* (Ohio, Ohio State University Press, 1974). Atiyah later offered a theory of agreement as 'conclusive admissions', which sought to give normative effect to agreements without generating a duty of performance: PS Atiyah, *Promises, Morals and the Law* (Oxford, Clarendon Press, OUP 1981) 184ff. See P Jaffey, *The Nature and Scope of Restitution* (Oxford, Hart Publishing, 2000) 132–33.

[40] Or 'unjust enrichment' claims based on the receipt of a benefit.

[41] Atiyah, *The Rise and Fall of Freedom of* Contract, above n 39, at 764ff; Gilmore, above n 39, at 87.

[42] This approach is set out in Jaffey, above n 39, ch 2; P Jaffey, 'A New Version of the Reliance Theory' (1998) 49 *Northern Ireland Legal Quarterly* 107.

[43] See further Jaffey, above n 39, at 397–400.

The reliance approach appears to account for another recognised claim in contract that cannot be explained in terms of a right-duty primary relation consistently with the monist principle. Sometimes C has a claim to recover a payment made under the contract in advance of performance when D has failed to perform.[44] This claim cannot be understood to arise from a primary duty of performance, because it does not serve to secure to C the benefit of the primary relation: the remedy does not represent the value to C of the performance of the duty owed to him. Its effect is to restore C to the position he was in before he made the payment, and this may not be the position he would have been in if the contractual duty had been performed. To explain the claim in terms of a primary right-duty relation would be to commit the dualist fallacy. The claim must arise from a primary right-liability relation, and again it can be explained in terms of the protection of contractual reliance. In making the payment C has relied on the assumption that D will perform, and the claim protects C's reliance. The difficulty in accounting for this claim as a claim arising from a breach by D of a duty to perform the contract presumably explains why it has often been regarded as a non-contractual claim, in particular an unjust enrichment claim.[45]

A common objection to a reliance approach in contract is that the standard measure of compensation is the expectation measure, which is the amount necessary to put C in the position he would have been in if the contract had been performed, and this might appear to be justifiable only on the basis that D had a duty to perform. If contract law only protects reliance, then C should be limited to the lesser reliance measure. The conventional answer to this objection is that the expectation measure is an appropriate proxy measure of C's reliance loss, taking account of C's opportunity cost, though it may be true that the reliance theory cannot account for the availability of the expectation measure in all possible cases.[46]

---

[44] The traditional position is that the claim is available only on a 'complete failure of consideration', though this is under challenge: below p 213.

[45] The same argument applies to the claim for a quantum meruit, ie a claim for reasonable payment for work done in part performance of the contract. The point is particularly clear in the case of frustration, which clearly does not involve a breach of duty by D: below p 214.

[46] The opportunity cost argument was advanced by Fuller and Perdue, above n 37. It works well in the case of a competitive market; in other cases it may be justifiable because of the difficulty of proving actual reliance loss. There are cases where C recovers explicitly for expenditure incurred in reliance on the contract, though the reliance measure here is conventionally taken to be a proxy for the expectation measure, where the expectation measure is difficult to prove. *Anglia Television v Reed* [1972] 1 QB 60. The reliance loss should also be capped under the reliance theory to reflect the contractual allocation of risk: see

Two Measures of Damages and the Dualist Fallacy

Another example of the dualist fallacy is provided by Stapleton.[47] Stapleton rejects the monist approach in favour of dualism (though not using these terms). She denies that the issue of the measure of compensation should be 'packed into the definition of the entitlement' (ie the primary relation). The 'measure of damages element' must be separated from 'the definition of the remaining content of that obligation'.[48] More particularly, she distinguishes between two measures of compensation for a breach of duty: the 'normal expectancies' measure and the 'entitled result' measure. The appropriate measure is understood to be a remedial question that is independent of the content of the primary duty.

But consider Stapleton's illustration of the distinction between the two measures. D is employed by C to value a picture. He incompetently values the picture at £100 when its actual value is £25. The picture is available for £60 and C buys it. The 'normal expectancies' measure is based on what would have happened if the valuation had been competently done (and so would have been, we presume, accurate), and as a result the picture was not bought. C would not have spent £60 on buying the picture and would not have ended up as the owner of a picture worth £25. The measure of compensation is £60 − £25 = £35. The 'entitled result' measure is based on what the position would have been if the picture had actually been worth the amount at which it was valued by D. C would have had a picture worth £100, and the measure of compensation is the difference between this value and the actual value of the picture C is left with: £100 − £25 = £75. Stapleton takes these to be different possible measures of compensation for the wrong committed by D. But in fact, the different measures follow from different primary relations, and once the primary relation is determined the measure follows directly.

If the primary relation is the duty to make a careful valuation, the measure of loss is arrived at in the normal way by comparing C's actual position with the position he would have been in if this duty had been performed, ie the 'normal expectancies' measure. If the

Jaffey, above n 39, at 46. Otherwise reliance damages would be inconsistent with the monist principle.

[47] J Stapleton, 'The Normal Expectancies Measure in Tort Damages' (1997) 113 *Law Quarterly Review* 257.

[48] Ibid, 260.

primary relation is a duty to ensure that the picture is worth what it is valued at, the measure of loss depends on C's actual position compared with the position he would have been in if the picture had been worth the valuation, ie the 'entitled result' measure. There is no contravention of the monist principle, once the primary relation is understood.

There is a complication to add, though it does not affect the main point concerning the monist principle and the dualist fallacy. Since the primary relations in this example are contractual, according to the argument above they are likely to be right-liability relations rather than right-duty relations. In particular, in connection with the supposed duty to ensure that the picture is worth what it is valued at, if there were such a duty it would be a strict liability duty.[49] It is impossible for D to perform this duty: he is not capable of procuring that the picture actually has the value that he ascribed to it. As I suggested in chapter 1, a supposed strict liability duty should generally be understood as a primary liability. Even if contractual primary relations are in general right-duty relations, a provision of this sort—a warranty—should be understood to give rise to a primary liability relation, according to which the warrantor accepts the risk that the value is less than the amount warranted.

Contract law is not the principal subject of this book, though it is relevant to a number of issues that arise in subsequent chapters. In particular it is relevant to the discussion of fiduciary relationships in connection with the trust in chapter 5. More generally, the discussion of contract illustrates the monist principle and its implications. It shows that it is mistaken, though it may be commonplace, to consider primary and remedial relations in isolation from each other. In requiring consistency between the two relations, the monist principle imposes a discipline that can require reassessment of either or both relations, including the theoretical basis of the primary relation. This point is important in other areas of private law, including property.

Discretionary Remedialism

Sometimes the court is said to have a discretion. It is notoriously difficult to say precisely what this means. It is clear that there is no discretion when a rule can be applied mechanically without evaluative judgment. But this is very often not the case, because to formulate a rule with the necessary degree of precision and comprehensiveness,

---

[49] Stapleton describes it as a 'strict obligation': ibid.

involving anticipating all possible contingencies, is often either impossible or undesirable. This is the problem of 'incomplete speci-fication'. Sometimes, faced with an incompletely specified rule, a court will refine the rule by way of analogical reasoning to take account of the novel circumstances. But often the rule will be left incompletely specified, so that its application involves issues of eval-uative judgment that are left tacit and treated as matters of fact. For example, a court might treat the issue of whether someone is an 'employee' as simply a question of fact, though it may involve eval-uative issues and competing interests.[50] However, this is not gener-ally regarded as an exercise of discretion.

By contrast, it seems that the judge is understood to have a discre-tion where, say, he has to decide what claim is in the circumstances fair and just, or what the best interests of the child require in all the circumstances, or how to divide up the wealth of a married couple on divorce.[51] There is room for argument as to whether there is really a difference of kind or only of degree between the two types of case, or, if they are different in kind, what the real distinction is between them. It might be said that in the former cases there is a 'weak' dis-cretion and in the latter cases a 'strong' discretion.[52] It seems that a dis-tinction of some sort is generally presupposed in private law, though maybe only one of degree, because it seems to be generally thought that in private law claims do not or should not arise as a matter of judi-cial discretion, even though some degree of evaluative judgment is clearly sometimes involved in the application of rules. I will distin-guish for convenience between rules and discretion, though this is not really a satisfactory way of expressing the distinction.[53]

Sometimes a court is said to have a remedial discretion. This implies that the primary relation is a matter of rules, but the remedy or remedial relation is discretionary. This is the traditional under-standing of the remedial jurisdiction of equity. As discussed below in chapter 4, traditionally it has been said that, whereas the common law is rule-based, equity tends to give judges a discretion, and remedies provide the best example of this. It is generally said that claims in pri-

---

[50] Cf above p 2, n 3.

[51] The last case is considered briefly below p 252.

[52] Dworkin, above n 4, at 31–39. According to Dworkin, in the case of a weak discre-tion there is a binding legal standard that the judge must use his judgment in applying, whereas in the case of a strong discretion the judge has to first formulate the standard he is to apply; and in the case of a weak discretion one party has a right to a decision in his favour, whereas in the case of a strong discretion neither party can be said to have such a right.

[53] Since the discretion is conferred by a rule.

vate law, which are generally a matter of common law, do not arise as a matter of discretion, but that with respect to remedies originally developed in the law of equity, including injunctions and specific performance, the remedy is discretionary. More recently, it has been suggested that in some circumstances there is or ought to be a discretion to impose a 'remedial constructive trust', another equitable device.[54] Some commentators defend discretionary remedialism on the basis that it provides a desirable flexibility,[55] though others object to it on the ground that it involves excessive uncertainty. Nowadays it is accepted that there are 'settled principles' governing the award of discretionary remedies, which are apparently understood to govern the exercise of the discretion without eliminating it.[56]

In any case, discretionary remedialism clearly offends against the monist principle. To have a rule-based primary relation and a discretionary remedy is an example of the dualist fallacy: it would be inconsistent to say, for example, that there is a primary duty to perform a contract but a remedial discretion whether to award specific performance to enforce the duty. There may be room for argument about whether a test of adequacy of damages is discretionary or not,[57] but, whether it is or not, on the reliance approach above the issue of adequacy relates to the primary relation, and the remedial relation follows from the primary relation in accordance with the monist principle.

The objection is made to discretionary remedialism in connection with the so-called 'remedial constructive trust' that it involves a discretion whether to recognise and enforce C's property rights by an order to return property to him, which amounts to a discretion to uphold or cancel established property rights. As considered further in chapter 6, this is actually just to say that, by failing to provide a remedy that protects and fulfils the primary right, the law offends against the monist principle. By analogy with the property case, it has been argued that a discretion to award specific performance in contract amounts to a discretion to cancel an accrued right.[58] Again the issue

---

[54] Below p 177.

[55] S Evans, 'Defending Discretionary Remedialism' (2001) 23 *Sydney Law Review* 463; cf DM Jensen 'The Rights and Wrongs of Discretionary Remedialism' [2003] *Singapore Journal of Legal Studies* 178.

[56] See eg *Cooperative Insurance v Argyll* [1998] AC 1, 9, per Lord Hoffman.

[57] 'Adequacy of damages' is to some degree evaluative—it involves weighing the risk of undercompensating C against the risk of overburdening D—but it is arguable whether one would describe it as discretionary.

[58] eg, D Friedmann, 'The Efficient Breach Fallacy' (1989) 18 *Journal of Legal Studies* 1; SM Waddams, 'Restitution as Part of Contract Law' in A Burrows (ed), *Essays on the Law of Restitution* (Oxford, Clarendon Press, 1991) 208–09.

is really whether the monist principle is respected. But here, as discussed above, if the primary relation is a primary liability relation, the non-availability of specific performance is not inconsistent with the primary relation and does not involve cancelling or curtailing C's primary right.

Some commentators reject discretionary remedialism on the ground that it involves the cancellation of accrued rights, but nevertheless take a dualist position in general. For example, Birks rejects discretionary remedialism partly on this ground, but he also considers that there are substantive remedial issues that go beyond identifying and implementing the primary relation (which appear not be confined to the issue of hardship in the sense discussed above).[59] But this position also conflicts with the monist principle and is mistaken according to the argument above.

'Freestanding' Remedies

Above I have assumed that C has a primary right, and the issue has been whether and to what extent the primary right determines the remedial right or remedy. Curiously it has sometimes been suggested that the courts may be able to award a remedy in the absence of any primary right at all—what might be called a 'freestanding' remedy. It is said that although in general an injunction serves to protect C's primary right, sometimes a court may award an injunction though it does not protect any right of C's, for example in order to prevent D from behaving unconscionably towards C.[60] It is difficult even to make sense of this, and it is certainly at odds with the approach taken above. One would surely want to say that C has a primary right that D should not behave in this unconscionable way towards him, which the injunction enforces. If the court considers an injunction appropriate, why does it not formulate the position in terms of a primary relation? The answer seems to be that the power to award an injunction is conventionally a matter of equity, and generally where equity grants an injunction it is in respect of a primary right at common law, so that the equitable law concerning the injunction has developed as a purely remedial body of law detached from primary rights. But, however the position is expressed, in reality if a remedy is awarded there must be a primary right that it protects, in accordance with the

---

[59] P Birks, above n 6.

[60] *South Carolina Insurance Co v Assurantie Maatschappij de Zeven Provincien NV* [1987] AC 24. PH Pettit, *Equity and the Law of Trusts* (Oxford, OUP, 10th edn, 2006) 569.

monist principle. The idea of freestanding remedies, or remedies dissociated from a primary right, is a version of the dualist fallacy.

Sometimes, as I have mentioned already, it is said that where a claim arises from an event that is clearly not a breach of duty—where, on my approach, it is a primary liability claim—the claim is a primary right.[61] This is said, for example, in the case where there is an invalid transfer of C's property to D, and C has a claim against D arising from D's receipt, which is not a breach of duty.[62] This comes from the failure to recognise the primary liability relation. It also amounts to a freestanding remedy, a remedy arising out of a vacuum, and it illustrates the dualist fallacy.

NON-REMEDIAL RESPONSES: PUNISHMENT AND DISGORGEMENT

Remedies and Non-remedial Responses

'Remedy' has been used above in a strict sense, to refer to a measure whose purpose is to correct the injustice done to the claimant C, meaning injustice in terms of the primary relation (the monist principle). Thus where the primary relation is a duty owed by D to C, the injustice is the breach of duty to C (and its consequences), and the remedy is an injunction to procure the fulfilment of the duty, or pecuniary compensation that puts C in the position he would have been in if the duty had been performed. The remedy or remedial relation serves to protect or fulfil the primary relation. Where the primary relation is a right-liability relation, the injustice is not a wrong or its consequences, but again it is defined by the primary relation, and the remedial relation protects and fulfils the primary relation.

'Remedy' is sometimes used more loosely to refer to any measure dispensed by a court in legal proceedings, including measures that do not serve to protect or fulfil the primary relation, or to do justice to C in this sense. An example is punishment, which in civil proceedings takes the form of punitive or exemplary damages. Punishment is sometimes loosely understood to refer to any response to a wrong that causes loss or harm to D. This encompasses remedies in the strict sense; and indeed sometimes a remedy is described as punitive simply because of the excessive burden it places on D.[63] But in fact not

---

[61] Above n 6.

[62] Below p 93.

[63] One might say that a remedy is punitive when it is excessive on the ground of hardship in the sense considered above.

all deliberately caused harm constitutes punishment; punishment is harm caused to D because he has committed a wrong, for the reason that he ought to suffer because of his wrongdoing. Some would say that the suffering is justified as a deterrent, as a means of promoting compliance with duties for the benefit of the public, and others that it is intrinsically right that D should suffer for his wrongdoing: these are the utilitarian and retributivist conceptions of punishment. In any case, the purpose is not to protect or fulfil the primary relation. One might say that punishment is defendant-oriented or public-interest-oriented rather than claimant-oriented. A remedy in the strict sense is not punitive (however burdensome to D), because its rationale is to satisfy C's primary right, not to cause D to suffer, even if the award of remedies also has a deterrent effect on potential wrongdoers.

Another non-remedial response is disgorgement. 'Disgorgement' is sometimes used to refer to any measure by which D gives up something he has received, and no doubt this is a reasonable usage as a matter of ordinary English. But I will use it more narrowly to refer to a measure by which D gives up a benefit received as a result of a wrong, specifically on the ground that he should not be permitted to keep the benefits of wrongdoing.[64] Disgorgement in this sense is not a remedy in the strict sense because its rationale is not to fulfil or protect C's primary right. By contrast, take the case where C's claim is to recover property or wealth invalidly transferred to D, or equivalent value.[65] This is not a claim for disgorgement because, although the effect is to remove a benefit from D, the rationale is to satisfy C's primary right, not to prevent D from profiting through a wrong. (D may or may not have committed a wrong and this is not relevant to the claim.) This can be described as restitution, and it is a remedy in the strict sense.[66] Disgorgement in the strict sense is really a component of punishment. It amounts to what is really the threshold punishment, since due punishment should presumably always entail, at a minimum, removing the benefit of wrongdoing, and disgorgement secures this for the same defendant-oriented or public-interest-oriented reason as punishment. Thus it is apt to describe disgorgement as 'quasi-punitive'. From the retributivist standpoint, disgorgement gives effect to the principle that profiting through a wrong is intrinsically bad, and from the utilitarian standpoint it

[64] Disgorgement is not a legal term of art and is possibly not a felicitous expression, but there is no established expression with this meaning.

[65] Considered in chs 3 and 6.

[66] As to the usage of 'restitution', see below p 216.

removes the incentive for wrongdoing by removing the profits of wrongdoing.

Punishment in the form of punitive or exemplary damages is available in limited circumstances in civil proceedings, though where it is allowed it is often considered to be anomalous.[67] At common law, disgorgement is not explicitly awarded, though where punitive or exemplary damages are awarded on the 'profit motive' ground, where the defendant committed the wrong with a view to pecuniary profit,[68] it seems clear that the rationale is principally to remove the profits of wrongdoing.[69] However, equity has been prepared to impose disgorgement through an account of profits or constructive trust, relying on the principle that a wrongdoer should not profit through his wrong. Thus disgorgement is generally available for wrongs that developed in equity, including breach of trust and fiduciary duty, breach of confidence, and breaches of intellectual property rights.[70]

It might appear that according to the monist principle the non-remedial responses of disgorgement and punishment should never be available in private law. Some commentators do indeed insist that this is the correct position.[71] Conversely, other writers have pointed to the fact that disgorgement and punishment are or ought to be available in support of a dualist approach to remedies.[72] In my view, neither of these positions is correct. The issue has to be considered in connection with the function of civil proceedings. I will come back to this below.

Punishment and Disgorgement in Contract

First, there is a point to be made in connection with primary right-liability relations. A pre-condition for imposing punishment or disgorgement is, of course, that the defendant must have committed

---

[67] *Rookes v Barnard* [1964] AC 1129; *Cassell v Broome* [1972] 1 All ER 801.

[68] *Rookes v Barnard* [1964] AC 1129, 1226 per Lord Devlin.

[69] Unfortunately the position at common law is confused by the misconception that claims arising from 'waiver of tort' and claims for payment for the unauthorised use of property involve disgorgement, or at least that they are all examples of 'restitution for wrongs': see below p 235.

[70] *Attorney-General for Hong Kong v Reid* [1994] 1 AC 324; *Attorney-General v Guardian Newspapers (no 2) (Spycatcher)* [1990] 1 AC 109.

[71] eg, A Beever, 'The Structure of Aggravated and Exemplary Damages' (2003) 23 *Oxford Journal of Legal Studies* 87; EJ Weinrib, 'Punishment and Disgorgement as Contract Remedies' (2003) 78 *Chicago-Kent Law Review* 55, 77 and 'Restitutionary Damages as Corrective Justice' (1999) 1 *Theoretical Inquiries in the Law* 1.

[72] Tilbury, above n 10, at 19.

a wrong. In other words, the primary relation must be a right-duty relation, not a right-liability relation.[73] The point can be illustrated again by reference to contract law, where the availability of disgorgement has been a matter of controversy in recent years following the decision of the House of Lords in *Attorney-General v Blake*.[74]

Traditionally disgorgement has not been available in contract law. One might put this down to a general aversion to disgorgement in private law, at least at common law, but it appears to be accepted that even if disgorgement and punishment can be justified in other areas, there is a particular objection to it in contract law. Even in jurisdictions where punishment and disgorgement are available in tort, it seems that they have generally been excluded from contract.[75] In *Blake* it was accepted that disgorgement is appropriate in contract in limited circumstances, though there remains some controversy over what these are. The position for disgorgement can be explained in the same way as the rule for specific performance discussed above: in general non-performance of a contract is not wrongful, because generally the primary relation in contract is a right-liability relation. But sometimes a contractor incurs a duty of performance, and so acts wrongfully by not performing. In such cases, as discussed above, the contractor should be ordered to perform; but, if this is no longer possible, he should be subject to disgorgement if he has profited through the breach of contract, and possibly outright punishment.

According to the reliance theory, this is the case where it is only through actual performance of the contract, and not through a payment of compensation, that the other party can be protected in respect of his reliance on the contract. Some examples were mentioned above in connection with specific performance.[76] Say that, as in *Blake* itself, C entrusts D with confidential information in connection with D's performance of the contract. D has a duty to keep the information confidential, because clearly only the actual maintenance of confidentiality can protect C's reliance. Furthermore, once the information has been disclosed, an order of specific performance cannot now restore its confidentiality. But D should not be allowed to retain any profit he has made through a wrongful disclosure.

---

[73] Save that there could be a breach of a remedial duty to satisfy a claim arising from a primary liability claim.

[74] [2001] 1 AC 268.

[75] eg US law: see eg *Oki America v Microtech Intern* 872 F.2d 312 (9th Cir 1989). Various explanations of this have been suggested, as discussed in Jaffey, above n 39, at 394–400.

[76] See above, n 35.

Similarly, to take an example mentioned above, if D has agreed to provide supplies of a product to C for his business, and C adapts his business so as to become dependent on supplies from D, at least without adequate notice to enable C to make other arrangements,[77] D would act wrongfully if he withheld supplies without giving adequate notice. If C cannot get an injunction in time to compel D to resume supplies, or is for some reason denied one, D should at least be forced to disgorge any profit he has made as a result. On this understanding, the 'damages are inadequate' test is in principle applicable to disgorgement as well as specific performance, and there is some support for this in the decision in *Blake*.[78]

In connection with specific performance, as discussed above the 'damages are inadequate' test is generally understood as a test to determine whether specific performance is available as a remedy for D's breach of duty, rather than a test to determine whether there is a primary duty or a primary liability. But, with respect to disgorgement, it is clear that if the 'damages are inadequate' test applies it cannot be concerned with what remedy is appropriate as a response to a breach of duty. Disgorgement is not a remedy at all, and it cannot be explained as an alternative remedy where compensation is inadequate. The test must be concerned with whether or not D had a duty to perform and so acted wrongfully by not performing. If it is the same test that applies in connection with specific performance, this confirms the argument above that in connection with specific performance the test is concerned with the content of the primary relation.

Civil Proceedings and Private Law

To return to the issue of the general availability of punishment (including disgorgement) in civil proceedings, the important point is that the structure of the legal proceedings that is appropriate for dispensing remedies is different from the structure of proceedings that is appropriate for the imposition of punishment. With respect to a claim for a remedy, the proceedings should be essentially even-handed as between C and D with respect to procedural and evidential rules. This is because the injustice inflicted on C if the claim is mistakenly denied is comparable to the injustice inflicted on D if the claim is mistakenly upheld. By contrast, with respect to punishment the proceedings should be biased in favour of avoiding the mistaken

---

[77] *Freeman & Mills v Belcher* 900 P 2d 669 (Cal 1995). See further Jaffey, above n 35.
[78] [2000] 3 WLR 625, 639 per Lord Nicholls.

infliction of punishment—they should give special safeguards to the defendant. Furthermore, the award of a remedy is something that it is reasonable for the claimant C to bargain over or waive, and so one would expect the proceedings to be in his control, whereas with respect to punishment the proceedings should be in the control of officers acting in the public interest in the name of the state. Also, the proceeds of disgorgement or punishment, if it takes a pecuniary form, should in principle go to the state rather than the victim of the wrong, since they are necessarily a windfall to the victim, because they go beyond what is necessary to satisfy his primary right. Thus one can see that the basis of the division between civil and criminal proceedings is that different forms of legal proceedings are apt for administering the different types of response. Civil proceedings are essentially concerned with providing remedies and criminal proceedings with imposing punishment. Consequently, the imposition of punishment or disgorgement in civil proceedings runs the risk that the defendant will not receive the appropriate procedural protection. This is the 'procedural objection' to dispensing punishment or disgorgement in civil proceedings.

One might object that remedies (in the strict sense) in civil proceedings have a deterrent function. Indeed it may be considered unnecessary to recognise a wrong as a crime for the very reason that damages in civil proceedings in respect of that wrong are generally sufficient to act as a deterrent, so that in a sense deterrence is a recognised aspect of civil justice. But it is still the case that the measure of damages awarded is entirely determined by its function as a remedy and the nature of the proceedings reflects this function.

The basic structure of civil and criminal proceedings can be explained in terms of this analysis, but in practice it is difficult to maintain a strict segregation between remedy and punishment. The problem is the need also to ensure what might be called the 'full legal response' to a wrong. The full legal response means both a remedy in accordance with the monist principle, and also disgorgement and punishment insofar as they are appropriate. There are practical, institutional difficulties in combining strict segregation with the full legal response.[79]

Some wrongs recognised in the civil law are also crimes, which means that in principle the civil court can administer the remedy and

---

[79] See further Jaffey, above n 39, at 376–83.

the criminal court can impose a punishment and disgorgement,[80] and the full legal response can be achieved consistently with maintaining strict segregation. But some civil wrongs are not recognised as crimes, and others may not be properly enforced as crimes. Here if the defendant has made a profit from his wrong, or he deserves to be punished for it, the full legal response will not be achieved if punishment and disgorgement are excluded from civil proceedings. One might say that this means simply that these wrongs should also be recognised as crimes so that the full legal response can be achieved through criminal proceedings. For some wrongs, however, this may be a very costly way of dealing with an occasional problem, and it may also attach an excessive stigma to that type of wrong in general. In such cases, there is much to be said for imposing punishment or disgorgement through civil proceedings,[81] particularly disgorgement since it is intrinsically limited in severity, provided that it is possible to provide adequate procedural and evidential safeguards.[82]

English law reflects this tension between maintaining strict segregation and securing the full legal response. Punishment is sometimes imposed through punitive or exemplary damages, but as mentioned above it is often considered anomalous or objectionable in civil proceedings,[83] generally on the basis of the procedural objection that there are insufficient safeguards for D, and also because C should not get a windfall.[84] The same applies to disgorgement at common law, though in equity it is available as a matter of course, and the procedural objection seems not to have been recognised or even acknowledged.[85]

A Misconceived Argument against Non-remedial Responses in Private Law

The argument above should be distinguished from a more uncompromising argument for the exclusion of non-remedial responses from private law. It is sometimes said that the very structure of private law precludes punishment and disgorgement.[86] This could be

---

[80] Punishment by way of a pecuniary penalty or fine should in principle be measured to exceed any measurable benefit to the offender: see M Wasik, 'The Hodgson Committee Report on the Profits of Crime and their Recovery' [1984] *Criminal Law Review* 708.

[81] Where punishment by way of a fine or pecuniary penalty is adequate.

[82] It follows that on this approach the appropriate scope of the criminal justice system involves certain practical empirical questions, as noted by Beever, above n 71, at 104.

[83] See further Jaffey, above n 39, at 374.

[84] There is now a statutory confiscation jurisdiction under the Criminal Justice Act 1988.

[85] As discussed in ch 4.

[86] Beever, above n 71, at 106–10; Weinrib, 'Punishment and Disgorgement as Contract Remedies' and 'Restitutionary Damages as Corrective Justice', above n 71.

understood to reflect the procedural argument above, but in fact the argument goes further. It is said that it is a mistake to think that punishment or disgorgement can ever be justified for breach of a duty in private law quite apart from procedural issues. The argument is that D's duty is owed to C, and consequently all that C is entitled to is the benefit of the duty owed to him. Since punishment and disgorgement do not serve to fulfil or protect the primary duty they should not be available as a response to the breach of a duty in private law.

This is a misapplication of the monist principle above. The monist principle holds that a remedy should give effect to the primary relation. A measure that purports to be a remedy but is not consistent with the monist principle is illegitimate. But the monist principle does not preclude a response that does not purport to be a remedy and is justifiable on a different basis. Whether such a response is appropriate does not depend on whether it protects and fulfils the primary relation since this is not its function. Thus the monist principle does not preclude a non-remedial response of punishment or disgorgement, and where punishment or disgorgement is recognised to be available, this is not contrary to the monist principle and it does not support a dualist approach to remedies.[87]

The argument for the complete exclusion of punishment and disgorgement from private law appears to have been influenced by the conflation of two quite different distinctions. The first distinction is between remedies and punishment, which are respectively, as discussed above, the private and public interest responses to a wrong. The second distinction is between private and public wrongs. A private wrong is the breach of a duty owed by one individual to another in private law, for example in contract or tort, and a public wrong is the breach of public duty, owed to the community or public at large, personified by the state, for example a duty to pay tax, or to comply with planning rules. If the public interest response of punishment is equated with public wrongs, and the private interest response of a remedy with private wrongs, the implication is indeed that there can be no punishment in private law. And in fact, ever since Blackstone, it has often been said that criminal law is about public wrongs and civil law about private wrongs.[88]

---

[87] Cf Tilbury, above n 10.

[88] This traditional view associated originally with Blackstone is found in *Halsbury's Laws*: see M Jefferson, *Criminal Law* (London, Longman, 7th edn, 2006) 12–13.

But, in the case of a public wrong, if punishment is justified it is not because the duty was owed to the community; it is because the wrong should attract punishment, in the public interest, according to the applicable principles of deterrence or retribution. The public interest equally requires punishment for a private wrong in accordance with the same principles. The fact that the duty is owed to another person does not preclude punishment. Indeed the standard crimes of murder, rape, assault, and theft are breaches of a duty owed to the victim. They may also give rise to civil proceedings for a remedy, and it seems to me unnecessary and implausible to argue that if the victim takes civil proceedings in such cases the claim is in respect of the breach of a different duty from the duty whose breach constituted the crime.[89] To the contrary, there is, in principle, a single wrong and a single duty, and it is a private duty.[90] In the case of a private wrong that is not recognised as a crime but for which punishment is appropriate, the issue in civil proceedings is whether it is unjust to impose punishment for the wrong on the basis of the procedural objection discussed above.

THE MONIST PRINCIPLE, CORRECTIVE JUSTICE, AND PRIVATE LAW

The Monist Principle as the Principle of Corrective Justice

Some statements of the principle of corrective justice suggest that it is no more than the monist principle. For example, one simple definition of corrective justice is that it requires the court to '[aim] to correct the injustice done by one party to the other', so that 'the remedy responds to the injustice and endeavours, so far as possible, to undo it'.[91] If injustice means injustice according to the primary relation, this is the monist principle. (Correcting an injustice is generally understood to mean remedying a wrong, implying that the primary relation is always a right–duty relation, but as discussed above there can also be primary right–liability relations, for which the causative event is not a wrong.)

---

[89] ie, essentially the same duty, though possibly defined in rather different ways, through different conventional-justificatory categories.

[90] Cf Beever, above n 71, at 108.

[91] EJ Weinrib, 'Corrective Justice in a Nutshell' (2002) 52 *University of Toronto Law Journal* 349, 350. See more fully EJ Weinrib, *The Idea of Private Law* (Cambridge Mass, Harvard UP, 1995).

The principle of corrective justice is often equated with the moral principle that a wrongdoer is responsible for remedying his wrongs, or that he has a duty of repair,[92] and in consequence it is thought to be implicit in corrective justice that D is liable for the full amount necessary to remedy the loss, so as to put C in the position he would have been in if D had performed his duty and not acted wrongfully. This is of course the usual rule for compensatory damages. It is sometimes explained by saying that the loss must in the end be borne either by the victim C or the wrongdoer D, and D should bear it because he is the wrongdoer. This may be appealing but it is not self-evident that it should apply in all circumstances. The monist principle also supports full compensation in this sense as the usual rule, but as discussed above it does not exclude the possibility that this measure of compensation should be reduced in order to avoid excessive hardship to the defendant. (As noted above, where there is a primary liability relation that imposes the risk of loss on D, the monist principle requires that D should be liable for the whole loss.) More generally, the point here is that the monist principle is not based on a moral principle of responsibility for remedying wrongs; it is a logical principle, concerned with the consistency of the primary and remedial relations. It can exclude certain remedies or measures of compensation on the ground of inconsistency with the primary relation, but it does not show that D should always be liable to pay compensation in the full measure of the loss caused to C by D.

It is sometimes said that corrective justice serves to remove wrongful *gains* as well as wrongful losses.[93] This is not intended to refer to disgorgement (in the sense explained above), because disgorgement is not a matter of justice as between the parties but of promoting the public interest in compliance with the law. It is said instead that a gain made through the wrong is something that is not rightfully D's vis-à-vis C; D's retention of it disturbs the mutual entitlements of the two parties (as defined by the primary relation). This has caused some difficulty in accounting for the law as it is, because there certainly seem to be ordinary cases in contract or tort where the law remedies a loss but leaves D with a benefit, and if D's benefit is removed it is generally thought to be the incidental consequence of remedying C's loss, not the object of the remedy.[94] According to the monist principle, a remedy protects and fulfils the primary relation, and usually this

---

[92] eg, J Coleman, *The Practice of Principle* (Oxford, OUP, 2001) 15.
[93] eg, Weinrib, 'Corrective Justice in a Nutshell', above n 91, at 354.
[94] I am disregarding disgorgement here.

is achieved by compensating for C's loss, whatever D's benefit may have been, because usually the rationale of the primary relation is to protect C against loss. However, there are cases involving primary liability relations where the primary relation is not concerned simply with protecting C against a loss. For example, as discussed in chapter 3 and in later chapters, in the case of ownership the primary right can generate a claim to recover property invalidly transferred to D, which depends on the benefit received by D as well as the loss to C. There are other cases, not concerned with property, where the receipt of a benefit generates a claim for the benefit received by D or part of it, and these are often described collectively as unjust enrichment claims.[95] (As already mentioned and as considered in chapter 8 and elsewhere, it is a mistake to think that they form a justificatory category.)

Private Law

The monist principle provides a minimalist interpretation of corrective justice (though one that reflects the natural meaning of the expression). Corrective justice is generally offered as a characterisation of private law, and there is clearly more to private law than the monist principle.[96] There is another, quite distinct concept of corrective justice. It is often said that, according to the principle of corrective justice, private law is bilateral or 'correlatively structured'.[97] This seems to be equivalent to saying that private law takes the form of primary legal relations between C and D, as I have assumed above. There are some principles that in their nature generate bilateral relations between individuals. These include the principles underlying the categories of contract, tort, and private property. This is why they form the justificatory categories of private law, and why they can be enforced through civil proceedings for remedies.[98] This

---

[95] In order to deal with the case where gain and loss are unequal, Weinrib says that what is important is 'normative' gains and losses, which do not necessarily correspond to factual gains and losses. This seems to undermine the theory: see eg P Cane, 'Corrective Justice and Correlativity in Private Law' (1996) 16 *Oxford Journal of Legal Studies* 471, 483.

[96] Also corrective justice in the sense of the monist principle can apply in public law along with civil and criminal proceedings.

[97] Weinrib, 'Corrective Justice in a Nutshell', above n 91, at 350. Also Coleman, above n 92, at 13.

[98] This approach to private law can be contrasted with the understanding of private law offered by some versions of law and economics, according to which its function is to maximise aggregate utility. This might be taken to imply that that there are only public duties, or on a reductionist view no legal relations in the ordinary sense at all: see above p 29. This does not sit very comfortably with the idea that civil proceedings serve to provide a remedy

is the appropriate sense of 'corrective justice' when it is used to characterise private law.[99] Some writers prefer the expression 'commutative justice' or 'transactional justice' or 'interactive justice' to refer to private law characterised in this way,[100] to avoid the association with corrective justice in the first sense.

There are other general principles or theories of justice that do not generate legal relations between individuals. This is generally the case of principles of distributive justice concerning the allocation of resources across the whole community, according to criteria such as satisfying need or rewarding desert or reducing inequality of wealth. These cannot be adequately implemented without state systems for taxation and social security or welfare benefits, including the provision of benefits such as education and medical treatment, which may generate legal relations between individuals and the state in public law.

The relationship between corrective and distributive justice has long been a matter of debate. Sometimes it is thought that corrective justice serves to restore a state of affairs that is in principle a matter of distributive justice. The implication seems to be that a primary relation is a matter of distributive justice and the remedial relation arising from it is a matter of corrective justice, which relegates corrective

at the instigation of a claimant: they have to be interpreted as proceedings taken by a private individual on behalf of the state to sanction the breach of a public duty, or to deter specified conduct, and the benefit that C receives by way of damages has to be understood as an incentive to potential claimants to perform this public service: Coleman, above n 92, at 13–24.

[99] According to Weinrib, private law, as a system of corrective justice, has a formal or autonomous character, which means that it is not concerned with benefits and burdens, or considerations of welfare, or consequentialist considerations, or public policy, or even any moral considerations at all: Weinrib, 'Corrective Justice in a Nutshell', above n 91, at 353. But this certainly does not follow from the fact that private law takes the form of bilateral legal relations based on general moral principles. Even arguments of public policy can be incorporated into private law, at least to the extent that they concern matters that D can reasonably be expected to take account of it or bear the risk of vis-à-vis C: see Dworkin, above n 4, at 294ff. Possibly the idea that private law has a formal or 'autonomous' character comes from the logical character of the monist principle; or it may draw on the idea of 'formalism' in the sense of 'mechanical jurisprudence', excluding analogical reasoning, as discussed above p 4. Weinrib also contends that because of the symmetry of correlative relations only considerations that bear on both parties can be relevant to the content of the primary relation, so that, for example, D's cost of precautions, which are relevant only to him, cannot be relevant to the content of his duty: Weinrib, 'Corrective Justice in a Nutshell', above n 91, at 351. But the primary legal relation involves an accommodation of the conflicting interests of the parties and so necessarily takes account of matters peculiar to each party.

[100] J Finnis, *Natural Law and Natural Rights* (Oxford, OUP, Clarendon Press, 1980) 178–79 uses 'commutative justice'. 'Transaction' must be understood to include involuntary transactions.

justice to the ancillary or even trivial role of enforcing distributive justice. This is, however, corrective justice in the sense of the monist principle, and it makes no sense to contrast this with distributive justice. In the more important sense of commutative or transactional justice, or corrective justice as private law, corrective justice is independent of distributive justice. The general principles behind the justificatory categories of private law generate their own primary and remedial relations, and they are not designed to allocate resources according to principles of distributive justice. Their function is to provide a resolution to particular problems arising from interactions or transactions between different people or groups.[101] They may favour certain activities, or a certain organisation of society, but it is not their function to apply a principle governing the distribution of wealth and opportunities, and any undesirable distributive effects can in theory be reversed through the arrangements made by the state outside private law concerning the distribution of wealth and opportunities. Private law in this sense is indifferent to principles of distributive justice, and the enforcement of a private law claim may uphold a state of affairs that is unfair according to principles of distributive justice.[102]

JUSTIFICATORY AND REMEDIAL CATEGORIES CONFLATED

Remedial principles or rules determine what remedy should be available, given the primary relation: they take us from the primary relation to the remedial relation. Examples of possible remedial rules are the rule that if the defendant D has committed a breach of duty and the circumstances are unchanged he should be ordered to perform the duty, or the rule that the measure of compensation should be the amount necessary to put the claimant C in the position he would have been in if the duty had been performed. On the monist approach, remedial principles or rules simply give effect to the monist principle, together with any qualification based on the hardship argument, and the category of remedial principles and rules is much

---

[101] See above p 10.

[102] However, the monist principle would not preclude taking wealth into account in determining the measure of compensation in the light of the issue of hardship. This is not to say that there cannot be rules designed to promote distributive justice regulating private law, but they do not emerge from the principles underlying the justificatory categories and so would normally be statutory.

smaller than under the dualist approach that I rejected above, under which the primary relation leaves open the nature of the remedy, to be determined by, say, a remedial discretion, or a supposed remedial rule that provides that a primary duty should be enforced by injunction if 'damages are inadequate'.

Examples of the Remedy-as-justification Fallacy

The 'remedy-as-justification' fallacy was mentioned in chapter 1. It consists in defining a justificatory category in terms of a type of remedy or remedial principle. There is a danger of committing the remedy-as-justification fallacy where the law is expressed simply in terms of the necessary conditions for a certain remedy to be available, so that the primary relation is omitted and concealed. This is an obvious possibility where a remedy is understood as a 'freestanding' remedy that does not enforce or protect a primary right at all.[103]

An example of the remedy-as-justification fallacy mentioned in chapter 1 is the implied contract fiction. The fiction that the claim to recover a mistaken payment is contractual or quasi-contractual arose because the form of remedy—payment of a certain sum—is the same as for the claim to recover a genuine contractual debt, so the old form of action for the recovery of a contractual debt provided a convenient means to secure the remedy in connection with a mistaken payment. Thus the true justificatory category of the claim to recover a mistaken payment was obscured and liable to be misunderstood.

The exposure and elimination of the implied contract fiction has been claimed as an achievement of the modern law of restitution or unjust enrichment. But ironically it appears that this modern development has replaced the old fiction with a more systematic case of the remedy-as-justification fallacy. As mentioned in chapter 1, the law of restitution developed because various claims arising from the receipt of a benefit by D, which historically were treated quite separately, were thought to be appropriately treated together under a common framework. Ostensibly what these claims have in common is the form of remedy—the transfer from D to C of the benefit received by D, or its value, or some part of its value. But their common treatment presupposes that they form a justificatory category. This is the theory of unjust enrichment, and it implies that there is an underlying principle of unjust enrichment. But if there is actually no such principle, the obvious inference is that the theory of unjust

---

[103] Above p 56. For an example see below p 122.

enrichment is based on the mistake of assuming that claims for a certain type of remedy necessarily form a justificatory category. The consequence is liable to be incoherence in the form of false assimilation and false differentiation. Some examples of this are considered later.[104]

Consider also the possible category of 'compensation claims'. The law of compensation claims consists of the remedial rules that determine when compensation is due and what the measure is. But say the law of compensation claims were taken to be a justificatory category. This category would comprise, not just these remedial rules, but the rules governing the primary relations that determine when a claim for compensation arises. As discussed in chapter 1, treating such a category as a justificatory category would mean working on the assumption that these rules drawn from contract and tort are based on a single general justifying principle, and so can sensibly be governed by a common framework. The effect would be to eliminate or disguise the differences between the rules in contract concerning, say, when a contract has been made, whether it has been breached etc, and the rules in tort that determine whether there was a tortious duty of care and whether it has been breached etc. If contract and tort are actually distinct justificatory categories this would clearly be misconceived, and it would cause false assimilation. At the same time it would cause false differentiation by recognising spurious distinctions within contract and tort according to whether the remedy is compensation or not.

This might seem to be an unlikely example of the conflation of a remedial category with a justificatory category. But contract law and tort law have sometimes been defined as being concerned with, respectively, expectation damages and 'status quo' damages (including reliance damages).[105] This is exactly the same error of defining justificatory categories by reference to a type of remedy. It is true that contract law is generally concerned with the conferral of benefits and tort law with the avoidance of harm, so generally expectation damages will be appropriate in contract and status quo damages in tort. But this is not always or necessarily the case. For example, one might have a duty in tort to go to someone's assistance, and the compensatory remedy then would be expectation damages. In contract, it is

---

[104] Below p 227.

[105] For a reference to this approach, see A Burrows, 'Contract, Tort and Restitution—A Satisfactory Division or Not?' (1983) 99 *Law Quarterly Review* 217, 253–55. Cf Stapleton, above n 47.

thought that claims for reliance loss are proxy claims for expectation loss,[106] but this should not be taken to be the case simply as a matter of definition. The position should in principle be established by reference to the underlying principle and its limitations, and not by an artificial exclusion based on the standard form of remedy.

Along the same lines, it is sometimes said that tort law is based on the principle that a wrongdoer should pay compensation for his wrongs, and this principle is taken to be equivalent to the principle that agreements should be performed as the basis for contract.[107] This is sometimes expressed as the 'duty of repair' or 'corrective justice' principle of tort law, as mentioned above. But unlike the contract principle, this is a purely remedial principle concerning the relationship between primary and remedial relations. As suggested above, it might be understood to be a version of the monist principle. It says nothing about what counts as a wrong or why, and it cannot be the basis for a primary relation in a justificatory category. This understanding of tort law amounts to a version of the remedy-as-justification fallacy. Corrective justice in this purely remedial sense cannot be the basis for distinguishing tort from other justificatory categories such as contract,[108] and it obscures the issue of the justification for claims in tort law.[109]

Punishment and Disgorgement Conflated with Justification

A similar type of mistake can arise in connection with the non-remedial response of punishment or disgorgement. As mentioned above, disgorgement is not generally available at common law, but it is available in equity and in particular for breach of fiduciary duty.[110] However, it has always been controversial exactly what a fiduciary relationship is and when one arises. This is a question of its justifica-

---

[106] Above p 46.

[107] A Burrows, *The Law of Restitution* (London, Butterworths, 2nd edn, 2002) 1; Coleman, above n 92, at 15.

[108] Sheinman criticises Coleman for contrasting corrective justice as the basis of tort law with retributive justice as the basis of criminal law, restitutionary justice as the basis of the law of restitution, and the law of the market as the basis of contract law: H Sheinman, 'Tort Law and Corrective Justice' (2003) 22 *Law & Philosophy* 21, 47.

[109] Thus it is not surprising that Coleman has struggled to explain how any particular wrongs can arise from the principle of corrective justice. He suggests, above n 92, at 32, that some wrongs are a matter of corrective justice and others are not and that a 'paradigm case' of a corrective justice wrong is provided by assault and battery, but he does not suggest anything in the nature of a fundamental principle or theory to explain the paradigm case and denies that this is necessary. See the comments in Sheinman, ibid.

[110] Disgorgement for breach of fiduciary duty is considered further below, p 146.

tory basis, and is discussed briefly in chapter 5. This uncertainty has left room for what has been described as a 'result-oriented' or 'conclusory' finding of a fiduciary relationship, where the court deems a relationship to be fiduciary in order to be able to impose disgorgement.[111] This is a version of the same remedy-as-justification fallacy, or here the 'response-as-justification' fallacy, and it tends to obscure the issue of the justificatory basis of the fiduciary relationship.

A similar issue arises in connection with punishment and the definition of criminal law. It was argued above that the difference between civil and criminal law is that they are concerned with different types of response, which call for different types of procedure. For example, the wrong of assault can generate a response in both civil law and criminal law, a remedy in civil law and a punishment in criminal law. This is the procedural definition of criminal law.[112] But criminal law often appears to be understood as a conventional-justificatory category, to be distinguished on this basis from civil law and in particular tort law. This is the assumption underlying much of the controversy in the literature over the definition of criminal law, meaning presumably the identification of a fundamental principle or distinctive type of justification that can show what sort of duties arise in criminal law, and how they are different from duties in tort law or other parts of civil law.[113] One suggested answer was mentioned above, namely that criminal law is about public wrongs and civil law is about private wrongs. But according to the procedural definition, criminal law is not properly understood as a justificatory category. The duty breached in criminal law in the commission of the crime of assault is in principle the same as the duty breached in the commission of an assault in civil law, the two duties having in principle the same content and the same justification.[114] For the sake of coherence they should be considered together when the issue arises of when the duty arises and what it requires. The treatment of criminal law and tort law in isolation from each other, as separate justificatory

---

[111] See *LAC Minerals v International Corona Resources* (1989) 61 DLR (4th) 14, 30, per La Forest J; see also below p 146.

[112] See AP Simester and GR Sullivan, *Criminal Law Theory and Doctrine* (Oxford, Hart Publishing, 2nd edn, 2003) 1; G Williams, 'The Definition of Crime' (1955) *Current Legal Problems* 107.

[113] For an account of different approaches to this question see L Zedner, *Criminal Justice* (Oxford, Clarendon Law Series, OUP, 2004) 58–63.

[114] Subject no doubt to additional considerations in criminal law concerning the degree of culpability necessary for punishment to be justified and additional requirements for certainty and clarity.

categories, is liable to cause false differentiation. This is really a systematic version of the response-as-justification fallacy.

The same objection would apply to the theory that criminal law is a based on a principle of retribution, if this is understood to imply that it is a justificatory category based on such a principle, that is to say that a principle of retribution underlies and explains the body of rules that determine what the duties are whose breach is punishable through criminal proceedings as a crime. Although a principle of retribution might be able to explain which wrongs should be punished and with what degree of severity, it surely cannot explain why particular duties arise. In other words, retributivism can be a theory of punishment, but not a theory of criminal law, if this comprises (in tandem with tort law) the law concerning what duties there are whose breach can constitute a crime.[115]

TWO FALLACIES OF REMEDIALISM

By 'remedialism' I mean an approach that concentrates exclusively or excessively on remedies, and so obscures or curtails the proper role of primary relations and their basis in justificatory categories. This chapter has considered two 'remedialist fallacies'. The first is the dualist fallacy. The dualist fallacy involves an inconsistency between primary and remedial relations. It is committed where, in determining the remedy to award, the court offends against the monist principle by contradicting the primary relation or by reopening an issue resolved in the primary relation. A typical case is where the court holds that a claim arises from a breach of duty but in refusing to award an injunction or specific performance it relies on arguments that imply that there was no such duty. The dualist fallacy is closely related to the failure to recognise primary liability relations: where the court declines to award specific performance or an injunction the true reason is often that the primary relation was a right-liability relation not a right-duty relation. A particular version of the dualist fallacy is discretionary remedialism, where, ostensibly at least, the primary relation is rule-based and non-discretionary but the remedy is discretionary. The dualist fallacy was discussed in connection with

---

[115] A similar point is made by P Cane, 'The Anatomy of Private Law Theory' (2005) 25 *Responsibility in Law and Morality* (Hart Publishing, 2002) 188, commenting on M Moore, *Placing Blame* (Oxford, Clarendon Press, OUP, 1997) 30–35; and also by Sheinman, above n 108, at 47, commenting on Coleman, above n 92.

contract law, but it is important in other contexts, including property law, as will appear in the next and subsequent chapters.

The second fallacy of remedialism is the remedy-as-justification fallacy. The remedy-as-justification fallacy is committed where a remedy or remedial principle is treated as the basis for a justificatory category. An old example is the implied contract fiction, which assimilated the claim to recover a mistaken payment to the claim to recover a contractual debt, the original rationale being that in both cases the appropriate remedy was the recovery of a sum of money. The remedy-as-justification fallacy distorts analogical reasoning and causes incoherence because it subverts a sound justificatory classification. In my view, as discussed further in chapter 8, the modern development of the law of unjust enrichment was prompted by this fallacy. Partly for this reason, the remedy-as-justification fallacy is also important in property law.

3

Property and Property Claims

Private Property

Property law addresses the problem of how to allocate the benefit of 'things' or resources. This is a functional definition of property law in the sense referred to in chapter 1.[1] Traditionally the most important such things have been land and goods, and in ordinary usage property law most often refers to land law and the law of goods or chattels. For some people, strictly speaking property is confined to tangible things, and is used of intangible things, such as contractual rights or choses in action, or intellectual property, only in an extended or figurative sense. I will take the view that property can include intangible things, including money, as discussed below.

The characteristic feature of a system of private property is the right of ownership, which is the exclusive right to all the benefit of a particular thing or 'object of property', encompassing the right to control it and determine how it is used or disposed of, and the right to benefit from it through use or exploitation by sale or licensing.[2] One can conceive of a private property system consisting only of rights of ownership, so that there are only discrete units of property each controlled by an owner who is entitled to all the benefit of it.[3] But in reality there are bound to be, in addition, 'lesser property rights', which confer an entitlement to some specific aspect of the benefit of an object of property belonging to someone else, in derogation of his right of ownership, so that the benefit of things is divided up in more complex ways. In the case of land, this is neces-

---

[1] Above p 10.

[2] Various commentators have said that the right of ownership is a standard or ideal type or organising idea behind private property, because it epitomises the idea of allocating the benefit of things to particular individuals: eg J Waldron, *The Right to Private Property* (Oxford, Clarendon Press, 1988) 38; JW Harris, 'Who Owns My Body' (1996) 16 *Oxford Journal of Legal Studies* 55, 56.

[3] Waldron, ibid.

sitated by the interdependence of land use. In land law, an easement is a right to make some limited use of land owned by another person, eg for access; and a restrictive covenant gives a benefit to a neighbour in the form of a constraint on use by the owner. Another lesser property right is the charge, which secures a debt of the owner by giving the chargee the right to recover the debt through the forced sale of the property in the event of default. The right of ownership and lesser property rights together form the private property system, based on the idea of dividing up the benefits of things and allocating them to individuals.

It will be helpful to mention a couple of points of terminology. First, the word 'owner' is often used to refer not only to someone who has a right of ownership in the sense above, but to someone who holds a lesser property right, and for convenience I will sometimes follow this usage. Secondly, the word 'property' is commonly used to refer to the 'thing' or object of property, the benefit of which is allocated to the owner by the property right, as well as to property law and property rights, and I will also follow this usage where convenient, though some commentators insist that only the latter usage is correct.

The Justificatory Category and the Fundamental Principle of Private Property

I have already suggested that private property law forms a justificatory category in private law, analogous to contract and tort, which means that private property law is a body of law based on a general moral principle capable of generating claims by an owner against recipients or users of property. This will seem unexceptionable to some, and simplistic or misconceived to others.

It is helpful to begin by considering what the underlying principle might be. There is a tradition in property law theory concerned with what has been described as a principle of 'justice in acquisition'.[4] This is a moral principle by virtue of which someone can come to own something that was previously unowned, for example by being the first person to appropriate it, or occupy it, or work on it. Assuming also a power of transfer of property, such a principle could account for the rights of ownership of all owners on the basis that all private property has been validly acquired by a first owner or by a valid transfer directly or indirectly from a first owner. This would provide a basis for private property law; it would be the basis for a body of rules

---

[4] R Nozick, *Anarchy, State and Utopia* (Oxford, Blackwell, 1974) 150ff.

governing claims by an owner against recipients and users of the owner's property.

However, it has never been clear exactly what the principle of justice in acquisition might be. Simply being the first to appropriate or occupy or work on property seems to be a doubtful basis for an exclusive right to it. According to Locke's famous labour theory, if O works on land, for example by cultivating it for farming, he should be entitled to the product of his labour in the form of a right of ownership of the land because he has mixed his labour with the land.[5] But the mixing argument seems to be no more than a persuasive metaphor in support of an intuition. It is sometimes said that the true principle is a matter of moral desert: the property right that O acquires is what he deserves as a reward for his work in cultivating the land.[6] But there are problems with this argument as well. Why does a principle of desert justify a property right rather than some other form of reward for working on property, for example a payment from the state? If there is an intrinsic link of some sort between the work on property and the property right that it gives rise to, why does an employee working on land not acquire the same right? Also, if desert is measured relative to the value of the work as a contribution to society, this must presumably depend on how the economy is organised overall, and cannot be determined by considering the work in isolation, as the principle seems to imply. And why should the desert argument prevail over the interests of other people based on need or equality?[7]

It seems doubtful whether this approach can be sustained as the basis for a justificatory category of private property law, and I will not pursue it further. It can be contrasted with a 'global' theory of property, which is concerned not with the right of a particular owner in respect of a particular object of property, but with the allocation of property rights in general. It must specify the sorts of things that should be recognised as objects of private property rather than regulated as communal or state property; what types of property right can subsist in them, their scope and incidents and how they are acquired; when property rights should be transferable, and so capable of being bought and sold and forming the subject matter of a market. Also, a global theory of property encompasses the rules on taxation, which in effect qualify or limit rights of ownership of property. It is difficult

---

[5] See Waldron, above n 2, ch 6, discussing Locke, *Two Treatises on Government*.

[6] See eg SR Munzer, *A Theory of Property* (Cambridge, CUP, 1990) ch 10.

[7] See generally Waldron, above n 2, at 201–07.

to see how a principle along the lines of the labour or desert principle or any principle of justice in acquisition can account for these aspects of a real system of private property law.

However, it is not clear that a global theory can account fully for a crucial and distinctive feature of private property. From the point of view of a claimant-owner, the underlying justification for a claim against another person in private law, in respect of property of his that has been taken from him, does not lie in the global theory of property, or the various policies or principles underlying it. From his standpoint, private property law calls for something in the nature of the principle of justice in acquisition that generates rights in respect of a particular object against other people, as a result of particular events in the history of the object.[8] An adequate theory of private property must have this dimension as well.

I will say that a global theory provides a 'background theory' or 'background law' of property. The background law provides a general framework for private property, but it does not provide the basis for a particular owner's claim in respect of the particular thing that he owns. The basis for this is the following principle, which I will call the reliance principle of private property, or the private property principle for short. The principle is that, as against anyone else, O should have the benefit allocated to him by a property right, as specified by background property law, because he has acted in reliance on the assumption, in accordance with background property law, that he has or will have the property right. The reliance may be expenditure of labour or money in acquiring, making, adapting or improving property, or the opportunity cost of not acquiring other property.[9] This is the general moral principle justifying a particular person's right to particular property as against everyone else. The private property principle empowers O to exploit resources for his own benefit, though benefits accrue to others from the operation of the principle. The principle is a principle of autonomy, like the contract principle, which empowers people to coordinate their behaviour for mutual benefit.

---

[8] ie, it is an 'historical entitlement theory' in Nozick's terminology: Nozick, above n 4, at 150ff.

[9] JW Harris, *Property and Justice* (Oxford, OUP, 1996) 321–23, discusses the reliance interest with particular reference to Bentham, who emphasised the importance of protecting expectations: J Bentham, *The Theory of Legislation*, Part 1, ch 10. There seems to be no reason to say that reliance provides a basis for protection only as against someone who induced it, as in the case of estoppel. Neither does it seem a good objection that expectations may sometimes be frustrated by a change in the law.

The principle of private property is reminiscent of the labour or desert principle, but it does not generate a 'pre-institutional' or pre-legal right to private property,[10] which is what is aimed at in the debate alluded to above concerning a principle of justice in acquisition; to the contrary, it presupposes and operates on the basis of background property law. It is not a matter of reward for O based on desert, but of O's entitlement, on the basis that he has acted in reliance on background property law.[11] It is consistent with very different bodies of background property law, and background property law channels O into acting in particular ways under the private property principle, for example according to the types of property right that are recognised and how they are acquired.

Thus it seems to me that private property is a justificatory category based on the reliance principle of private property. The primary relation is a right of ownership or some other property right, which generates claims in accordance with the monist principle. Reflecting the nature of the property principle, these claims arise to secure to the owner O the value and benefit of the object of property or some aspect of it in accordance with his property right. The causative events from which the claims arise are events by which the benefit of the property accrues to another person, namely invalid transfers of property and unauthorised uses of property; and the remedies are the recovery of the property invalidly transferred and reasonable payment for unauthorised use. I will refer to these claims as property claims or property-based claims. Historically the common law has tended not to recognise explicitly a category of property claims or property-based claims. There are so-called 'proprietary claims', but as discussed below this conventionally refers to something else. Particular examples of property-based claims have sometimes been described or misdescribed as claims in tort, constructive trust, quasi-contract, and more recently restitution or unjust enrichment.

These property-based claims are claims in corrective justice in both the senses considered in chapter 2.[12] First, a claim arises in accordance with the monist principle, that is to say, in response to causative events determined by the primary relation, namely invalid

---

[10] At least, it is not necessary for present purposes to consider whether there is any role for the principle in the pre-institutional context.

[11] ie, it is a matter of a quid pro quo or what is earned, not a reward. 'Desert' is sometimes used in this entitlement sense: see Waldron, above n 2, at 201.

[12] Above p 67.

transfers and unauthorised uses, in such a way as to protect and fulfil the primary relation.

Secondly, it might be said that property is not a matter of corrective justice or private law in the sense of giving rise to bilateral relations between parties, because it is a matter of distributive justice.[13] On the approach above, distributive justice is relevant to what I have called background property law. Background property law, including the law of taxation, can take account of considerations of distributive justice such as need and equality as well as desert, and it can also take account of considerations of efficiency, such as how to accommodate and coordinate the use of land by different people, and how to promote commercial activity. There must certainly be room for considerations of this sort in a theory that can plausibly explain a modern property system, but they are not matters of corrective justice or private law in the bilateral relations sense. But the reliance principle of private property, operating on background property law, generates bilateral primary relations between the claimant-owner and other parties, from which property-based claims arise.

Also it is sometimes thought that there are no bilateral relations in private property law because a property owner has a primary right against 'all the world' not just against another particular person.[14] But, although it is true that a property right is a right against 'all the world' (as considered further below), this does not imply that there is not still a bilateral relation between O, the owner, and a particular person, D, who turns out to be the recipient of an invalid transfer or an unauthorised user, even though an identical relation subsists between O and other parties. The same issue arises with respect to tort law. I will come back to this feature of property rights, which is often discussed in connection with Hohfeld.[15]

Objects of Private Property

An important issue is what types of thing should be objects of private property, as opposed to being subject to common ownership or state ownership.[16] As mentioned above, this is a matter for background property law, not the private property principle itself. It depends on

[13] It is sometimes suggested that corrective justice has no application to property law: see eg P Cane, 'The Anatomy of Private Law Theory' (2005) 25 *Oxford Journal of Legal Studies* 203, 211.

[14] A Clarke and P Kohler, *Property Law* (Cambridge, CUP, 2005) 155.

[15] Below p 90.

[16] Waldron, above n 2, at 40–41.

empirical issues concerning the link between the benefits to be obtained from a thing and the investment of money and labour in it, as well as issues of efficiency and distributive justice. These matters are sometimes controversial of course, but it is not necessary to pursue them here. However, it is useful to consider a prior issue, concerned with what is capable of being an object of property.

The Fallacy of Labour as an Object of Property

It is sometimes thought that labour is an object of property belonging to the person who expends it, so that a contract by which C agrees to do work for D involves a transfer of C's labour to D in return for payment. But labour is not an object of property. Everyone should of course be free to decide whether and how to apply his labour for profit, and one might wish to express this by saying that C is entitled to his labour. But C's freedom to decide when and how to apply his labour for profit depends on his rights in tort not to be assaulted, imprisoned or coerced, and his power to contract.[17] These rights do not depend on O's having acted in reliance on the assumption of having or acquiring a right over his person or labour in accordance with the private property principle. The private property principle is concerned with things that exist separately from owners or right-holders. This is the 'separability condition' for objects of property.[18] Thus it is unnecessary and misleading to describe labour as an object of property in order to account for the legal protection it attracts.[19]

As we will see in chapter 8,[20] the law of unjust enrichment often implicitly commits the fallacy of treating labour as an object of property, because it generally equates a claim for payment for the expenditure of labour with a claim to recover a transfer of property.[21]

Contract Rights as Objects of Property

It is sometimes thought that an object of property must be a tangible thing and that there cannot be intangible property.[22] In particular,

---

[17] As to tort, see below, p 103.

[18] See JE Penner, *The Idea of Property in Law* (Oxford, Clarendon Press, OUP, 1997) ch 5. Harris, above n 9, ch 1.

[19] The idea of labour as an object of property is common in the political philosophy literature on property in the Lockean tradition: eg JO Grunebaum, *Private Ownership* (London, Routledge & Kegan Paul, 1987).

[20] See below p 221.

[21] See eg J Gordley, *Foundations of Private Law* (Oxford, OUP, 2006) 423–26. See further below p 234.

[22] Or that intangible property is in some sense not true property: eg Waldron; above n 2, at 33–37; T Honoré, 'Ownership' in *Making Law Bind* (Oxford, Clarendon Press, 1987) 181–82.

there has been controversy over contractual rights as a form of property. But there is nothing in the concept of property or the private property principle to justify a limitation to tangible things.

A contract gives rise to a legal relation between the contracting parties. An ordinary contract right is purely a matter of contract law. It is not a property right or an object of property. But sometimes the purpose of a contract is to generate a right that is capable of being entirely dissociated from the right-holder or creditor under the original contract and transferred to and held by other people against the debtor.[23] Such a right acquires an independent existence: it satisfies the separability condition. In such cases the contract generates an object of property, amenable to the operation of the private property principle.[24] This may be the case, for example, with respect to rights to payment under ordinary commercial contracts, cheques and other financial instruments.[25] The expression 'asset' encompasses contractual rights as objects of property as well as tangible things. An ordinary bank account is not transferable in the ordinary way, by a transfer of the contractual right, but it is an object of property nevertheless, because transfers can be made from the account by way of a deduction from the balance and a corresponding credit to another account, or a payment in cash.[26] This common type of case is considered further below.

Where contract generates an object of property, the content of the right is set by the contract, as a matter of contract law, but the position of the creditor as against third parties, including the validity of transfers, and claims arising from an invalid transfer, for example a transfer induced by mistake or deception, is in principle a matter of property law, just as for invalid transfers of tangible things. Property and contract remain distinct justificatory categories, concerned with discrete sets of issues, though they are dependent on each other.[27]

[23] Strictly speaking, the requirement is negotiability, meaning that the transferee is not affected by any claim that the debtor may have had against the transferor, and the transferor need not be involved in the transferee's pursuing the claim against the debtor.

[24] Sometimes referred to as a receivable or credit or book debt. Some such rights are embodied in a document. The expression 'chose in action' appears to extend to rights in contract and tort that are not objects of property.

[25] By contrast, it would not be the case where the personal relationship between the parties or the identity of the other party is important, as generally for contracts for personal services or employment contracts: see Penner, above n 18.

[26] This does not of course mean that C owns any of the bank's property, or literally has 'money at the bank'. The object of property is the contractual right itself, not the debtor's estate or any part of it. The status of the contractual right as an object of property does not depend on the presence in the debtor's estate of tangible things. The contractual right could be a right to services if it were such as to be transferable. Cf Penner, above n 18, ch 6.

[27] Cf above, p 32.

Abstract Value

Originally tangible things may have been desired only for their tangible qualities, but they can also serve as a store of value, relying on their marketability. One might say that where the property is held for its value in exchange—as an investment—the object of property is the exchange value of the tangible thing, rather than the thing itself.[28] This may seem an entirely artificial distinction, but consider the position in the case of a fund. A fund is a fluctuating set of specific assets (including tangible things and contractual rights as objects of property), which can each be sold and replaced, without affecting the continued existence of the fund itself. The ultimate objects of property are no doubt the specific assets that make up the fund, but for some purposes it may be useful to treat the 'abstract value' of the fund, or some part of the abstract value of the fund, which is not defined by reference to any specific asset in the fund, as the object of ownership, rather than the specific assets that make it up. The distinction between abstract value or wealth and specific assets is important, particularly in the remedial context. Even in the absence of a fund, the object of a remedial property right may be abstract value in the defendant's estate rather than a specific asset. This is an important issue in the law of tracing, as discussed in chapter 6.

Money

The origin of money lies in tangible things that are valuable as such and can be held and exchanged. But nowadays the value of money in the form of a coin is not the value of the coin as a tangible thing but its nominal value for the purpose of exchange, based on the general recognition of a convention that it has such a value. Money is essentially abstract value, but in the form of coin it is tied to a specific tangible thing so that it functions as a tangible object of property. The practical advantage of this is purely evidential, that is to say, proving the ownership of the abstract value.

Money can also take the form of a contractual right as an object of property, as some of the examples mentioned above illustrate. A banknote originally constituted a transferable contractual right against the bank that issued it, for the payment of the stated sum. At one time the contractual debt could have been satisfied by payment in coin, but nowadays the promise to pay declared on the face of the note is

---

[28] See B Rudden, 'Things as Thing and Things as Wealth' (1994) 14 *Oxford Journal of Legal Studies* 81. A fund requires 'separation of title', as considered in ch 5.

a fiction, and the banknote does not represent a contractual right at all. Just like money as coin, it is valuable by virtue of the general acceptance of a convention by which it has the value stated.

Sometimes money is distinguished from property, in particular where it is intangible, but there is no reason why money, whether tangible or not, should not be regarded as property. Claims arising from invalid transfers of money are property-based claims just like claims arising from invalid transfers of tangible property. In a sense, money is the archetypal form of property. Money exists in accordance with a convention by virtue of which people can rely on it as an object of value that can be kept and exchanged and so is worth receiving in return for the provision of goods and services; in other words, the rationale of the convention is to create a thing for the very purpose of recognising it as an object of property to which the private property principle applies.

Intellectual Property

Intellectual property rights are property rights in intangible things produced by labour, especially creative labour, such as information, inventions, ideas, artistic and literary works and reputation. Again, although there is controversy over this, there is no reason to doubt that intellectual property is a genuine form of property.

A distinguishing feature of intellectual property is that it is non-exclusive: it is capable of being used by any number of different people at the same time, unlike tangible property or other types of intangible property, including money. One consequence of this is that the standard property-based claim in respect of intellectual property is not the claim to recover an invalid transfer but the claim for payment for unauthorised use.[29] Also, sometimes it is argued that intellectual property should not be recognised at all because, being non-exclusive, its use does not interfere with the creator's use. But this does not mean there should be no intellectual property rights. It does not negate the argument that they are justified as a reward for certain types of productive activity and an incentive to pursue them; but it means that, because intellectual property is capable of being used simultaneously by many people, an exclusive right imposes a greater cost on the rest of society, and this needs to be taken into account in determining what sort of intellectual property rights are justified. It may also account for the fact that with limited exceptions

---

[29] Expressed as damages measured by reference to a notional licence fee: see below n 73.

intellectual property rights have been recognised only by statute and not at common law.[30]

Transfer and Grant

A property owner can generally make a grant of a property right in respect of some aspect of the object of his right of ownership, carving out a part of his own interest. Generally the only limitation is that the property right granted is in the form of a recognised property right. Whereas contracting parties can create contractual rights having whatever content they choose, owners of property can grant only the particular types of property right that are recognised in the law, such as a lease, a charge, an easement, or a restrictive covenant. This is the 'limited number' or 'numerus clausus' principle.[31]

Also, a property owner can generally transfer his property right to someone else. Transferability is sometimes said to be a defining feature of property rights.[32] It is true that an object of property must be capable of being owned by different people in accordance with the separability condition, so it is always possible for the law to provide that a right of ownership is transferable; and one might doubt whether it is apt to describe a property right that is not transferable as a right of ownership.[33] Lesser property rights may be in their nature restricted with respect to transferability—for example, a right in land may be tied to a neighbour's property and so not freely transferable.

However, there may be good reason for the law to withhold a power of transfer, even where transfer is in principle possible.[34] The private property principle does not restrict the possible scope or incidents of property rights, including transferability. This is a matter of background property law. The issue is liable to depend on the value placed on having a market, for which transferability is a prerequisite. But for certain types of property, a power of transfer is necessary, in the nature of the type of property. As considered above, it must be

---

[30] *Victoria Park Racing v Taylor* (1937) 58 CLR 479, at 509, per Dixon J. Cf *International News Services v Associated Press* 248 US 215 (1918) according to which US law has taken a different path.

[31] See eg B Rudden, 'Economic Theory v. Property Law: The "Numerus Clausus" Problem' in J Eekelaar and J Bell (eds), *Oxford Essays in Jurisprudence: Third Series* (Oxford, OUP, 1987) 239; *Hill v Tupper* (1863) 2 H&C 121; 159 ER 51.

[32] See the discussion in S Worthington, *Equity* (Oxford, OUP, 2nd edn, 2006) ch 3.

[33] Presumably one might say that, as a matter of usage, if a property right is not transferable it lacks one of the hallmarks of a right of ownership, and must be a lesser property right.

[34] Waldron, above n 2, at 341–43.

the case for money; and a contractual right must be transferable for it to be capable of being an object of property.[35]

The reliance principle of private property explains another important feature of property law that is relevant later. The recipient of a valid transfer or grant of a property right derives his property right from the transferor's power of transfer or grant, but his right is also directly supported by the private property principle: the principle can operate with respect to acquisition by transfer or grant as well as acquisition by way of first ownership of a thing. The recipient's reliance is clear where he has given consideration for the transfer or grant but, just as in the case of first ownership, he may incur reliance in other ways, for example by making alterations to property, or by incurring expenditure on the assumption that his wealth has increased as a result of the receipt, or simply in the form of an opportunity cost if he refrains from acquiring other property.

If the transfer or grant to the recipient was valid, there is no need to invoke this argument in support of his property right. But it is worth noting that one can never be absolutely sure that the right of a grantor or transferor is not vitiated by an invalid transfer at some stage in the chain of owners that preceded him. The argument based on the recipient's reliance (including previous recipients) provides a basis for upholding the current disposition of property rights, notwithstanding the risk of some defect in the chain.

By the same token, and of more practical importance in the law, the principle of private property should operate to give protection in the form of a property right to someone who has acted in reliance on the reasonable belief that he has acquired or will acquire a property right, when in fact there has not been a valid transfer or grant to him. There are various doctrines that might be explained in this way,[36] including adverse possession, prescriptive easements, proprietary estoppel,[37] and bona fide purchase.[38] These doctrines are sometimes thought to be anomalous and at odds with the nature of private property law, because they have the effect of generating a property right in derogation of an existing right of ownership, without a valid transfer

---

[35] This may be why it is sometimes thought that transferability is a necessary feature of property rights.

[36] Though they do not necessarily confer the property right that was assumed or expected. These doctrines are not always explained in this way.

[37] See below p 253.

[38] See below p 140.

or grant.[39] It might be thought that property rights cannot really be vulnerable in this way, because they are in their nature too robust to yield to a simple reliance interest.[40] But in these types of case the recipient's reliance interest is an interest of the same type as the original owner's, and what is at stake is how to weigh one party's reliance interest against the other's,[41] in relation to the benefit of property.

SOME OTHER ASPECTS AND THEORIES OF PRIVATE PROPERTY

The 'Bundle of Rights' Theory of Property

In a well-known article,[42] Honoré identified the various incidents or components of a right of ownership in a standard case, as follows: the right to possess, the right to use, the right to manage, the right to receive income, the right to the capital, the right to security, the right of transmission or transfer, and absence of term (indefinite duration). These different aspects of the benefit of an object of property encompassed in the right of ownership amount to a specification of what a right of ownership, as an abstract right, comprises in concrete terms with respect to a typical form of property.

In practice, particular incidents or components will be missing, because the owner has made a grant of a property right in respect of some part of his interest, or has acquired his right of ownership already subject to such a grant. Sometimes the benefit of an object of property has been divided up in such a way that it is difficult to say who, if anyone, is properly described as the owner of the property, as in the case where a freehold is subject to a long lease. More generally, the benefit of an object of property can in theory be carved up in innumerable ways, even if there are a limited number of possible types of lesser property right, and there may be a very complex allocation of rights. Thus from the simple fact that someone is an owner or has a property right, one cannot infer, without further specification, what

---

[39] One can distinguish between the creation of a lesser property right, as generally in proprietary estoppel and prescriptive easements, and the elimination of a lesser property right in the process of acquiring ownership, as in bona fide purchase.

[40] See eg Clarke and Kohler, above n 14, at 412, discussing the suggestion that adverse possession is 'tantamount to theft'. Similar objections have been made to the acquisition of easements by prescription, and here the objection is reflected in the fiction of presumed grant: ibid, 490ff.

[41] Singer treats reliance as a 'counter-principle' in competition with the right of ownership: JW Singer, 'The Reliance Interest in Property' (1988) 40 *Stanford Law Review* 611.

[42] Honoré, above n 22, at 165.

aspects of the benefit of the object of property he is actually entitled to.[43] For this reason it is commonly said that property is simply a 'bundle of rights'.[44] The bundle of rights theory of property has been taken to imply that there is no determinate content to property at all. In any particular case, one has to simply establish the particular components of an owner's or right-holder's bundle. The idea of the bundle of rights is often traced to Honoré, whose objective was to reach a satisfactory definition of the concept of ownership, but it has led in the opposite direction to the idea of the fragmentation or disintegration of private property.[45] This seems to be one reason for the widespread scepticism about property as a coherent category of private law. But the coherence of private property as a justificatory category comes from the reliance principle of private property, not the particular types of property right that are recognised in the law or their incidents, or other matters of background property law, and it is not undermined by the variety or complexity of the arrangements of property rights that can be found in practice.

Property and Persons

Sometimes a contrast is drawn between property rights and rights against persons. This is sometimes expressed in terms of a contrast between the law of property and the law of 'obligations', the latter meaning traditionally contract and tort, and for some writers also restitution or unjust enrichment or aspects of it. It is certainly true that property law is concerned with things as objects of property, as discussed above. This means, for example, that if an object of property is destroyed, any property right in it is necessarily extinguished. It is sometimes said that the property right is 'exigible' against the thing,[46]

---

[43] eg, Singer, above n 41.

[44] eg, Munzer, above n 6, at 23. 'Bundle of rights' is also used to refer to the different Hohfeldian modalities of legal relation involved in property law—claim-rights, powers, liberties and immunities; and also to the indefinite number of distinct, co-existing parallel rights envisaged by Hohfeld: WH Hohfeld, *Fundamental Legal Conceptions as Applied in Judicial Reasoning* (D Campbell and P Thomas (eds), Aldershot, Ashgate Publishing, 2001) originally published (1913) 23 *Yale Law Journal* 16 and (1917) 26 *Yale Law Journal* 710. These usages are not always distinguished. Thus the bundle of rights is sometimes said to be based on a combination of Hohfeld and Honoré: see Munzer, ibid, 22ff. 'Bundle of rights' is used in a further distinct sense: see below n 53.

[45] See eg T Grey, 'The Disintegration of Property' in *Nomos XII: Property* (New York, New York University Press, 1980) 69; K Gray, 'Property in Thin Air' [1991] Cambridge Law Journal 252, 305.

[46] P Birks, *An Introduction to the Law of Restitution* (Oxford, Clarendon Press, rev edn, 1989) 49–50.

and this has important practical implications.[47] However, assuming that 'right' means a conclusive right in the sense of chapter 2 (as will generally be the case in ordinary legal usage),[48] it makes no sense to say that a property right is a right in a thing *as opposed to* being a right against a person. The law consists of rules that generate legal relations between people, who bear the rights, duties or other incidents of the rules. A property right is a right against other people in, or in respect of, a thing. One can say that private property law, and the private property principle, are directed in the first place at things, but also generate legal relations between people in respect of things,[49] whereas the principles behind contract and tort are not directed at things, but only at people's behaviour and responsibilities. One reason why the primary legal relations subsisting between an owner and others may not be apparent is that they are primary right-liability relations, as discussed further below.

The expressions *'in rem'* and *'in personam'* are sometimes used to express this distinction, an *in rem* right referring to a property right and an *in personam* right to a right in contract or tort (or some other part of private law outside property law). Used in this way, the expressions *in rem* and *in personam* relate to justificatory categories. '*In rem*' relates to the justificatory category of property, and *'in personam'* to the other justificatory categories in private law. Unfortunately there is a quite different usage of the expressions '*in rem*' and '*in personam*' which is liable to be confused with this first usage.

A Right 'Against the Whole World'

According to this second usage, an '*in rem* right' means a right good against everyone, or 'all the world', or against an indefinite number of people. In this second sense of '*in rem*' it is contrasted with '*in personam*' in a different sense: here an *in personam* right is a right good against a particular person or definite number of people rather than an indefinite number. This second distinction between '*in rem*' and '*in personam*' is sometimes expressed as the distinction between 'absolute' (*in rem*) and 'relative' (*in personam*) rights.[50]

[47] Below p 159.

[48] Above p 36.

[49] In AM Honoré, 'Rights of Exclusion and Immunities Against Divesting' (1959–60) 34 *Tulane Law Review* 454, Honoré defends the view that a property right is a right in respect of a thing *as opposed to* being a right against persons. Sometimes Honoré seems to suggest that there is a primary right in a thing but not against a person, which generates a remedial right or remedy against a person: see at 463–64. If so, this is an example of the dualist fallacy. Cf P Eleftheriadis, 'The Analysis of Property Rights' (1996) 16 *Oxford Journal of Legal Studies* 31.

[50] Honoré, 'Rights of Exclusion and Immunities Against Divesting' ibid, 453–54.

A property right is also *in rem* in this second sense. A property right determines who has the benefit or some aspect of the benefit of a thing that anyone might benefit from, and gives it to that person over everyone else. Thus it generates claims against everyone else, including 'strangers', meaning people with whom the owner or property right-holder had no prior relationship.[51] But it is not only property rights that are *in rem* in this sense. Primary rights in tort such as the right not to be assaulted or the right not to be defamed are not property rights but they are *in rem* rights in the sense that they are good against all the world (though the claim arising from such a right is a right against a particular person). A contractual right to performance is *in personam* in this second sense, being binding only on the other party or parties to a contract. But consider the power to make an offer of a contract: this power can be exercised vis-à-vis anyone—it is *in rem* in this sense.

It is unfortunate that '*in rem* right' is used in these two different senses. Both usages seem to be very long-standing, though presumably the first usage, meaning a property right or right in a thing, is the original one, and seems a more natural usage of the expression. I will refer to the second sense, meaning a right good against all the world,[52] as the Hohfeldian sense of *in rem*, though this usage was not original to Hohfeld (and indeed it departs from Hohfeld's approach in one respect that some commentators have emphasised though it is not important for present purposes).[53]

Hohfeld insisted that '*in rem*' was used correctly only to mean a right good against all the world. Thus it might appear that he rejected altogether the traditional idea of a body of property law that generates

---

[51] Thus a property right 'runs with the property'. But a property right may fall to a defence of bona fide purchase and it may generate a personal claim against a recipient or a claim in respect of different assets or abstract value, the original property right lapsing. Thus in my view a property right cannot be equated with an 'immunity to divesting' as argued in Honoré, ibid.

[52] Hohfeld, above n 44, at 55.

[53] This is that Hohfeld thought that, properly understood, an *in rem* right was not a single right of C good against an indefinite number of people, but an indefinite number of distinct bilateral relations or 'multital' relations, each comprising the right of C correlated with the duty of another person: Hohfeld, ibid, 53. (This is also sometimes referred to as a 'bundle of rights'.) This he took to be required by the doctrine of correlativity, on the basis that a single right must be correlated with a single duty. This aspect of Hohfeld's approach has been widely criticised. In fact it is doubtful whether the doctrine of correlativity requires this. Correlativity follows from the fact that a rule in private law affects two classes of people. A rule can confer a right on a single person that is correlated in this sense with an indefinite number of duties, because it can constrain an indefinite number of people for the benefit of a particular person.

property rights in things. Along with the idea of fragmentation of property mentioned above, this has been influential in promoting scepticism about property as a coherent category in private law. Hohfeld objected to the first usage of *in rem* for the reason mentioned above, that to say that there is a right in a thing, if used in contra-distinction to a right against a person, makes no sense because all rights are one side of a legal relation with another person. As pointed out above, the argument is mistaken. There is no reason to think that property law, in the sense above meaning a justificatory category of the law concerned with rights in things, is a deficient or incoherent concept. And in fact Hohfeld did not actually deny the existence of property rights—he referred to them in passing using the expression 'real right'.[54] It would be better to say that Hohfeld thought that *in rem* in the second sense, meaning a right good against everyone, was the significant feature of property rights, though not unique to or definitive of them. In other words, he did not actually deny that there was a category of private property law in the traditional sense of the law of rights in things; he took the view that it was not a significant category, compared with the categories of *in rem* and *in personam* in his preferred sense.

Hohfeld's approach to property and his understanding of *in rem* rights is explicable in the light of his general approach to the law, which was touched on in chapter 1.[55] His concern was with modalities rather than justificatory categories. The modalities of legal relation discussed in chapter 1 were the right-duty relation, power-liability relation, right-liability relation, etc. The distinction between an *in rem* right and *in personam* right in the second sense preferred by Hohfeld is also a distinction of modality, though it is an independent distinction of modality, so that right-duty or power-liability relations can be *in rem* or *in personam* in this sense. *In rem* and *in personam* in this sense are means for expressing a range of different types of pro-position and, unlike 'property' or 'property right' or '*in rem*' in the associated sense, they are not tied to any particular principle or justificatory category. They arise not only in private property, but in tort and contract as the examples above show.[56]

---

[54] Hohfeld, above n 44, at 69.

[55] Above p 20.

[56] The point is illustrated by the comparison Hohfeld makes between a contractual duty not to enter land arising from a contract with the owner, and the duty of a stranger not to enter land arising from the right of ownership: Hohfeld, above n 52, at 56. He points out that the contractual duty not to enter the property is intrinsically—ie, in terms of the con-tent of the duty and the correlative right—identical to the duty of the stranger that arises by

As discussed in chapter 1, the reason for Hohfeld's preoccupation with modalities was that he was concerned not with analogical reasoning with respect to unsettled law, but with being able to state settled law with precision, and modalities are crucial tools for this purpose. Justificatory categories are important with respect to justification and analogical reasoning, but they are not strictly necessary for the purpose of making a statement of settled law, and when used in this context they serve only to identify a body of law for convenience of exposition.[57]

PROPERTY-BASED CLAIMS

Thus property is in my view a justificatory category, based on a general moral principle, the private property principle as explained above. 'Property-based' claims are claims arising in this justificatory category. The primary right from which such claims arise is a property right, generally a right of ownership. I will consider two types of property-based claim arising from a primary right of ownership: the claim to recover an invalid transfer of property or its value, and the claim for reasonable payment for the unauthorised use of property.

The Property-based Restitutionary Claim

The Nature of the Claim

The standard property-based claim is a claim to recover property invalidly transferred, or its value. An invalid transfer is a transfer that was not made pursuant to a valid exercise by or on behalf of the owner C of his power of transfer, which means the exercise of the power of transfer was vitiated by mistake or duress or some other 'vitiating factor', or the transfer was effected by someone other than

---

virtue of the right of ownership. The difference between the two, according to Hohfeld, is only extrinsic, by which he meant that in the former case only the contractor has the duty, whereas in the latter case the same duty is shared by everyone apart from the owner (this is the *in rem/in personam* distinction in the Hohfeldian or modality sense). But the crucial difference between the two types of case that Hohfeld ignores is the nature of the justification for the legal relation.

[57] This does not mean that it is not necessary to state of a right that it is in respect of a thing in order to describe the content of the right. The point is that the general significance of this fact is that it places the right in a justificatory category, and Hohfeld was not concerned with justificatory categories. Honoré emphasises the social significance of property rights as compared with Hohfeld's concept of the *in rem* right, Honoré, 'Rights of Exclusion and Immunities Against Divesting' above n 49, at 468.

C without his authority—for example by an agent or trustee acting beyond his authority, or by a stranger.

If there is an invalid transfer to D, C must (prima facie at least)[58] have a claim to recover the property or its value. C's primary right is his right of ownership or other property right—the right to all the benefit or some particular aspect of the benefit of the property as against the whole world—which generates as a result of the invalid transfer a remedial right against D to recover the property or its value. This is in accordance with the monist principle, by which the claim serves to fulfil or protect the primary right. The claim is a property-based claim, in the sense that it falls in the justificatory category of property. I will refer to it as the property-based restitutionary claim or claim to recover an invalid transfer, 'restitutionary' conveying simply that the remedy is the recovery of a transfer. The basic features of this generic claim will be outlined here; it has various conventional forms in the common law and equity, which will be considered more fully in chapter 6.

The claim does not arise from a breach of duty. Neither the invalid transfer itself, nor the receipt by D, is a breach of duty by D. One can hardly say that D had a duty not to receive an invalid transfer of property, since the transfer was not under his control and he may have no way of knowing whether it was invalid. (If it is a duty, it is a strict liability duty.)[59] It is the mere fact of the receipt of a transfer that generates the claim to recover the property from D. Thus as mentioned previously the primary relation is a primary liability relation. C's primary right is a right to the property that does not correspond to a duty in other parties but to a liability, by virtue of which a recipient becomes liable to a claim to recover property invalidly transferred. The primary liability relation simply allocates the right to the benefit of the property to the owner C, and so subjects anyone else to the risk of a claim in the event of the receipt of an invalid transfer.

For the same reason, strictly speaking a remedial duty to return the property cannot arise from the moment of the receipt of the invalid transfer. In fact C's claim to recover the property is correlated not with a duty to return it on the part of D, but with a liability to surrender it, and the claim arising from an invalid transfer is not a right in the strict sense correlated with a remedial duty, but actually a legal power, correlated with a remedial liability. The power is exercised by

---

[58] ie, subject to bona fide purchase and subject to reduction of the measure in the light of change of position: see below pp 140, 160.

[59] See above p 23.

following the requisite procedure, in the form of legal proceedings and execution of judgment, for securing satisfaction of the claim by the recovery of the property or its value from D's estate.[60]

This is not to say that D does not generally incur a duty with respect to C's property, for example a duty not to take it, or not to dispose of or consume it if it has been received through an invalid transfer.[61] It is just that it is the invalid transfer itself, and not the breach of any such duty, that generates the claim to recover the property. A different type of claim can arise from the breach of such a duty, and it is important to distinguish between the two types of claim, and the circumstances that give rise to them. Confusion has indeed arisen in the literature and in the case law between the claim to recover an invalid transfer and the claim arising from D's breach of a duty not to dispose of or consume property belonging to C that has been invalidly transferred to D, which is, properly understood, a claim for compensation for loss, not a claim to recover property or its value. They are, respectively, claims in property and in tort. This point is discussed below and in chapter 7.

Proprietary and Personal Claims

A 'property-based' claim is not the same thing as a 'proprietary claim' as this expression is usually used. The claim to recover an invalid transfer is property-based, but as the law stands it is not necessarily a proprietary claim. Whereas 'property-based' signifies the justificatory category of the claim, 'proprietary claim' is used in contrast with 'personal claim' to refer to a type of remedy. C has a 'proprietary claim' when he has a remedial property right in property in D's estate. By contrast a personal claim is a claim against D, but not a remedial property right in any part of D's estate; the typical examples of a personal claim are the claims for damages and the claim for the payment of a debt. The claim arising from an invalid transfer is found as a proprietary claim and also as a personal claim: sometimes C has what amounts to a claim of ownership of the property invalidly transferred to D, and sometimes C has only a personal claim for the value of the property transferred. It can be very important in practice which is

---

[60] The is not the same as saying that a right of action involves a legal power to take proceedings in conjunction with a remedial right correlated with a duty to return the property. C's claim is itself a power. See further, P Jaffey, 'Hohfeld's Power-Liability/Right-Duty Distinction in the Law of Restitution' (2004) 17 *Canadian Journal of Law & Jurisprudence* 295.

[61] As a general rule, D does not have a duty to return the property, since the property might be large and unwieldy so that a duty to return it would be unfairly burdensome: see below p 202.

available. If D is bankrupt, C will be able to recover only a proportion of the full measure of a personal claim, but a proprietary claim
will be unaffected by D's bankruptcy because the asset that is the
object of the claim, being C's property, is outside D's estate in bankruptcy. Either a proprietary or a personal claim is explicable as a claim
that arises to protect and fulfil the primary right of ownership in
accordance with the monist principle, though as argued in chapter 6
the monist principle really requires a proprietary claim.[62] For present
purposes, the point is that, as mentioned above, the question whether
the claim is proprietary or personal in the remedial sense is different
from the question whether the claim is property-based, in the sense
that it falls in the justificatory category of property. A personal claim
can be a property-based claim in this sense, though it is not itself a
property right.[63]

It appears that some writers, focusing on the proprietary claim,
think of property in a purely remedial sense, so that it appears to be
a remedial rather than a justificatory category. This tends to fit in with
a sceptical attitude to the concept of property as a justificatory category. The issue is important in connection with the availability of
proprietary claims, as discussed in chapter 6.

An Unjust Enrichment Claim?

It is sometimes suggested that the claim to recover an invalid transfer
is a restitutionary or unjust enrichment claim. As pointed out above,
it is reasonable to describe the claim as a restitutionary claim in a
remedial sense, simply to signify that the remedy is the recovery of
the transfer. And it is reasonable to say that the claim removes from
D what would otherwise be an unjust enrichment. Restitution and
unjust enrichment here refer to the remedial relation subsisting after
the invalid transfer. Neither usage is inconsistent with the analysis of
the claim as property-based, meaning that the claim arises in the justificatory category of property. But both 'restitution' and 'unjust

---

[62] See below pp 161, 172.

[63] Sometimes a distinction is drawn between a 'proprietary claim' and a 'proprietary
remedy'. Here 'proprietary claim' might be interpreted to mean a property-based claim, and
'proprietary remedy' the remedial assertion of a property right. I have preferred to use
the expression 'property-based' to indicate the justificatory category because of the strong
remedial association of the expression 'proprietary', and I will use 'proprietary claim' in the
customary remedial sense. I used a different terminology in P Jaffey, *The Nature and Scope of
Restitution* (Oxford, Hart Publishing, 2000) chs 9, 10, namely 'proprietary' meaning
property-based and '*in rem*' to refer to a proprietary claim, though I believe the approach is
otherwise consistent.

enrichment' have come to be used, in effect, though it may not be expressed in this way, to refer to a justificatory category, so the implication is that the claim falls into the category of restitution or unjust enrichment as opposed to being property-based. The sceptical approach to property mentioned above may have encouraged the idea that the basis of the claim cannot be property, but if it is not property it is difficult to see what other general principle or type of justification could explain it. This raises the question whether there is a genuine justificatory category of restitution or unjust enrichment at all, which will be considered in chapter 8. As I have suggested already, the best way to understand the influence of the analysis in terms of a justificatory category of restitution or unjust enrichment is that it has arisen from the remedy-as-justification fallacy.

The unjust enrichment approach might be thought to gain support from the following argument. As mentioned above, sometimes the claim is personal not proprietary. This means that ownership of or 'title to' the property passes to the recipient D. Thus it might be said that because it passes title the transfer must be valid, and the claim arises because although valid the transfer was nevertheless vitiated. For example, it has been said that if C makes a transfer under the influence of a fundamental mistake title does not pass, but if the mistake is not fundamental then title does pass though the mistake still vitiates the transfer and gives C a personal claim to recover the value transferred.[64] In this type of case it might be thought that because the transfer was valid to pass title, and C's right of ownership has therefore been extinguished, the claim cannot be a property-based claim. It must have some other justificatory basis, which, some commentators have inferred, is the principle of unjust enrichment.

This line of argument seems to have been influential,[65] but it is misconceived. The problem lies in an ambiguity in the expression 'invalid transfer'. If a transfer is 'vitiated', it is necessarily invalid in the sense that there was no valid exercise of C's power to transfer as owner. But it may be that, though the power is invalid in this sense,

---

[64] See eg D Fox, 'The Transfer of Legal Title to Money' [1996] RLR 60. On this basis, it might appear that an unjust enrichment claim is a personal claim and the property-based claim is a proprietary claim. But in the unjust enrichment literature it is sometimes said that where C's title initially passes to D, C may then acquire a new title in the same property on the basis of which he can make a proprietary claim. Alternatively, it is said that sometimes where C initially retained title but title was lost after receipt by D, the claim is a property-based claim and not an unjust enrichment claim. See below p 232.

[65] It seems to be generally accepted among writers on restitution and unjust enrichment.

title nevertheless passes.[66] This does not mean that the claim is not property-based. It means only that, since ownership of the property has passed, the claim must be a personal claim to recover its value, not a proprietary claim in the form of continuing ownership of the property transferred. In other words, the issue is not the justification for the claim but the type of remedy. The original right of ownership is still the primary right from which the claim arises, and its basis is the private property principle. Where it is held that a transfer passes title but that a claim nevertheless arises, the concern must be not with the justification for the claim but with the protection of third parties dealing with D who might be prejudiced by C's retention of title to the property, ie by a proprietary claim.[67] Thus this misconceived line of argument seems to have arisen from the remedial understanding of property mentioned earlier.[68]

The mistaken tendency to characterise the claim as a restitutionary or unjust enrichment claim may be related to the fact that it is a primary liability claim. If the primary right-liability relation is overlooked, it appears that the claim arises not from a relation subsisting before the transfer at all, but just from the receipt of the benefit. It is as if nothing before then is relevant, and the justification for the claim is said to be simply unjust enrichment. But the receipt of the benefit is significant only by virtue of a relation subsisting before the receipt, namely the primary right of ownership of the property.

It is of course sometimes accepted under the unjust enrichment approach that C's primary right of ownership is relevant to the claim. However, it is apparently assumed that the claim does not arise directly from this right of ownership, but from a principle of unjust enrichment that determines how the right of ownership is to be protected.[69] But any such principle is redundant; the primary right of ownership is enough to account for the claim. It is an example of the dualist fallacy to think that although the right from which the claim arises is the right of ownership, the claim does not arise directly to protect and fulfil this right, but on the basis of a remedial principle of

---

[66] This must presumably be the understanding of the case where title passes to D only because the property transferred is untraceable, on receipt or subsequently. The problem here is the failure to recognise the possibility of abstract value as an object of property as discussed in ch 6.

[67] Cf cases of voidable title: see further Jaffey, above n 63, at 324.

[68] Above pp 95–6.

[69] See eg D Friedmann, 'The Protection of Entitlements via the Law of Restitution—Expectancies and Privacy' (2005) 121 *Law Quarterly Review* 400.

unjust enrichment that determines in what way and to what extent it will be protected.

The claim to recover an invalid transfer discussed above can arise in respect of various types of property, for example tangible things, coins and banknotes, and contractual rights. But the most common type of case nowadays may be the claim arising from an unauthorised transfer of money in the form of abstract value from one bank account to another, which takes effect as a deduction from C's credit and an increase in D's. If the transfer is made without authority from C's account, the transfer is invalid and C has a claim against D arising from his right of ownership of the contractual right as an object of property.[70] It seems that the language of property has traditionally been used in connection with claims to recover transfers of tangible property, like land and goods,[71] whereas the terminology of restitution and unjust enrichment developed and has been more common in connection with transfers of money, whether of cash or of money held by way of a contractual debt. The reason for the use of unjust enrichment terminology rather than property terminology in these cases may be the assumption that intangible value, and particularly abstract value, cannot be the object of a right of ownership. But as discussed above, there is no reason to take this view. Money, including money held by way of contractual debt, is a form of property, and the claim to recover the money arises from the primary right of ownership of the contractual right as an object of property.

The Property-based Unauthorised Use Claim

Say D uses C's property without permission. Generally it appears that C has a claim for reasonable payment.[72] I will refer to this as the unauthorised use claim or use claim for short. Reasonable payment means a sum assessed according to what might have been reasonably

---

[70] One might object that if C's bank makes a transfer without proper authorisation, the effect is just that the balance on C's account is unchanged, and the bank has lost money to D; there is no transfer from C to D at all. But if C's bank relied on the ostensible authority of C's agent or trustee to make the transfer, it is entitled to reduce the balance on the account, so that the money comes from C and not from the bank, and if there was no *actual* authority to make the transfer under the terms of the agency or trust, C has a claim against D arising from the invalid transfer. There are many cases of this sort, particularly where a trustee makes an invalid transfer of trust funds held at the bank: see Jaffey, above n 63, p160–62.

[71] Though this is treated as a matter of property torts, as discussed in ch 7 below.

[72] This is recognised for land, goods and intellectual property. A representative case is *Strand Electric & Engineering v Brisford Entertainments* [1952] 2 QB 246. For money, this is a matter of interest.

agreed as a licence fee if D and C had negotiated a licence for the use of C's property. Thus it has sometimes been referred to as 'licence fee damages'. The measure will generally be some proportion of D's profit (exceeding any loss that C has made). The claim seems to be justifiable, but it has proved surprisingly difficult to characterise and explain.[73]

The underlying problem is that the claim appears to arise from a duty not to use the property—it is invariably so understood—and yet the remedy of reasonable payment is not explicable as a remedy for a breach of duty under the monist principle. The appropriate pecuniary remedy for a breach of duty is compensation for loss, and the reasonable payment measure is not a measure of compensation for loss. D's unauthorised use may not have caused C any loss: it may not have caused any damage to the property, and it may not have disturbed C in his use of it, or prevented C from licensing its use to anyone else, since C may not have intended to use or license it. If there have been any such losses, compensation for them is recoverable on the normal measure of compensation for breach of duty, not by way of the reasonable payment measure which is not apt to cover such losses anyway.

It has been argued that the claim can be explained as a compensation claim under the so-called 'opportunity to bargain' argument.[74] The argument is that before the unauthorised use, C could have insisted that D pay him a licence fee. By using the property without taking a licence, D has deprived C of the possibility of agreeing a licence fee, and C's loss is the lost 'opportunity to bargain'. But this makes sense only on the basis that D had a primary duty to take-a-licence-and-use-the-property (as if he had already contracted to take a licence) and failed to do so. Then a reasonable licence fee could be awarded as compensation for loss, consistently with the monist principle. But clearly D had no such duty, since he was entirely free not to use the property at all and not to take a licence, and on this basis the lost opportunity is worth no more than any loss of licence fees caused by D's interference with C's licensing of third parties, which would be covered by an ordinary compensation claim.

---

[73] It has received considerable attention in the restitution and unjust enrichment literature: see generally A Burrows, *The Law of Restitution* (London, Butterworths, 2nd edn, 2002) ch 14.

[74] RS Sharpe and SM Waddams, 'Damages for Lost Opportunity to Bargain' (1982) 2 *Oxford Journal of Legal Studies* 290.

Some judges and many commentators have described the use claim as a restitutionary or unjust enrichment claim,[75] and it is often described as a claim for 'restitutionary damages'. Often this appears to be intended in a purely remedial sense, to mean that the remedy is based not on the loss to C but on the benefit received by D through the wrong. But this does not explain how it arises from the breach of duty. It is sometimes thought to be a case of disgorgement, based on the principle that a wrongdoer should not profit from his wrongdoing. D acts wrongfully by using C's property without permission and is forced to make the payment to C as a means of removing the profits of wrongdoing.[76] But disgorgement should remove all the profits of the wrong, whereas the measure of reasonable payment is carefully calculated as some (generally quite small) proportion of D's benefit. This makes no sense as disgorgement. Furthermore, as discussed in chapter 2, when disgorgement is in issue one would expect to see some reference to whether it is anomalous or inappropriate in civil proceedings, but no concern along these lines has surfaced in connection with this claim, in the case law or the literature.

It appears that the claim is sometimes understood as a claim to reverse an invalid or wrongfully procured transfer from C to D. (The expression 'restititionary damages' appears to be understood by some writers to encompass without distinction both the remedy of reasonable payment for unauthorised use and the remedy of recovery of a transfer.)[77] But a use is not the same thing as a transfer, and the unauthorised use claim is different from the claim to recover an invalid transfer considered above. There is a transfer from C to D when property that was originally in C's possession or control comes into D's possession or control. Use does not entail a transfer. If it did, then whatever C lost through the transfer could be compensated for by way of a compensation claim for the breach of the duty not to use the property, as a well as by the recovery of the invalid transfer. The tendency to equate the use of property with a transfer of it, often by thinking in terms of a figurative loss or 'subtraction' from C, is a common error in the restitution and unjust enrichment literature, and presumably comes from focusing on the fact of benefit to D and the assumption that all

[75] See Burrows, ibid; EJ Weinrib, 'Restitutionary Damages as Corrective Justice' (2000) 1 *Theoretical Inquiries in Law* 1.

[76] See eg Burrows, above n 73, at 460. This is part of the tendency to conflate the use claim with disgorgement; see also below p 235.

[77] J Edelman, *Gain-Based Damages* (Oxford, Hart Publishing, 2002) 66–69.

claims arising from a benefit should be treated in the same way under the category of restitution or unjust enrichment.

Another way of interpreting the claim as a restitutionary or unjust enrichment claim is suggested by Weinrib.[78] He argues that the use claim arises because C's primary right against D includes a right to the value that can be realised through the use of the property.[79] Because this right to the 'opportunity to gain' is an incident of C's right, it should be reflected in the duty correlative to the right. Consequently D's duty is not merely a duty not to cause harm, but a duty not to benefit through use,[80] and the remedy therefore includes a right to the benefit made by D. But, in accordance with the monist princi- ple, the pecuniary remedy for a breach of duty is the amount that so far as possible represents what the performance of the duty was worth to C. Any further 'supra-compensatory' sum paid to C in conse- quence of D's breach of duty cannot be justified as a response to the breach (unless it amounts to disgorgement, which is explicitly not what Weinrib intends).[81] If in breaching the duty D prevents C from realising an opportunity for profit, or diverts to himself an opportun- ity for profit, then D's benefit will also be C's loss, and is recoverable as such. But if the breach of the duty does not affect C, as in the case of an unauthorised use that does not deprive C of personal use or of the prospect of profit through licensing, then the loss caused is nil, and this is the case even if the duty is a duty not to profit and D has profited by the breach.[82]

The answer to the problem lies in the monist principle. Although D does generally have a duty not to use C's property, it is not a breach of this duty that generates the unauthorised use claim. The claim for reasonable payment cannot be explained, consistently with the monist principle, on the basis that it protects or fulfils a primary rela- tion consisting of a duty not to use the property. Only a claim for compensation for loss would achieve that (or, for the future, an injunction against unauthorised use). All the arguments above, in

---

[78] Weinrib, above n 75. The argument echoes Birks's concept of anti-enrichment wrongs: P Birks, *An Introduction to the Law of Restitution* (Oxford, Clarendon Press, rev edn, 1989) 328.

[79] Weinrib, above n 75, at 8–12.

[80] Weinrib, above n 75, at 24.

[81] Weinrib, above n 75, at 6.

[82] There is something curious about Weinrib's 'duty not to profit'. Where there is a duty not to do X, where X is some activity that could generate a profit, the 'duty not to profit' seems to elide the duty not to do X with the question whether there should be claim of prof- its made through doing X.

assuming that the claim arises from a breach of this duty, commit the dualist fallacy.

But Weinrib is right in recognising the importance of the right to use-value. The primary right from which the claim arises is C's primary right of ownership—his primary right to all the benefit and value of the property, including the right to the use-value of the property, meaning its value through use. This is a primary right-liability relation. It represents an allocation to the owner as opposed to anyone else of the right to benefit from the property. In accordance with the monist principle, a claim arises against an unauthorised user by virtue of the unauthorised use, whether or not it happens to be wrongful, just as the claim to recover an invalid transfer considered above arises from the receipt of a transfer. Generally unauthorised use will indeed be wrongful, but this is not the basis of the claim. When D uses the property, the benefit he receives comes from a combination of the use-value of the property and his own action in using it. C's right to the use-value of the property entails a right to the proportion of D's benefit attributable to the use-value of the property, which can be measured as a reasonable 'licence fee' for the use of the property.

It is not surprising that the primary relation is assumed to be the duty not to use the property, not only because of the usual assumption that claims always arise from a breach of duty, but because generally where the claim arises D will indeed be in breach of such a duty. However, sometimes there may be no duty to refrain from using C's property. For example, it may be that if it becomes crucial in an emergency for D to use C's property in order to avoid injury or damage, D is at liberty to use the property, but nevertheless a liability to make a reasonable payment for the unauthorised use arises. A possible example of this is considered below.

PROPERTY AND TORT

Property and Tort as Distinct Justificatory Categories

It is sometimes said that property rights are protected by remedies in restitution or unjust enrichment. The analysis above shows that this is misleading.[83] The claim to recover an invalid transfer and the claim for reasonable payment for unauthorised use are property-based

---

[83] Above pp 96, 101.

claims, not restitution or unjust enrichment claims. The primary right is a right of ownership and the claim arises from it in accordance with the monist principle.

It is also said that property rights are protected by remedies in tort, or that the remedial part of property is tort,[84] or to the same effect that property is a 'facilitative' or 'productive' category, protected by tort as a 'remedial' or 'protective' category,[85] or that property is defined in terms of trespassory rules,[86] or tortious duties of non-interference.[87] The implication is that the scope of property rights is defined by a duty in tort. This is also misconceived, though by contrast with the case of restitution or unjust enrichment, there is of course a genuine justificatory category of tort law. Property law and tort law are distinct justificatory categories. The function of tort law is to determine the extent to which D should be constrained in his activities in order to protect C against harm or intrusion, or, more broadly, the extent to which he should be responsible for a loss that an act or activity of his causes to C. The basic principle is (I have suggested) something along the lines of a principle of reasonable care or a principle of responsibility.[88] An important part of tort law is to determine what sorts of harm to C should be recognised and weighed into account in determining D's duty of care. C clearly has an interest in not being physically harmed. He also has an interest in freedom from physical constraint, in his reputation, and in the privacy of personal information. The interests recognised in tort law also include C's interest in his property. This calls for an independent, prior definition of the scope of C's property right, and this is supplied by property law.

Consider a case of negligence where C suffers damage to his property from D's negligent driving. C's claim arises from D's breach of his duty to take reasonable care to avoid harm to C, including harm to his property. Clearly the duty of reasonable care is not correlated with the right of ownership. C's property right counts, in tort law, as an interest that is weighed into account in determining D's duty of reasonable care and C's correlative right in tort law. In a case of trespass, where C has a claim for compensation arising from loss caused

[84] eg, P Cane, 'Corrective Justice and Correlativity in Private Law' (1996) 16 *Oxford Journal of Legal Studies* 470, 475–76; Friedmann, above n 69.

[85] See eg Cane, ibid; Friedmann, above n 69.

[86] Harris, above n 9, at 24.

[87] Penner, above n 18, at 139.

[88] See above p 10.

by D's encroachment on property or use of it, it might seem more plausible to say that D has breached a duty in property law correlated with the right of ownership, rather than a duty in tort. Again, however, it is best understood as a duty in tort protecting an interest in property. The duty in tort does not correlate with or define the scope of the property right, but presupposes it; it prescribes what is actually required of D, and this is not the same thing as defining the scope of C's property right. The duty in tort cannot be equated precisely with non-encroachment. For example, in principle D's duty should depend on what D knows or can reasonably be expected to know, so that D does not commit a breach of duty if he cannot reasonably be expected to know that the property in question is private property belonging to someone else.[89] But the scope of the property right clearly does not depend on what D knows or ought to know. Furthermore, in exceptional circumstances there may be considerations that outweigh C's interest in his property so that D does not in those circumstances have a duty in tort to refrain from using the property. For example, in an emergency where it is crucial for D to use C's property to avoid damage or injury, he may be entitled to do so. If so, this is not because use of the property does not in the circumstances fall with the scope of the property right, but because in the circumstances there is no duty in tort not to use it. In such a case, although there is no breach of a duty in tort, there may nevertheless be a claim for reasonable payment for unauthorised use. Of course, this approach depends on the distinction between right-duty and right-liability relations. Without any recognition of a right-liability relation, it would make no sense to say that the scope of the right of ownership could be defined without determining at the same time the duty against trespass.

This approach casts light on the famous and controversial case of *Vincent v Lake Erie*.[90] D moored his boat at C's dock in a storm. He did so without permission, in order to save his boat from damage. Some damage was caused to the dock, and C was held entitled to compensation, but the claim cannot on the face of it be explained as a claim based on a wrong by D, because the court held that D was entitled to act in the way that he did in order to protect his boat from damage. This seems to create a problem, because if D did not act wrongfully, it appears that he should not have been liable to pay

[89] See further below p 194.
[90] 109 Minn. 456, 124 N.W. 221 (1910).

compensation. On the argument above, even though he did not act wrongfully by using C's property, D can be subject to an unauthorised use claim arising from C's primary right of ownership of the dock, which is a property-based claim, not a tort claim. One would have to say that the compensation measure was in the circumstances an appropriate measure of payment for the unauthorised use, which seems not unreasonable in the circumstances.[91]

Compare the case where D is caught in a storm and knocked against C's dock as a result of a gust of wind, despite the fact that he at all times showed a reasonable standard of care and skill in his control of the boat. I take it that there would be no claim for compensation, because the only possible claim is the tort claim based on negligence. There is no question of a property-based unauthorised use claim, because D made no unauthorised use of the dock.

The same issue of the relationship between property law and tort law arises in connection with the restitutionary claim to recover an invalid transfer. As mentioned above, where D receives property through an invalid transfer, D can incur a duty not to consume or dispose of the property. This is a duty in tort and it is not the basis for the claim to recover the invalid transfer. Again, because D may not know whether he has even received a transfer, and if he does he may have no reason to know whether it is invalid, it is better to say that D has a duty to take reasonable care not to destroy or dispose of property invalidly transferred to him. Some confusion in the case law, both in the common law of tort and in the law of equity, has resulted from the failure to recognise the distinction between the property-based restitutionary claim to recover invalidly-transferred property and the tortious claim in respect of the wrongful disposal or consumption of invalidly-transferred property.[92] This issue is considered at more length in chapter 7.

Thus it is misleading to say that property rights are protected by remedies in tort, if this is understood to mean that the scope of a right

---

[91] See also P Jaffey, 'Duties and Liabilities in Private Law' (2006) 12 *Legal Theory* 137. In the usual case reasonable payment includes an element for wear and tear, and where the measure is set after the event and the measure of such loss is known the measure should be set to at least match it; and arguably where the use is in an emergency the fee should not exceed it.

[92] One could postulate a regime for a certain type of property under which a stranger is always free to use the property but incurs a liability to pay for any use he makes of it. This might be appropriate for intellectual property, on the basis that the rationale of an intellectual property right is not to enable the owner to control or restrict usage, but to secure to him the value of the subject matter of the right, eg, an invention in the case of a patent.

of ownership or property right is defined by a duty in tort. The scope of the property right is defined by a right–liability relation, not a duty. The duty in tort is not correlated with or definitive of the scope of the right of ownership; it takes account of C's interest in property as explained above. The difference is also reflected in the characteristic remedies for claims in tort and property arising in accordance with the monist principle. In property law it is a claim for the recovery of property or its value arising from an invalid transfer, or a claim for reasonable payment for unauthorised use, whereas in tort it is a claim for compensation for a breach of a duty not to act in a way that will intrude on or damage the property, or not to consume or dispose of it if it has reached D's hands.

To say that tort is the remedial aspect of property is an example of the dualist fallacy because it implies that, instead of arising simply to fulfil and protect the primary right of ownership in accordance with the monist principle, the remedial right depends on a separate body of tort law that determines what the appropriate level of protection should be for the primary right. At the same time it confuses the distinction between property and tort as justificatory categories with the distinction between primary and remedial rights. These distinctions are not arbitrary or pedantic. They serve to separate out distinct types of issue and so avoid inconsistency and incoherence.

Non-property Interests Conflated with Interests in Property

The previous section concerned the case where a property right is recognised as an interest protected in tort. A different issue is where tort law protects an interest that is not a property right at all, but is mistaken for or treated as a property right. Say D discloses personal confidential information concerning C's relationship with his spouse, so causing distress and embarrassment to C. Recognising that C has a claim for compensation does not entail recognising information as an object of private property. The claim does not depend on showing that C is entitled to all the value and benefit of the information as an object of property. It is not relevant to show that C has invested his labour and money in creating the information, in the expectation of a right to all the benefit of it, and so has acquired a property right in it. This is not the rationale of the claim. The rationale is to protect C's interest in privacy, and the issue raised is whether C has such an interest and whether it is outweighed by D's interest or the public interest in the disclosure of the information. This is purely a matter of tort law, and does not involve property law at all.

Compare this with the case where C has built up confidential commercial information valuable to his business, and D discloses it. It might appear that this is the same as the previous case. But here, if C is entitled to have the information kept secret, it is because he is exclusively entitled to the benefit of the information in his business or as a tradeable commodity. Without this there would be no basis for complaining about the loss. Thus here the confidential information is an object of property, more precisely a form of intellectual property. Furthermore, it does indeed seem plausible in this case to say that C devised and collated the information in the expectation of an exclusive right to all the benefit of it, in accordance with the principle of private property. This is a question of background property law.

If C is the owner of the confidential information, C may have, in addition to or instead of a claim for compensation for loss, a claim for payment for unauthorised use of it.[93] By contrast, one would not expect an unauthorised use claim to arise in the case of personal information, because the claim is not based on C's ownership.[94] Similarly, if C is the owner of confidential information he may well have a power to license its use or to sell it, whereas an interest in privacy that gives rise to a duty in tort not to disclose personal information would not support a power to sell or license it.[95]

The 'law of confidential information' is a recognised conventional-justificatory category: there is an established body of law that lays down a uniform set of conditions for a claim for 'breach of confidence'.[96] But, as anticipated in chapter 1,[97] it is not a true justificatory category: it has parts drawn from different justificatory categories, and their common treatment under a single framework is liable to involve false assimilation. A claim for breach of confidence may be a claim in tort to protect an interest in privacy, or a claim in tort in respect of confidential information as an object of property; or it may be a property-based claim for reasonable payment for the unauthorised use of the confidential information. Furthermore, a claim for breach of confidence can be a claim arising from a contract

[93] As mentioned above, this is the characteristic claim in respect of intellectual property.

[94] Or at least, if such a claim were to arise, one would have to infer that C also has a right of ownership over personal information.

[95] As opposed to a power to waive a right of privacy. Cf's Honoré's distinction between a true property right and a 'simple right' which is 'protected by law but is not alienable or transmissible': above n 22, at 180–81.

[96] See eg *Coco v Clark* [1969] RPC 41.

[97] Above p 34.

or fiduciary relationship.[98] Thus it is unhelpful to ask, 'Is confidential information property?'; or to ask what the true basis of the law of confidential information is—whether it is tort or property or equity (meaning fiduciary law).[99] It is not a single category at all in the important justificatory sense.[100]

The same issue comes up in connection with reputation. The law of defamation is not based on the idea that C is entitled to all the value and benefit of his reputation as an object of private property, in order to give him a return on the effort he has put into acquiring it. If this were the case, one would expect him to have an unauthorised use claim for reasonable payment when his reputation is used for profit without permission, and be able to license and sell his reputation as a commodity. In fact there is only a claim for compensation, and this should be understood as compensation for damage to a personal interest not damage to reputation as an object of a property. Although one can describe reputation as a thing, it is a mistake to think that it is, by virtue of the law of defamation, a limited form of private property, or analogous to private property, or that it is just a matter of a change of terminology to express the law of defamation in terms of private property.[101] The mistake is to think that the law of property encompasses any rules relating in any way to things, as opposed to rules based on securing the benefit or some aspect of it to a right-holder in accordance with the reliance principle of private property.

By contrast, in some jurisdictions the law allows a celebrity an unauthorised use claim in respect of his fame and empowers him to license its use for commercial purposes, in advertising and sponsorship. In other words, it recognises the celebrity's reputation as an

---

[98] Fiduciary relations are discussed in ch 5.

[99] See eg W Cornish and D Llewelyn, *Intellectual Property* (London, Sweet & Maxwell, 5th edn, 2003) para 8-50. Sometimes breach of confidence is treated as part of the law concerning injunctions, which suggests the remedy-as-justification fallacy and obscures the justificatory basis: see eg PH Pettit, *Equity and the Law of Trusts* (Oxford, OUP, 10th edn, 2006) 629.

[100] In the recent development of the English law of privacy, the courts have insisted that privacy is protected by the law of confidential information, but that there is no right of privacy. This obscures the nature of the claim. It is really a tort claim in respect of an interest in privacy: see P Jaffey, 'Rights of Privacy, Confidentiality, and Publicity, and Related Rights' in P Torremans (ed), *Copyright and Human Rights* (The Hague, Kluwer Law International, 2004) 157.

[101] As Waldron seems to suggest, *The Right to Private Property*, above n 2, at 322, 324; see also Honoré, 'Ownership' in *Making Law Bind*, above n 22, at 179–81; Clarke and Kohler, above n 14, at 372.

object of property. There may be good reasons for recognising this form of property. But this development has sometimes been made by supposed analogy from purely tortious cases, in privacy or defamation, so as to suggest that the fundamental difference between recognising an interest attracting protection in tort and recognising an object of property has not been appreciated. In other words, it involves false assimilation. It would also be a mistake to recognise a celebrity right or 'right of publicity' as a right based on the 'principle of unjust enrichment', or as a right against misappropriation or unfair competition,[102] since any of these formulas simply evades and conceals the real issue, which is whether it is right to recognise reputation as an object of property.

---

[102] In addition, as mentioned earlier, generally the recognition of intellectual property is left to Parliament.

4

Law and Equity

Important parts of English property law developed in equity. This chapter will consider the relationship between the common law and equity, and the next chapter will consider equity's greatest contribution to property law, the trust. The main argument of this chapter is that the historical division of English law into common law and equity had the fortuitous effect of facilitating the recognition by English law of new concepts in property law and new types of property right, including the trust, but nevertheless the full understanding and further development of these concepts is nowadays being frustrated by the continuing resistance of equity lawyers to the elimination of equity as a distinct category in the law.

'Equity' is used in a technical sense to refer to a category of English law. The nature of this category and its connection with 'equity' in its ordinary sense of fairness or justice is a matter of some controversy, which I will come back to. It is helpful to begin with a rather schematic account of the historical development of the law of equity in English law. Equity emerged during a period when the common law courts were unduly rigid in their approach, or subject to improper influence, and litigants took to appealing to the Crown against decisions of the common law courts. These appeals were delegated to the Chancellor, who asserted a power to overrule the decisions of the common law courts when they operated unfairly, and in due course this practice grew into a recognised jurisdiction exercised through the Chancellor's court, the court of Chancery. In time the Chancery court developed a body of case law, expressed in a distinct terminology with a distinctive set of concepts, which became known as the law of equity. In consequence there were two court systems, the common law and equity, operating in parallel and administering their own bodies of case law. For a time the two court systems were in genuine conflict, in the sense that they might give judgments at odds with each other and there was doubt as to which was to prevail and be enforced by the state. But in due course it became clear that in the case of dispute the decisions of the Chancery courts had precedence.[1]

This left the law in a curious state. The common law courts might deny that a claim was available on certain facts, but the Chancery courts would recognise a claim. Or the common law might recognise a claim but confine the claimant to a certain remedy, and the claimant could take further proceedings in equity to obtain a better remedy. Or the common law might allow a claim, but the courts of equity would issue an order preventing the claimant from enforcing it. There remained the appearance of two bodies of law in conflict: a proposition of the common law made without qualification by common law judges, and relied on by them in issuing decisions that purported to be definitive, might be contradicted by a proposition of the law of equity that was actually enforced as the law of the land. But, once the relationship between the two systems was established, the real position was that the common law and equity were not separate bodies of law in conflict, but different parts of a single body of law, each constituting one stage in a two-stage process of determining the law. A proposition of the common law, though apparently definitive, had to be understood as implicitly subject to equity, and so was not contradicted by equity but taken by equity as a provisional decision to be modified as appropriate. The common law could not be taken as a complete statement of the law, and the law of equity could not be understood without first understanding the common law that it qualified or supplemented.

The divided system carried considerable costs to litigants. A litigant might have to take more than one set of proceedings, and he might find that he had taken proceedings in the wrong court and had to start all over again. Legal costs were increased by the need for specialised knowledge of the two different systems.[2] The Supreme Court of Judicature Acts 1873–75 mitigated these problems by bringing together the two bodies of law in a single court system, so that both the common law and equity could be applied in the same proceedings. This was 'procedural fusion', or the fusion of the administration of law and equity. Since then the issue that has troubled courts and writers is whether there should also be 'substantive fusion': should the

[1] The 'triumph of equity' is attributed to *The Earl of Oxford's case* (1615) 1 Rep Ch 1.

[2] The same problem also arose purely at common law in connection with the forms of action; above p 18.

common law and equity be preserved as separate bodies of law, or should they be integrated into a single expanded body of law, so that it would cease to be of any significance whether any part of the law is a matter of common law or equity (except as a matter of convenience in exposition in tracing its origin and development). This raises the question of the nature of equity as a body of law and its relationship to the common law.

A Methodological Distinction

The separate courts of equity arose because of the need to get around the rigidity and arbitrariness of the common law courts. Equity was an institutional device to deal with an institutional problem. Once the procedural distinction was removed, and the two bodies of law were brought together to be dealt with by the same courts, could there be any reason to preserve a two-stage process instead of integrating law and equity into a single body of law? One possible answer is that law and equity had developed differences in general approach to regulation and adjudication, which I will refer to as methodology. One can distinguish between various distinct though related points.

First, it might be said that the law of equity has a moral basis—it does justice or equity in the ordinary sense—whereas the common law is morally arbitrary or has some other sort of basis. It is certainly true that originally equity was precipitated into existence by injustice in the common law, and that it sought to achieve a just outcome that the common law failed to provide. This was reflected in the idea that the law of equity was based on 'conscience', meaning that the Chancellor relied on his own moral sense of right and wrong. But it seems clear that the reason why equity emerged was not that the common law had a rival objective of some sort. It would be difficult to see what other goal the common law might be thought to have, though there is certainly the possibility of divergent views on what justice requires in any particular case. The problem was that the common law fell short of its aim of doing justice because of institutional problems. In fact, whereas the modern common law has moved towards a structure based on its underlying moral principles, through the modern justificatory categories of contract, tort and property (or, as many would say, unjust enrichment), equity's morally charged but vague expressions such as 'conscience', 'unconscionability', 'good faith' and 'clean hands' continue to obscure the moral basis of equitable doctrines.[3]

Sometimes it has been said that the common law administers justice by applying binding rules drawn from precedent—'justice according to law'—whereas the justice administered in equity is unmediated by any requirement to apply binding rules established by precedent and the judge is free to apply directly his own sense of right and wrong. This seems to have been a true reflection of the early role of equity, and for this reason equity came to be described pejoratively as 'varying with the length of the Chancellor's foot'.[4] But in modern times the courts of equity have been emphatic in rejecting this characterisation and insisting that a court of equity 'is not a court of conscience', meaning that equity is a body of law based on precedent just like the common law,[5] and 'conscience' and 'unconscionability' and similar expressions are technical expressions whose meaning is determined by precedent. In any case, it is open to question whether there is any distinction nowadays between the common law and equity on this question.

A related idea is that equity is open to change and development, whereas the common law is rigid and unchanging. On this view, the difference between the common law and equity concerns the freedom of the courts to develop the law through analogical reasoning. No doubt equity was originally far more flexible than the rigid common law that prompted its emergence, and it seems that the idea of the common law as an immutable body of law and equity as capable of change and development persisted into modern times,[6] though at one time it was the Chancery courts that notoriously became associated with the type of rigid and legalistic approach that had originally afflicted the common law courts.

In quite recent times this point has been considered in connection with the development of the equitable law of constructive trusts to protect spouses and cohabiting partners.[7] In this context, one view expressed was that nowadays the creation of new rights and remedies is a matter for Parliament, and not the courts.[8] In part this may reflect

---

[3] Exemplified in some of the 'maxims of equity': see eg JE Martin, *Hanbury & Martin Modern Equity* (London, Sweet & Maxwell, 17th edn, 2005) 27.

[4] *Table Talk of John Selden* (ed Pollock, 1927) 43; PH Pettit, *Equity and the Law of Trusts* (Oxford, OUP, 10th edn, 2006) 4.

[5] *Re Telescriptor Syndicate Ltd* [1903] 2 Ch 174, 195, per Buckley J; Pettit, ibid, 5.

[6] See eg *Re Hallett's Estate* (1880) 13 Ch D 696, 710, per Jessel MR.

[7] This is considered below p 252.

[8] *Western Fish Products Ltd v Penwith DC* [1981] 2 All ER 204, 218, per Megaw LJ; Pettit, above n 4, at 5–6.

the ethos of mechanical jurisprudence in the sense discussed in chapter 1, according to which the judicial role is conceived purely as a matter of finding and applying settled law.[9] In the light of its origins, it may have been a particular concern to emphasise this point in connection with equity. In fact the modern position seems to be best captured by the following much quoted passage:

> [I]n the field of equity, the length of the Chancellor's foot has been measured or is capable of measurement. This does not mean that equity is past childbearing; simply that its progeny must be legitimate—by precedent out of principle.[10]

As this statement suggests, nowadays it is difficult to see any real difference between the common law and equity in terms of their freedom to develop through analogical reasoning.

Equity as a Discretionary Jurisdiction

Lastly, and most commonly, it is said that equity is characteristically discretionary. One version of this approach is the idea that in equity there is a general discretion to disapply or override a common law rule in particular circumstances in which it operates unfairly. This is sometimes explained in terms of the Aristotelian concept of equity, which is understood as a response to a problem arising from the generality of rules. A rule may be a good rule, with a sound rationale, and carefully drafted to take account of various considerations, but it is inevitable that, because it has a fixed verbal form, it will in some unforeseen circumstances fail to reflect its rationale, or fail to take account of relevant considerations, and so operate unfairly.[11] Thus one might argue that, whatever the care and competence with which rules are devised, there is always the need for a general overriding discretion to disapply a rule in particular circumstances, and this is the role of a separate law of equity.[12] In reality, in the historical emergence of equity it was surely concerned not with essentially good rules that fell short of perfection, but crude and arbitrary rules that needed to be negated and supplanted by different ones in general or over a wide range of operation. In any case, there is nowadays no general power in equity to depart from common law rules in this way, save by way of refining rules through analogical reasoning, which works in the same way in equity and at common law.

---

[9] Above p 4.

[10] *Cowcher v Cowcher* [1972] 1 WLR 425, 430, per Bagnall J.

[11] F Schauer, *Playing by the Rules* (Oxford, Clarendon Press, OUP, 1991) 100.

[12] eg, A Hudson, *Equity and Trusts* (London, Cavendish Publishing, 4th edn, 2005) 11.

It is better to put the point as follows. The law is sometimes discretionary, and sometimes it is based on strict rules. (As mentioned in chapter 2,[13] this may be only a matter of degree.) The issue is the scope for evaluation left to the judge in the application of the law. Discretion and strict rules are different regulatory techniques. They have different advantages and disadvantages, and there are different contexts where one or other may be preferable. Historically equity no doubt showed a preference for discretion. This would be the natural consequence of the origin of equity in the free exercise of conscience by the Chancellor.

But it is not clear that modern equity is systematically different from the common law in its approach to this issue. There are certainly aspects of equity that appear to be discretionary or have always been understood as discretionary. The traditional 'maxims of equity' appear to be quite open-ended and might be said to be discretionary.[14] Equitable remedies such as the injunction and specific performance are said to be discretionary, and the issue of discretion is an important aspect of the controversy concerning the so-called 'remedial constructive trust', which is considered in chapter 6.[15] But it is said that the discretion to award these remedies is exercised according to settled principles. It is doubtful whether there is any discretion in a strong sense.[16] Certainly it is far from clear that in cases like this the court is less constrained than it is in parts of the common law, as for example where it has to make a judgment of the standard of care in tort. Also, it is not generally thought that a discretion is involved in applying equitable rules that employ concepts such as unconscionability or bad faith.[17] And of course there are parts of equity that are notoriously dominated by strict rules, including much of the law governing the trust and equitable property rights.

Is a Two-stage Process Justified?

These possible methodological distinctions between common law and equity are clearly relevant to the origin and development of equity. They may have left their mark on the modern law of equity, but it seems very doubtful that any of them can provide a general definition or characterisation of modern equity, though maybe some

---

[13] Above p 53.
[14] Above n 3.
[15] Below p 177.
[16] Above p 54.
[17] Above, n 5.

equity lawyers would insist on this. In any case, even if there is still in the modern law a systematic difference between law and equity along these lines, the question remains whether it is justified to preserve it. What is the advantage of requiring a court to follow a two-stage process of adjudication, in which the law is first determined provisionally by reference to a body of law based on one method of regulation or adjudication, and then modified according to a different body of law based on a different method of regulation or adjudication, in order to reach the definitive position? Now that the institutional problems in the common law that led to the creation of a separate law of equity have long since been overcome, is there any reason why it would not be preferable simply to have a single stage of adjudication applying a single body of law, which can take account of the methodological issues as appropriate to particular parts of the law? With respect to discretion, as suggested above it is an important general question of regulatory technique in what circumstances and to what degree there should be a judicial discretion. This is an issue that the courts are inevitably faced with and it deserves direct and explicit consideration.[18] The association of discretion with the law of equity interferes with any such consideration. It ties the use of discretion to the accidents of history that allocated certain issues to equity, and it obscures these issues in the controversy surrounding the true nature of equity. In my view, these suggested methodological differences do not provide any reason for resisting the substantive fusion of law and equity.

EQUITY AS A JUSTIFICATORY CATEGORY AND THE ANTI–FUSION FALLACY

Equity as a Substantive Area of Law

The various doctrines that developed in equity form the substantive law of equity. This includes the law of trusts and equitable property rights, particular applications and developments of the trust in the form of company and partnership law and probate, fiduciary relationships, confidential information, equitable estoppel, relief from unfair contracts, and much of intellectual property law.[19] Sometimes references to the substantive law of equity present it as a justificatory

[18] See eg CR Sunstein, *Legal Reasoning and Political Conflict* (Oxford, OUP, 1996) ch 7.

[19] See the list of matters allocated to the Chancery Division by the Supreme Court Act 1981, s 61, though this is not exhaustive or determinative of the subject matter of equity.

category comparable to contract or tort. However, it is not apparent on what basis equity could really be understood as a justificatory category. One possibility might be a principle of unconscionability.

A Fundamental Principle of Unconscionability?

As mentioned above, the origin of the concept of 'conscience' in equity seems to be that the Chancellor was to consult his own conscience rather than the law in the form of binding precedent. But it is now often used in a quite different sense (though the difference generally goes unremarked) to refer to the conscience of the defendant D, as when it is said that D's 'conscience is affected', and this seems to be understood to imply that the claim is based on D's knowledge of relevant facts, meaning, by implication, his fault or culpability.[20] Some claims in equity are indeed based on D's knowledge or fault, but it is not true of all.[21] More generally, it is sometimes said that equity (or a part of equity) is based on a doctrine or a principle of 'unconscionability',[22] which seems to be invoked as if it were a general moral principle of the sort that might underlie a justificatory category. But it is not clear what this principle might be.[23] Unconscionability is a type of wrongdoing, but a wrong is a type of modality not a justificatory category. The connotation is of a serious or culpable wrong, but this gives no indication of what the principle might be. One might say that a body of law has developed to give content to the concept of unconscionability. But unless there really is an underlying principle of some sort around which the case law develops, the body of case law is a spurious justificatory category in the sense of chapter 1.[24]

It is sometimes said that unconscionability does have a more precise meaning than culpable wrongdoing: equity's role is limited to restraining the exercise of legal (as opposed to equitable) powers or rights, and unconscionability is the test of when D should be restrained.[25] Unconscionability, in other words, is the abuse of legal rights or powers. But this does not identify or even indicate a principle or type of justification for a claim. It amounts to saying only that equity is the second stage of a two-stage methodology of adjudica-

---

[20] A claim might be entirely in accord with the Chancellor's conscience—morally justified, as one would nowadays say—but not based on fault.

[21] eg, the important equitable proprietary claim considered in ch 6.

[22] See eg G Watt, *Trusts and Equity* (Oxford, OUP, 2nd edn, 2006) 13–16.

[23] See *Royal Brunei Airlines Sdn Bhd v Tan* [1995] 2 AC 378, 392, per Lord Nicholls.

[24] Above p 13.

[25] Watt, above n 22, at 13–14.

tion, so that equity is always set against the ostensible position according to the first stage–the common law–and as discussed above there is no reason to preserve this distinction.

On reflection it is surely quite implausible to think that equity is a justificatory category like contract, tort or property, based on a particular fundamental underlying principle. Its content depends on accidents of history and the particular shortcomings of the common law that prompted its intervention. For this reason the law of equity cannot be captured by a general formula; thus it is sometimes said that equity 'cannot be defined, only described'.[26] Its formal definition is that it is that body of the law that was enforced in the Court of Chancery before the Judicature Acts (including subsequent development of this law).[27] In the terms of the discussion in chapter 1, equity is a purely conventional category, so far as justification is concerned.

Substantive Fusion and Analogical Reasoning

Thus the law of equity contains material drawn from different justificatory categories, including contract, tort, and property. For example, there are doctrines of equity that enforce agreements, though not under the name of contract law. Fiduciary relationships are a good example, as considered later.[28] Similarly, some of the law of equitable estoppel appears to enforce agreements,[29] and sometimes when 'fraud' or 'unconsionability' is invoked in equity the fraud or unconscionability in question is reneging on an agreement.[30] These rules are not part of the conventionally-defined law of contract, but, if it is right that their justification lies in the principle that agreements should be fulfilled, they are part of the true justificatory category of contract.[31] Similarly, there are doctrines of equity that in substance generate claims in tort, though not traditionally so described. One recognised example is the claim for knowing or dishonest assistance.[32]

---

[26] RP Meagher, JD Heydon and MJ Leeming, *Meagher, Gummow and Lehane's Equity—Doctrines and Remedies* (Australia, London, Butterworths, Lexis-Nexis, 4th edn, 2002) para 1-010.

[27] Pettit, above n 4, at 1.

[28] See below p 144.

[29] See eg the discussion in Martin, above n 3, at 892.

[30] See below p 247.

[31] There are parts of equity that are complex in the sense that they combine parts derived from different justificatory categories, for example confidential information as discussed above p 108.

[32] See below p 199.

This has implications for analogical reasoning. Assuming that some doctrines of equity are indeed contractual or tortious in the justificatory sense though not part of the conventional category of contract or tort, it follows that analogical reasoning on relevant aspects of contract and tort should transcend the law-equity boundary to promote the coherence of the justificatory categories of contract and tort. Before procedural fusion, it is clear that this did not happen. Law and equity developed quite separately, with concepts and terminology and sometimes conflicting principles even when dealing with the same justificatory category. Indeed this was probably necessary in order for equity to appear to supplement the common law rather than simply contradict it. This segregation and independent development of law and equity has inevitably led to some incoherence and in particular false differentiation and false assimilation, in the senses explained in chapter 1.[33]

Since the Judicature Acts, equity and the common law have been applied together in the same courts and it has been practicable for analogical reasoning to operate across the two bodies of law. It should operate to eliminate false differentiation and assimilate rules concerning the same issue into a single body of law.[34] This is what is meant by substantive fusion. Substantive fusion is the natural consequence of the ordinary judicial function of analogical reasoning, once the misconception of equity as a justificatory category is overcome. The problem is that equity is invariably treated unreflectively as if it were a justificatory category, as where it is contrasted with contract as a body of rules generating a certain type of claim, or a claim is said to lie in equity but not in contract or tort. It is this implicit assumption that equity is a justificatory category, analogous to contract, tort or property, that inhibits analogical reasoning across law and equity. In other words, as suggested in chapter 1,[35] insofar as equity is treated as a justificatory category, it is a spurious justificatory category, which should be broken down and assimilated into the genuine justificatory categories of contract, tort and property. I will say that any argument based on the assumption that equity is a category of more than historical significance, or in particular that it is a justificatory category rather than a purely conventional category, commits the 'anti-fusion fallacy'.[36]

[33] See above p 6.
[34] For a similar integrationist view see S Worthington, *Equity* (Oxford, OUP, 2nd edn, 2006) esp ch 10.
[35] Above p 14.
[36] Cf the 'fusion fallacy' considered below, at n 45.

A number of objections might be made to this line of argument. To take again the case of contract, and assuming again that there are agreement-based claims in equity, one might say that this part of the law of equity, the 'equitable law of contract' (not usually so described of course), differs fundamentally from the common law of contract in crucial respects—it has never had any doctrine of consideration or privity, for example. Thus they are not really the same type of law at all, and should therefore not be assimilated. It is true of course that equity's treatment of agreements is different from the common law's—otherwise it would never have served any purpose—but, however different it may be, if it is based on the same general principle as the common law of contract it should in principle be assimilated into a single body of law to avoid false differentiation. Even striking differences such as the absence of a rule of privity or consideration do not indicate that there is a different general principle or distinctive type of justification behind this part of the law of equity, merely that equity has adopted a different position on certain issues that arise in implementing the principle though a body of rules.

There is a danger of a misunderstanding that makes substantive fusion appear to be potentially crude and regressive. One might think that substantive fusion forces the law to choose between the common law position and the equitable position, so that, for example, substantive fusion would mean either following the common law and sticking to the doctrines of privity and consideration (ignoring, for the sake of the illustration, the statutory reform of the doctrine of privity in English law),[37] or alternatively following equity and abandoning the doctrines of privity or consideration altogether. But of course the better position may be that the common law's doctrine of privity or consideration is generally sound, but equity is right to disapply it in particular circumstances. Thus one might argue that it is necessary to retain a separate law of equity so that this flexibility can be retained. But this crude choice is not at all what substantive fusion requires: I will call this misconception the 'crude fusion fallacy', and I will come back to it below. To the contrary, the effect of substantive fusion is to require the distinctions justifying different treatment of agreements in different circumstances to be identified and incorporated into a single body of law. Examination of the circumstances in which equity enforces an agreement in the absence of privity or consideration might assist in determining in what way the common

---

[37] The Contracts (Rights of Third Parties) Act 1999.

law doctrines should be qualified in other cases. The effect will be to form a single more sophisticated body of law, drawing on the insights of law and equity.

Remedies and Fusion

The areas of law that came to be dealt with in equity included certain types of remedy. Whereas the common law was for the most part confined to awarding damages, equity developed the power to award remedies unknown to the common law, including specific performance and the injunction.[38] A particular problem arises in connection with these equitable remedies. The traditional position is that the common law can specify a primary relation in tort or contract, but leave open the nature of the remedy for equity to determine—for example, it can specify a primary right-duty relation, but leave open the question whether there should be a remedy of specific performance or an injunction for a breach of duty. This enshrines the dualist fallacy in the law. (The division of the law into the two bodies of law and equity is also sometimes described as dualism, but of course this is a different usage from the usage in connection with remedies in chapter 2.) According to the monist principle, the choice of remedy in general follows from the nature of the primary relation, and substantive fusion of law and equity is a necessary step in allowing this to be properly understood and applied.

Even worse, it appears that sometimes the equitable remedy of the injunction is treated as a freestanding remedy, in the sense that the court considers whether the remedy is available in particular circumstances without ever formulating a primary relation at all. Thus it is said that an injunction may be awarded against D to prevent D from acting unconscionably towards C, though the injunction does not protect any right of C's.[39] This is also liable to lead to the remedy-as-justification fallacy, if a body of law builds up around the issue, in the form of a conventional-justificatory category with a framework and set of criteria for the availability of the remedy.[40]

---

[38] These remedies could be awarded because in equity enforcement measures could be taken against the defendant himself to coerce him into acting, as opposed to merely seizing property to secure a payment of damages or debt: see below p 141.

[39] See above p 56.

[40] It has sometimes been said that the common law remedy of damages (meaning compensatory damages) should not be available for an equitable claim such as breach of fiduciary duty or breach of confidence. The argument is presumably that, as a matter of precedent, equity has to rely exclusively on its own authorities and not on the common law's, and there is no authority for such a remedy in equity; and furthermore that it is impermissible to

A Problem in Achieving Substantive Fusion

Although substantive fusion is justified and is the natural consequence of ordinary analogical reasoning, this is not to say that it is a straight-forward process, and there is good reason to proceed with caution. Often where equity and the common law address issues from the same justificatory category, the analogy is concealed because of the difference in concepts and terminology. It is often far from clear which parts of equity and the common law are really addressing the same types of issue and should be assimilated through analogical rea-soning. For example, I suggested above that fiduciary relationships are a type of contractual relationship, but this is certainly controver-sial.[41] The difficulty is compounded by the fact that substantive fusion often involves assimilating two general regimes, not just spe-cific rules on a certain point. For example, the common law and equity each have general regimes governing property-based claims to recover invalid transfers—restitutionary claims—which operate in different types of situation. These are discussed in chapters 6 and 7. A problem here is that substantive fusion may involve a number of changes to distinct but interdependent rules, and in the nature of the judicial function this may be difficult to achieve through a series of separate decisions. This is the so-called problem of 'partial reform'.[42] However, 130 years after the Judicature Acts it seems clear that the lack of progress in substantive fusion is due not to these genuine dif-ficulties, but to misconceptions about the nature of equity and the nature of substantive fusion.[43]

A Comparison with the Theory of Unjust Enrichment

In this connection it is interesting to compare substantive fusion of law and equity with the modern development of a law of restitution

---

reason by analogy with the common law: see Pettit, above n 4, at 6–7. But this is entirely arbitrary and amounts to false differentiation. Even if equity were a separate justificatory category there would be no justification for it. The issue is in any case very artificial because although equity traditionally did not make an award described as damages it has always been able to award pecuniary compensation. Equitable remedies such as specific performance and the injunction have of course always been available for common law claims, as is now in some circumstances the account of profits, as held in *Attorney-General v Blake* [2001] 1 AC 268.

[41] See below p 144.

[42] See ch 1, n 14.

[43] Contrast the general absence of resistance to the elimination of any residual influence of the old forms of action, which had the same effect of obscuring justificatory categories and causing incoherence, as discussed in ch 1.

or unjust enrichment. Both of these projects involve far-reaching and sustained exercises of analogical reasoning. As mentioned previously, the argument for the development of a law of unjust enrichment—the 'theory of unjust enrichment'—is that there is a general moral principle of unjust enrichment, but historically it has been given effect in a limited and desultory way in different isolated parts of the law, and these should now be brought together to form a single coherent body of law. The argument for substantive fusion is to the opposite effect: equity is a conventional-justificatory category, but it is a spurious justificatory category; it is actually composed of parts drawn from different true justificatory categories, including contract, property and tort, and it should be broken down and its parts assimilated into those true justificatory categories.[44]

In my view, the argument for substantive fusion is sound, and the theory of unjust enrichment is specious. Recent developments might suggest the opposite: in a relatively short period of time there have been dramatic moves towards the recognition of a law of unjust enrichment, whereas substantive fusion appears to have moved slowly and faced greater resistance. If nothing else, this shows the difficulties that are involved in these issues.

DIFFERENT POSITIONS ON SUBSTANTIVE FUSION

There has been controversy over substantive fusion ever since the Judicature Acts were passed. I have argued for substantive fusion. A number of different approaches are found that are against substantive fusion or fall short of it. First, there is the view still sometimes described as orthodox, which is that there has only been and should only be procedural fusion. Substantive fusion is an error—the 'fusion fallacy'.[45] This approach was originally expressed in the form of a famous metaphor devised by Ashburner to describe the position after the Judicature Acts: 'the two streams of jurisdiction, though they run in the same channel, run side by side, and do not mingle their waters'.[46]

---

[44] The advancement of substantive fusion is sometimes given as one of the advantages of recognising a law of unjust enrichment. This is not however a good argument for the theory of unjust enrichment.

[45] Meagher, et al, above n 26, at para 2-100, where the expression is used to refer to the argument for substantive fusion based on the Judicature Acts.

[46] Ashburner's *Principles of Equity* (2nd edn) 18.

This position is indefensible, though it is possible to see what is behind it. First, it is argued that the Judicature Acts themselves do not require or authorise substantive fusion: their purpose and effect was procedural fusion.[47] This is no doubt quite correct; but the argument for substantive fusion does not rely on the Judicature Acts. The justification for substantive fusion is the value of coherence that lies behind analogical reasoning. Procedural fusion merely made explicit the need for substantive fusion and facilitated it by bringing the two bodies of law in front of the same judges. This point also shows why substantive fusion is necessarily a gradual process, not something that took effect, or could feasibly have taken effect, immediately and directly through the enactment of the Judicature Acts. (It seems that the expression 'fusion fallacy' was originally used to refer to the argument based on the construction of the Judicature Acts, not the coherence argument.)

Secondly, a general hostility to the whole idea of analogical reasoning may account for the opposition to substantive fusion. Some writers strongly opposed to substantive fusion may be inclined to think of the law as a more or less settled body of rules, and the freedom of judges to change it as very modest and incremental—a view tending towards mechanical jurisprudence in the sense discussed in chapter 1.[48]

The first approach above, that nothing more than procedural fusion is justified, is usually contrasted with the view associated with an equally famous dictum of Lord Diplock, referring to Ashburner's metaphor quoted above[49]:

> By 1977, this metaphor has in my view become most mischievous and deceptive. The innate conservatism of English lawyers may have made them slow to recognise that by the Supreme Court of Judicature Act 1873, the two systems . . . formerly administered by courts of law and Courts of Chancery . . . were fused . . . If Professor Ashburner's fluvial metaphor is to be retained at all, the waters of the confluent streams of law and equity have surely mingled now.

The problem with this is that it is patently not the case that the process of substantive fusion has actually run its course and assimilated equity into the common law, and some commentators have, in response to Lord Diplock, pointed to particular ways in which they

---

[47] Pettit above n 4, at 10. *MCC Proceeds Inc v Lehman Bros Int (Europe)* [1998] 4 All ER 675, 691, per Mummery LJ.

[48] Above p 4.

[49] *United Scientific Holdings Ltd v Burnley BC* [1978] AC 904, 925–26.

are clearly not substantively fused.[50] However, such examples do not undermine the argument for substantive fusion, though they may reveal that the courts have missed opportunities that they ought to have taken to advance it. Also, elsewhere in the same judgment Lord Diplock seemed to imply that substantive fusion was enacted by the Judicature Acts themselves,[51] and as mentioned above this is not the case.

A third view attempts what is said to be a middle course. A representative statement is the much-cited dictum of Somers J in *Elders Pastoral Ltd v Bank of New Zealand*[52]:

> [N]either law nor equity is now stifled by its origin and the fact that both are administered by one court has inevitably meant that each has borrowed from the other in furthering the harmonious development of the law as a whole.

What is not clear from the dictum, and may not be appreciated by some writers who have adopted it, is that this process will lead inexorably to the elimination of equity by analogical reasoning—to full substantive fusion and Lord Diplock's position. This is so because a harmonious or coherent system has no room for the division between law and equity, because it is arbitrary with respect to issues of justification.

Fourthly, some judges and writers have said that although law and equity should be moulded into a single body of law, this cannot involve the elimination of the distinction between legal and equitable property rights, so to this extent substantive fusion will always be incomplete.[53] This might be thought to be a version of the previous view. In any case, it is mistaken. In fact it arises from the 'crude fusion' fallacy mentioned above. I will come back to this in the next section in connection with property rights.

EQUITY AND PROPERTY LAW

Some of equity's most important contributions have been in the field of property law. One has been to develop distinct variants of types of

---

[50] eg, Pettit, above n 4, at 11.

[51] [1978] AC 904, 924.

[52] [1989] 2 NZLR 180, 193; see also J Martin, 'Fusion, Fallacy and Confusion: A Comparative Study' [1994] *The Conveyancer and Property Lawyer* 13.

[53] *MCC Proceeds Inc v Lehman Bros Int (Europe)* [1998] 4 All ER 675, 691, per Mummery LJ; A Burrows, 'We Do This At Common Law But That In Equity' (2002) 22 *Oxford Journal of Legal Studies* 1.

property right already recognised at common law.[54] Thus there are equitable as well as legal charges, easements and leases. Equity's version is recognisably the same type of property right as the common law's, but different in certain respects. First, it can be acquired in different circumstances—for example, in the absence of the formal requirements for a grant or transfer of the common law property right, such as a requirement of writing or a formal deed. Secondly, the content of the right may be different. For example, the implied terms in an equitable lease differ from the implied terms in a legal lease, and whereas a legal charge must be in respect of a fixed asset, an equitable charge can be a floating charge. Historically, one important and general difference between legal and equitable property rights is that a legal property right is binding on any stranger who receives the property, whereas an equitable property right lapses in favour of a bona fide purchaser for value ('equity's darling').

As I have just mentioned, sometimes it is said that substantive fusion would be a mistake because it would involve the elimination of the distinction between legal and equitable property rights, and this would mean adopting either the legal variant or the equitable variant of a certain type of property right and abandoning the other variant. This would surely be a backward step, because there is a role for both variants. The loss would be damaging because it would make the law cruder and less sensitive, and less able to deal appropriately with different situations. But substantive fusion would not require the law to choose between one or other variant of a certain type of property right. This is the 'crude fusion' fallacy mentioned above. In the end what is required is that the law specifies what types of property rights are possible, what their precise content is, when they can arise and when they are extinguished. Nothing of substance is contributed by classifying them in terms of their origins in law and equity, any more than it would be helpful to distinguish between legal contractual rights and equitable contractual rights in the contract examples discussed above. It is true that certainty and clarity are particularly important in the definition of property rights and so there is good reason to be cautious about changes in terminology, but equally there is the danger of confusion resulting from the anti-fusion fallacy as explained above. The point arises in connection with claims arising to recover invalid transfers of property, where it is a live and important issue, as considered at length in chapter 6.

---

[54] See eg A Clarke and P Kohler, *Property Law* (Cambridge, CUP, 2005) 311ff.

A particular objection to substantive fusion in connection with property rights relates to the trust. It is said that substantive fusion must be avoided because the abolition of the distinction between common law and equity would entail the abolition of the trust, since the trust depends for its very existence on the distinction between legal and equitable title.[55] In fact, as discussed in chapter 5, although the division between law and equity may have provided the means for the development of the trust, the trust can only be properly understood once it is dissociated from its historical origins in law and equity and understood in terms of its function and the justification for the rules governing it.[56] There is an irony in the fact that the division between law and equity arose from institutional failings and is indefensible in a rational system, and yet it led fortuitously to the recognition of the trust.

SUMMARY

The division between law and equity developed historically because of institutional failings in the common law, as a procedural device for circumventing injustice. In the modern law, the division is sometimes characterised in terms of a difference of methodology, typically on the basis that the common law is concerned with certainty and equity with fairness, or the common law with strict rules and equity with discretion. This suggests that the separation of law and equity is the basis for a two-stage process in adjudication. But the supposed methodological distinction is not an accurate reflection of modern law and equity, and in any case there is no good reason to preserve such a two-stage process. Sometimes the two-stage process corresponds to the division between primary and remedial relations, so that the primary relation is thought to be a matter of strict common law rules and the remedial relation a matter of discretion in equity. Here the dualism of law and equity entrenches the remedialist dualist fallacy discussed in chapter 2. Sometimes equity appears to operate as a conventional-justificatory category, analogous to contract and tort at common law. But the substantive content of the modern law of equity is largely a matter of historical accident. Equity is really

---

[55] See below p 151.
[56] The trust and the restrictive covenant are examples of property rights devised by equity.

more in the nature of a purely conventional category, not a category based on a certain general moral principle. Its treatment as a conventional-justificatory category is a source of incoherence in the law. It should be eliminated as a conventional-justificatory category by the ordinary development of the law through analogical reasoning.

5

The Trust

The law of trusts is several hundred years old, and it remains a vital instrument in many areas of commerce and finance. But despite its everyday importance and the scholarly attention it has received over many years, debate continues over the nature of the trust and how to define it. For most ordinary purposes it is enough to know the established rules of the law of trusts and the various applications of the trust that these rules allow for. But a full understanding of the trust also involves understanding the basis for these rules, which means principally identifying the justificatory category or categories of private law that contribute to the law of trusts.

A trust arises when a settlor transfers property to a trustee,[1] on the basis, accepted by the trustee, that the property is to be held by him on the terms specified by the settlor, which provide for how the property is to be held and distributed among the beneficiaries. As far as the settlor's interest in the property is concerned, the effect is that he has disposed of it just as if he had made an outright transfer of it as an ordinary gift or contractual payment. But the trustee does not become the owner of the property, or at least not in any ordinary sense. The trust property is under his control, and he has the power of an owner vis-à-vis third parties, but unlike a genuine owner he is not entitled to apply the property for his own benefit. He has a duty to hold it for the beneficiaries and distribute it to them in accordance with the terms of the trust.

The trust provides a means by which a property owner can allocate the benefits of property in ways that he could not do by way of an outright gift. As the settlor of a trust he can provide that property should be held and allocated by the trustee at a later time, or subject to a condition, or at the discretion of the trustee in the light of

---

[1] There is usually more than one trustee of an express trust, but for convenience I will generally assume that there is only one.

subsequent events; or income from the property can be allocated to one beneficiary for a period and then at the end of the period the capital value allocated to another. Also money from many settlors or contributors can be pooled and managed by a trustee on behalf of them all as beneficiaries, as where an unincorporated association or a pension or investment fund holds money for its members or investors. The trust, in other words, is a device by which the benefit of property can be allocated in complex ways, by virtue of its distinctive feature—the separation of the power to control property from the right to benefit from it.

The trust was an invention of the law of equity. Where S transferred property to T requesting him to hold it for the benefit of B, and T received the property on this understanding, originally the common law took the view that there had been a valid transfer of ownership from S to T, and T was now the owner of the property, free in law to use or dispose of the property for his own benefit. But equity, although accepting that T was the owner for the purpose of managing and dealing with the property vis-à-vis third parties, recognised a duty on the part of T, owed to B, to hold the property for the benefit of B. Thus B's rights against T under the trust are said to be equitable. B's claim is traditionally said to be based on 'conscience',[2] but as discussed in chapter 4 this does not disclose any distinct principle or type of justification for B's right.

Is the Trust a Matter of Contract Law?

One view is that the trust is in essence a contractual arrangement[3]: a trust arises from the trustee's agreement with the settlor to act as a trustee and carry out the terms of the trust, so that the basis for giving the trust legal effect is simply the contractual principle that agreements should be performed. In fact, although it is important to recognise the contractual dimension of the trust, contract cannot provide a complete account of it. It is worth considering why this is,

---

[2] *Westdeutsche Landesbank Girozentrale v Islington Borough Council* [1996] AC 669, 705, per Lord Browne-Wilkinson; A Hudson, *Equity and Trusts* (London, Cavendish Publishing, 4th edn, 2005) 51.

[3] See JH Langbein, 'The Contractarian Basis of the Law of Trusts' 105 (1995) *Yale Law Journal* 625; FW Maitland, *Equity: A Course of Lectures* (J Brunyate, rev edn, 1936).

and distinguishing between some good and bad reasons for conclud-
ing that the contractual analysis is inadequate.

One might object, first, that trust law is simply not part of contract
law, because trust law is not to be found in the books on contract,
and it is not described in the case law as being part of contract law.
But this shows only that trust law is not part of contract in the conventional sense. For present purposes, we are concerned not with the
conventional-justificatory category of contract, but the true justificatory category, that is to say with the question whether trust law can
be explained in terms of the general moral principle that agreements
should be kept.

For the same reason, it would not necessarily be a good objection
to point to rules of trust law that are inconsistent with recognised
rules of contract law. A trust confers enforceable rights on the beneficiaries even though they were not party to the agreement between
the trustee and the settlor, and have not given consideration; and
conversely the settlor himself cannot enforce the trust though he was
party to the agreement and may have given consideration.[4] But, if the
basis of these rules is, in the end, the agreement of the trustee to the
arrangement proposed by the settlor, then trust law is essentially
contractual nevertheless. As discussed in chapter 4 on equity, it is possible that equity developed a set of rules based on the same general
principle, but taking different positions from the common law. It
seems perfectly plausible to say that, given the way that a trust
operates, an arrangement by which the beneficiaries rather than the
settlor can enforce the duties that the trustee has undertaken is a legit-
imate way to give effect to the contractual principle; indeed it seems
the only viable way to give effect to the contractual principle in the
circumstances.[5] This would raise the question whether the differences are justified by differences between the types of case dealt with
in law and equity, or whether they are discrepancies that should be
eliminated,[6] but it does not show that the rules in equity are not
based on the same general principle.

Another objection might be that, although the trustee is bound by
the terms of the trust, much of the detailed content of his duties and

---

[4] A trustee may take up the trusteeship, as a replacement trustee or if the settlor has died,
without dealing with the settlor, though on terms stipulated by the settlor. Though there
may be no contract under the ordinary rules of contract law, his duty surely arises from an
agreement or voluntary undertaking in a broad sense.

[5] This is a natural extension of the argument for specific performance of agreements for
the benefit of third parties: see above ch 2, at n 35.

[6] See above p 121.

the rules governing the administration of the trust are not to be found in the terms of the trust accepted by the trustee, but in the general law, for example the rules concerning the administration of the trust, including the investment of trust property, and the exercise of discretion by trustees. But this also does not undermine the contractual thesis. In ordinary contract law as well, there are rules of general law that operate as 'default terms' to supplement the terms actually agreed.[7] This is inevitably the case, because it is not feasible or even possible for all eventualities to be provided for in advance by the parties in their agreement. The issue in the end is not whether the relationship is governed exclusively by terms actually agreed by the parties, but whether the basic justification for imposing liabilities or duties on the parties is the principle that agreements should be binding. Trust law also contains mandatory rules that override any inconsistent provisions actually contained in the trust instrument, but this is also a recognised feature of ordinary contract law, and is not inconsistent with the contractual thesis.

A trustee is subject to a duty to manage and allocate property because he has accepted the position and thereby undertaken to act as trustee. This duty is a matter of contract law, not in the sense that it is a part of conventional contract law, but in the sense that that it is based on the general principle of contract law, that agreements should be observed, and so is part of the true justificatory category of contract. When I refer below to the contractual dimension of the trust, it should be understood in this sense. Nevertheless, the institution of the trust cannot be fully explained as an aspect of contract law. The real shortcoming of the contractual thesis is that it cannot account for what I will call the property dimension of the trust.

THE PROPERTY DIMENSION OF THE TRUST

The Problem with the Contractual Analysis

When a trust is established, the trust property is transferred to the trustee, and the trustee's duties relate to this property. This is not inconsistent with the contractual thesis. A contractual duty can relate to property, as in the ordinary case of a contract for sale of goods, and contract law can explain why, in the ordinary case, the trustee is required to transfer the property in accordance with his agreement,

---

[7] eg, the implied warranties in sale of goods contracts.

even if ownership of the property has been validly transferred to him. Thus A could transfer specified property to B outright, subject to an agreement by B that he will transfer it at a later date to C, and B could have a legal duty arising from the agreement to transfer it to C.[8] This would look just like the creation and execution of a trust. Indeed generally where a trust is set up and the trustee carries it out in accordance with its terms there is nothing on the surface to show that anything other than contact law is relevant.[9]

But contract law cannot account for the position when the trustee goes bankrupt. Here the trustee's own property must be sold to satisfy his creditors, but the trust property is unaffected and kept separate to meet the claims of the beneficiaries under the trust. Although the trust property has been transferred to the trustee and no longer belongs to the settlor, is not the trustee's own property. There would be no justification for this on a purely contractual analysis. If the trust were purely a matter of contract, the trust property would become the trustee's own property when it is transferred to him. It would be available along with the rest of the trustee's own property to satisfy his liabilities, and the beneficiaries' claims against the trustee would be in competition with other claims against the trustee in his bankruptcy.[10]

The contractual analysis also cannot account for the claim that a beneficiary has against third parties or 'strangers', where trust property is transferred by the trustee to a recipient in breach of trust, that is to say, contrary to the terms of the trust, and beyond the trustee's legal power. The modern position is that a beneficiary has a claim against any recipient who is not a bona fide purchaser.[11] The recipient was not party to the agreement by the trustee, and so cannot be liable for breach of a contractual duty owed to the beneficiary (or settlor). Historically the claim was said to be based on 'conscience', but as considered in chapter 5 this does not disclose any genuine basis for a claim. Similarly it is no help in identifying the basis of the claim to say that the recipient is deemed to be a trustee or that he

[8] Subject to the privity point mentioned above.

[9] Langbein, above n 3, excludes the remedial role of the trust from his contractarian account.

[10] H Hansmann and U Mattei, 'The Function of Trust Law: A Comparative Legal and Economic Analysis' (1998) 75 *New York University Law Review* 434, 469; H Hansmann and R Kraakman, 'The Essential Role of Organisational Law' (2000) 110 *Yale Law Journal* 387. Also the trust persists in an interregnum between trustees.

[11] ie, a bona fide purchaser for value without actual or constructive knowledge (equity's darling). See further below, p 140.

has assumed the position of an express trustee or that he is a constructive trustee.[12]

In the early stages of trust law the claim may have been explicable on the basis that the recipient acted wrongfully through his complicity in the trustee's breach of duty, or through his interference in the trustee's performance of his duty, so it was a form of accessory liability. This may have been how the recipient's 'conscience was affected'. But the complicity analysis certainly cannot explain the modern law concerning the liability of recipients. A recipient can be liable though he has not caused or contributed to causing the breach of duty by the trustee through any dealings with him; he may be liable even if he has no knowledge of the breach of duty by the trustee (if he is not a purchaser). Indeed, the claim can arise against an indirect recipient who received the property through an intermediate who received it directly. Furthermore, the beneficiary's claim against the recipient is a proprietary claim, and this cannot be explained, consistently with the monist principle, as a response to a breach of duty by the recipient in the form of complicity in the trustee's breach of duty.[13] (There is a modern law of accessory liability that is much narrower and quite distinct from the liability of the recipient.)[14]

The only plausible basis for the recipient's liability is that the beneficiary has a property right in the property transferred, the property right being capable of binding strangers, just as this is the only plausible basis for the fact that the trust property, although under the trustee's legal control, is not available as part of his estate for the satisfaction of his liabilities. This is the property dimension of the trust.

The Property Dimension and 'Separation of Title'

As discussed in chapter 3,[15] a right of ownership gives the owner the exclusive right to the property, including the right to all the benefit, through personal use or through licensing or sale, and also control over the property, meaning the power to determine how the property will be used or applied. In a trust, by contrast, the power to control the property is separated from the right to receive the benefits of

---

[12] See G Watt, *Trusts and Equity* (Oxford, OUP, 2nd edn, 2006) 264–65. See also L Smith, 'Transfer' in P Birks and A Pretto, *Breach of Trust* (Oxford, Hart Publishing, 2002).

[13] See below p 161.

[14] 'Knowing or dishonest assistance': the leading case is *Royal Brunei Airlines Sdn Bhd v Tan* [1995] 2 AC 378. See below p 199.

[15] Above p 76.

its use or its value through licensing or sale. The right to benefit is allocated among the beneficiaries, but the trustee has the power of control, including the power to deal as owner with third parties in respect of the trust property and to dispose of property to third parties, though the proceeds of sale are subject to the trust and are held for the beneficiaries.

In the simple case of a 'bare trust', there is a beneficiary who is the 'beneficial owner' with the right to all the benefit of the property, or two or more beneficiaries who share the beneficial ownership. In more complex cases the beneficiaries do not have rights of beneficial ownership, but some other property right, as determined by the terms of the trust, that is to say, a right to some aspect of the benefit of the property, for example a right to the income of the property for life or for a period of years, or a right of remainder in the capital after the end of an income interest, or a conditional right to the property, etc. The various property rights of the beneficiaries encompass all the benefit of the property and so, as it were, add up to beneficial ownership, and collectively the beneficiaries are capable of acting as a beneficial owner.[16] The allocation of benefit among the beneficiaries—the content of the beneficiaries' property rights—is determined by the settlor in the terms of the trust. The presumption is that the settlor as a property owner has a power to dispose of his property, and therefore also the power to allocate the benefit of his property by way of a trust on such terms as he chooses.

Thus the property dimension of the trust is a set of property rights, representing an allocation into different components of the benefit and control of the trust property, which in absolute ownership, in the absence of a trust, are united in a single owner. The trustee has the power to control the trust property, and the benefit is with the beneficiary as beneficial owner or divided in some way among the beneficiaries.

Conventionally the trustee is said to have 'legal title'. Ostensibly this implies that he is the owner of the property. The origin of this usage is that when the trust first developed, the common law recognised the trustee as the owner. When equity held that he was obliged to hold the property for the beneficiaries, he nevertheless kept the title of owner in the common law courts, though in substance this now signified only the power to control the property and to deal with it in the interests of the beneficiaries. Conversely, a beneficiary

---

[16] *Saunders v Vautier* (1841) 4 Beav 115.

is said to have an 'equitable interest' or in the case of a beneficial owner 'equitable title'. For obvious reasons this allocation of property rights between the trustee and beneficiaries is sometimes described as a 'separation of title'.

The Two Dimensions of the Trust

Thus there are two dimensions to an express trust, the contract dimension and the property dimension. They are separate dimensions generating distinct primary relations and claims that together constitute the express trust. The beneficiary under a trust has both a property right and a contract right. These are distinct, and have different justificatory bases. There are also two important differences between the contractual right and the property right with respect to their modality, as opposed to their justificatory bases. In contract, the beneficiary has, first, an *in personam* right against the trustee, in the Hohfeldian sense that the right is good against only the trustee as the person who accepted the position and agreed to carry out the trust; and, secondly, the relation is a right–duty relation, the trustee having a correlative duty to manage the trust property and allocate it according to the trust. (I will come back to this in connection with the fiduciary character of the trust.) By contrast, the beneficiary's property right is *in rem*, in the sense that (subject to the point made below) it is capable of binding everyone; and the relation is a right–liability relation, the beneficiary's right correlating not with a duty but with a liability, as discussed in chapter 3.[17] The claim that arises against a recipient of trust property invalidly transferred is not based on a breach of duty by the recipient.

The Nature of the Beneficiary's Property Right

A number of different objections have been made to the idea that a beneficiary under a trust has a property right, and these raise some interesting points about the nature of a trust and the beneficiary's position under a trust. One issue relates to the nature of the rights of the beneficiary and the trustee. As mentioned in chapter 3, according to the *numerus clausus* principle, only certain types of property right are recognised in the law.[18] The trust involves distinct types of property right.[19] The trustee has a property right consisting of the power to control the use of the property and to transfer it. A right of

---

[17] Above p 94.
[18] Above p 86.
[19] S Worthington, *Equity* (Oxford, OUP, 2nd edn, 2006), 63.

beneficial ownership or a share of beneficial ownership differs from absolute ownership because it excludes this power over the trust property. More generally, a beneficiary's right can be any sort of right of payment from the trust. This becomes possible once the right to benefit is detached from possession and control. Then it becomes possible for a property right to consist of a right to benefit from the trust in any way in which the benefit of the trust property can be divided up and allocated by a trustee. In fact, a beneficiary can have a property right that does not entitle him to any determinate benefit at all, for example a conditional right, or a right under a discretion. Even such a beneficiary has a property right that can in principle be enforced against third party recipients or in the bankruptcy of the trustee to restore or protect the trust fund.

One reason why some writers reject the property right analysis may be that the beneficiary's right is not one of the standard property rights such as a right of ownership or a lesser property right such as a charge or an easement. This may be why it is said that a right to payment from the trust must be an *in personam* right against the trustee.[20] But although the trust necessarily involves allocation by a trustee, and the beneficiary has a contractual right against the trustee that he carry out the allocation, for the reasons given above a contractual right cannot adequately explain the trust; the beneficiary also has a property right in the trust property.

Also, although the beneficiary's property right is generally transferable, it may not be, and sometimes transferability is taken to be a necessary feature of a property right.[21] For example, the right to be considered under a discretion is not transferable, though on the analysis above it is a property right under the trust. Where the beneficiary's property right is transferable, the *in personam* right in contract against the trustee will be transferable with the property right. They will be transferred together as a compound right. In this case, the *in personam* contractual right becomes an object of property, in the sense discussed in chapter 3,[22] so that the beneficiary has a property right in the trust property and also a property right in the contractual right against the trustee.[23]

---

[20] eg, Hudson, above n 2, at 990–92.

[21] See above, p 86.

[22] See above, p 82.

[23] Writers who regard the beneficiary as having only an *in personam* right against the trustee may say that the right is also a property right or a sort of property right because it is transferable. This implies that the *in personam* right becomes an object of property if it is transferable, not that there is a property right in the trust property.

The Trust Fund as the Object of Property

Another issue concerns the object of a beneficiary's property right. At any one time, the trust property consists of specific assets such as tangible things, contractual rights to payment, and money as cash. When a trust is created the settlor's intention may be that the specific assets transferred to the trustee should be preserved by him and subsequently passed on to the beneficiaries. This might traditionally have been the case with respect to land or heirlooms. But more commonly the intention is to establish a trust fund.[24] As mentioned in chapter 3,[25] a fund is a fluctuating body of specific assets. Where there is a trust fund, the interests of the beneficiaries are in its pecuniary value as investments, and the trustee's responsibility is to preserve and enhance the value of the fund by selling items and reinvesting the proceeds as appropriate. A fund requires a separation of title, so that legal or control title can be with the trustee or fund manager and beneficial title with the beneficiary. It is one of the advantages of separation of title that it allows for the existence of a fund.

The trustee's legal title or power to control the trust property and deal with it must, in its nature, be in respect of specific assets. For example, he is entitled to be registered as the owner of a plot of land; he must be the creditor with respect to a contractual right of payment; and he has the right to possession of tangible things. But what is the object of a beneficiary's property right? Does the right subsist in the specific assets making up the fund for the time being, or is it in the abstract value or wealth of the trust fund? If the trustee exchanges a specific asset in the trust fund for a different asset, the object of the trustee's legal title has changed, but has the object of the beneficiary's property right changed or is it at all times simply the abstract value of the fund? The issue does not appear to be of any consequence if the trust is operating normally, because the trustee has the power to buy and sell assets for the trust fund and if the beneficiary's right is in a specific asset the trustee has the power to re-vest it in the new asset. But it seems better to say that the object of the beneficiary's right is simply the abstract value of the fund, because generally the purpose of trust is to realise the value of the trust fund and distribute it to the beneficiaries. This issue arises again in the next chapter in connection with the recovery of invalid transfers.

---

[24] ie, there is a 'duty to convert', according to the rule in *Howe v Earl of Dartmouth* (1802) 7 Ves 137.

[25] Above p 84.

In Rem *Rights and Bona Fide Purchase*

The most longstanding objection to the property right analysis relates to whether the beneficiary's right is *in rem*, in the Hohfeldian sense meaning good against people in general rather than against a particular person or persons. A property right is necessarily *in rem*. (Indeed in the literature on this issue 'property right' and '*in rem* right', in this sense, are generally equated, though as discussed in chapter 3 this is mistaken.)[26] Thus it is sometimes argued that since the beneficiary's right under a trust does not survive against a bona fide purchaser of the trust property from the trustee, it is not binding on everyone and so is not *in rem* and cannot be a property right.[27] By contrast, it is said, absolute ownership at common law binds everyone, because there is no bona fide purchase defence.[28]

The bona fide purchase rule protects a purchaser in respect of his reliance on the assumption that the transfer to him under the contract is valid. The interest of the purchaser in being able to rely on the validity of the transfer prevails over the countervailing interest of the beneficiary in his beneficial property. This is an example of the protection of the reliance of a recipient in the absence of a valid transfer or grant based on the private property principle, as discussed in chapter 3.[29] This does not imply that the beneficiary's property right is not *in rem*. At a certain level of specification or abstraction (in the sense discussed in chapter 2)[30] it purports or tends to bind everyone, though at the level of the conclusive or concrete right it is overridden by the conflicting interest of a bona fide purchaser in being able to rely on the validity of the transfer to him under his purchase contract. The difference between the common law and equity is not a matter of whether the right of a beneficiary in the trust property (as compared with a right of absolute ownership) is *in rem*; it is to do with the weight given to the interest of a bona fide purchaser as against that of a beneficiary (as compared with an absolute owner) in determining

---

[26] Above p 90.

[27] This side of the argument is associated with Maitland, above n 3. The opposite view that a beneficiary does have a property right is associated with AW Scott 'The Nature of the Rights of the *Cestui que Trust*' (1917) 17 *Columbia Law Review* 269. An account of the controversy is provided by DWM Waters, 'The Nature of the Trust Beneficiary's Interest' (1967) 45 *Canadian Bar Review* 221.

[28] Some say that the beneficiary's right under a trust is neither *in personam* nor *in rem*, but *sui generis*: PH Pettit, *Equity and the Law of Trusts* (Oxford, OUP, 10th edn, 2006) 83.

[29] Above p 87.

[30] Above pp 36, 42.

the concrete form of the beneficiary's right. In fact the common law also protects the bona fide purchaser in many situations, though it starts from the position that the property right is good against every-one.[31]

Conflict between Equity and the Common Law

Another old objection to the argument that the beneficiary's right is a property right is that it is only because the beneficiary's right is *in personam* that equity does not conflict with the common law. If the beneficiary's right is *in personam*, arising only from the trustee's agree-ment to act, then one can still say that the trustee is the genuine owner of the property. Thus one can say, at least with respect to the issue of property, that there is no conflict between common law and equity, the difference between the two being only that equity but not the common law holds the trustee bound by his undertaking as a mat-ter of contract law (or, traditionally, as a matter of 'conscience'). But as pointed out above this position became untenable once the bene-ficiary's right was enforceable against strangers. From then on bene-ficial ownership was with the beneficiaries, and the trustee had been stripped of all aspects of ownership save the owner's power to con-trol the property. But the idea that the beneficiary did not have a property right may have persisted as a convenient fiction to avoid the appearance of contradicting the common law's traditional description of the trustee as a legal owner or title-holder. In reality it is no longer helpful to refer to the trustee as an owner in any sense and legal title has to be understood in the limited sense explained above.

The equitable maxim that 'equity acts *in personam*' is liable to cause confusion on this point. The maxim is not meant to imply that the beneficiary's right is *in personam* in the sense just considered, nor is it a reference to the discretionary or 'fact-sensitive' nature of equity.[32] It is a reference to equity's so-called '*in personam*' *enforcement* jurisdic-tion. The orders of equity courts have traditionally been enforced by contempt proceedings against the defendant to compel him to do as directed.[33] By contrast common law damages awards have tradition-ally been executed by the seizure of the defendant's assets. This is why the court of equity could make orders of injunction and specific performance. It seems sometimes to have been thought that it was because equity's enforcement jurisdiction was '*in personam*' in this

---

[31] See below p 182.
[32] Cf Hudson, above n 2, at 29.
[33] Worthington, above n 19, at 15.

enforcement sense that there was no conflict with the common law's recognition of the trustee's ownership of the trust property: the trustee's duty to the beneficiaries was enforced by contempt proceedings against the trustee, without ever involving the trust property in the enforcement proceedings.[34] But the enforcement procedure is irrelevant to whether there is a conflict of substantive law, as to either property rights in the trust property or the trustee's duties in respect of it. It may originally have made sense to say that there was no conflict between law and equity because the beneficiary's primary right was an *in personam* right arising from the trustee's undertaking and not an *in rem* property right, but this has nothing to do with the means of enforcement, and there is no necessary link between the '*in personam*' enforcement jurisdiction and the *in personam* character of the primary right. When, in the course of the development of the trust, the beneficiary acquired a property right, this was not to do with any change in equity's manner of enforcement. When it came to enforcement, equity could still use its '*in personam*' enforcement procedure to protect the *in rem* property right. Conversely, an *in personam* right can of course be enforced by the seizure of assets to recover damages, which is the standard position at common law.

THE TRUST IN TWO DIMENSIONS AND IN ONE DIMENSION

Thus the trust has two dimensions, in contract and in property. The contractual dimension arises from the trustee's agreement to act as such, and the property dimension arises from the allocation of property rights resulting from the settlor's transfer. Claims arising in connection with the trust are in principle based either on contract or property, though equity has given these categories its own distinctive features.

It is illuminating to consider whether a trust or 'pseudo-trust' can subsist in one dimension without the other. Consider a purely contractual form of pseudo-trust. Here the property is transferred by the pseudo-settlor to the pseudo-trustee T outright and T owns it absolutely. This arrangement was referred to above in the discussion of the contractual dimension. T has a purely contractual duty to administer the property and distribute it among the beneficiaries,

---

[34] See Watt, above n 12, at 18.

enforceable by the beneficiaries.[35] But if T transfers the trust property to a third party in breach of contract, the beneficiaries have no cause of action against the third party unless the third party is complicit in the breach of contract; and the property forms part of T's ordinary estate, so that it is available to satisfy the liabilities of his creditors in his bankruptcy. This arrangement will look like a trust as long as nothing goes wrong. It may be that at one time this would have been a true description of the trust.[36] As mentioned above, even nowadays it is sometimes said that the beneficiaries' rights under the trust are only rights against the trustee personally. But this is not really a trust at all in the absence of the crucial property dimension. Another purely contractual arrangement would be where the pseudo-settlor S retains full ownership of the property himself but appoints T to act as his agent or pseudo-trustee to manage it. T will have a contractual relationship with S. If there is a contract to provide benefits to beneficiaries, it will presumably be with S rather than T. In any case, the property is not protected from S's bankruptcy, and the beneficiaries will have no claim to protect the property from third parties.

Could there instead be a legal relationship consisting of the property dimension of the trust alone, without the contract dimension? Could B have beneficial ownership in property that is in the control of R, without R having agreed to act as trustee and having thereby incurred a duty to manage and allocate the property? In fact this is a common situation. It sometimes occurs when there has been an invalid transfer of B's property to R.[37] B then has what is usually described as an equitable proprietary claim, or a claim under a constructive trust, as considered further in subsequent chapters. Thus there is no reason to call this a pseudo-trust. The role of the trust having only the property dimension is important, which suggests that it is the property dimension rather than the contractual dimension that is the essence of the trust (even if, as considered further in the next section, the name 'trust' is associated with the contractual dimension).

A crucial point in understanding this property-only form of the trust is that the recipient R is not subject to a duty, merely a liability in respect of the property. As discussed earlier, B's claim is actually a power correlated with R's liability.[38] However, if R comes to know

---

[35] This presupposes again that the privity problem is overcome.

[36] Also, this appears to be the legal arrangement under the 'fiducia' in some civil law jurisdictions: see Hansmann and Mattei, above n 10, at 443.

[37] Below p 156.

[38] Above p 94.

of the invalidity of the transfer, he will incur a duty not to destroy or dispose of the property. This is a duty in tort, and is much less demanding than the analogous contractual duty of an express trustee to manage and allocate the trust property. This form of trust or proprietary claim, and the related duty in tort not to consume or dispose of the property, are considered in the next two chapters.

'TRUSTING' AND FIDUCIARY RELATIONSHIPS AS THE BASIS OF THE TRUST

The Relevance of 'Trust' and Fiduciary Relationships

It might be thought that it is simply 'trusting' or trust in the ordinary sense that is the basis of trust law,[39] rather than (or in addition to) contract or property. Certainly one would expect to find a connection with the ordinary sense of trust. There is an obvious sense in which the settlor has placed trust in the trustee by delivering the property to him, and similarly the beneficiary has to trust the trustee to preserve the property until it is distributed. But trusting is itself not a source of claims independent of contract and property.

There is a type of relationship that is said to be based on trust, of which the trust, or the relationship between the trustee and the beneficiaries, is a standard example, namely the fiduciary relationship. The trustee is a fiduciary, and other types of fiduciary include company directors, partners and agents. In these cases the fiduciary has been entrusted with the management of the property or business or other affairs of the principal, and in consequence is in a position to exercise a power or discretion vis-à-vis the principal, who is accordingly in a position of dependency. The distinguishing feature of the legal treatment of fiduciary relationships is a duty on the part of the fiduciary to advance the interests of the principal, variously described as a duty of trust and confidence, a duty of loyalty, or a duty of good faith.[40]

However, one cannot say that simply trusting, in the ordinary sense, in itself provides the basis for a fiduciary relationship or a duty of loyalty, or a claim by the principal or beneficiary in a fiduciary relationship. In general, one can say that A places his trust in B where A acts on the assumption that B will act in certain way, and may suf-

---

[39] R Cotterell, 'Trusting in Law: Legal and Moral Concepts of Trust' (1993) 46 *Current Legal Problems* 75.

[40] See eg *Bristol and West BS v Mothew* [1998] 1 Ch 1.

fer a loss if he does not. It seems to be equivalent to saying that A relies on B, and I will refer to reliance rather than trusting, though a distinction between trust and reliance will be mentioned below. If A's reliance on B generates a claim, then presumably B bears the risk of A's reliance so that B has a responsibility to protect A against loss through his reliance, including by compensating A for any loss incurred as a result of his reliance, where B fails to act in the way that A has relied on him to act. But the fact that A has chosen to rely on B surely cannot in itself be the basis for imposing a duty or liability on B. A surely cannot impose a duty or liability on B merely by deciding that he will rely on B to behave in a certain way. This would be quite unfair to B, because B may have no knowledge of the way in which A is relying on him and the risk that he bears as a result, and even if he does know there is no reason why A should be able to impose this risk on him unilaterally. In some cases where A relies on B to act in a certain way B in any case has a duty to act in that way and A relies on B to comply with the duty—for example where A is a pedestrian and takes the risk that B, a driver, will comply with his duty to drive carefully. But here it is clear that A's relying on B is not the basis of B's duty to A. In general it must surely be the case that if A is to be able to rely on B's acting in a certain way, in the sense that A relies on B at B's risk, A must first secure B's agreement to accept responsibility for A's reliance. This means that B's responsibility for A's reliance arises from an agreement and is in principle contractual. Trust or reliance, independently of contract, cannot provide an explanation of the trust or a fiduciary relationship.[41]

Thus the duties of a fiduciary (including a trustee) arise not directly from reliance on him or the trust placed in him, but from his agreement to act as a fiduciary. Trust or trusting does not provide a basis for the trust that is independent of contract.[42] It is an aspect of the contractual dimension of the trust. However, there is something distinctive about the type of contract that is characterised as fiduciary, which justifies the association with the idea of trust. It is sometimes said that a fiduciary relationship arises where F has undertaken to act on behalf of P, in circumstances such as to give rise to a duty of loyalty.[43] This indicates the contractual nature of the fiduciary relationship, but it is

---

[41] I leave aside issues of trust in the context of public institutions.

[42] Again this does not mean that the fiduciary relationship meets all the conditions for a valid contract under the ordinary law of contract. On the approach set out in the text, see further P Jaffey, *The Nature and Scope of Restitution* (Oxford, Hart Publishing, 2000) ch 13.

[43] *Bristol and West BS v Mothew* [1998] 1 Ch 1, 18, per Millett LJ.

an unilluminating definition, if not an entirely circular one, since it provides no basis for saying when or why a fiduciary relationship arises, along with its concomitant duty of loyalty.

Disgorgement in a Fiduciary Relationship

A better answer to the question can be found in a distinguishing feature of the legal treatment of fiduciary relationships, including trusts. Because a fiduciary or trustee manages property or business or conducts affairs on behalf of the principal or beneficiary, he is likely in the course of his work as a fiduciary to encounter opportunities to depart from his duty to advance the principal's interests and make a personal profit instead. The rule is that if the fiduciary makes a profit through a breach of his duty of loyalty he is liable to surrender the profit to the principal. Sometimes this could be explained as a compensatory claim, if the fiduciary receives a profit that would have gone to the principal if the fiduciary had not committed the breach of duty; but generally it has to be understood as disgorgement, based on the principle that the fiduciary is not permitted to retain the benefit of his wrong, and this is how it is normally understood.[44] Disgorgement is a distinctive feature of the fiduciary relationship. In an ordinary contractual relationship, the traditional rule is that disgorgement is not available, and often the reason why a claimant tries to establish that a contractual relationship is also fiduciary is that disgorgement will be available. Sometimes it is even offered as a definition of a fiduciary relationship that it is a relationship that is capable of giving rise to a claim for disgorgement,[45] but this is again unilluminating or circular. Part of understanding fiduciary relationships lies in explaining why they differ from ordinary contracts in this respect.

The remedial regime for contract was touched on in chapter 2.[46] It was suggested there that it could be explained on the basis that contract law protects a contracting party in respect of his contractual reliance. It was argued that a contracting party D is responsible for the other party C's reliance, and this means that D does not generally have a duty to perform the contract. D has a duty to perform the contract only where, by virtue of C's contractual reliance, the circumstances are such that C would suffer uncompensatable reliance loss as

---

[44] See eg *A-G for Hong-Kong v Reid* [1994] 1 AC 324; *Murad v Al-Saraj* [2005] EWCA Civ 959.
[45] *Re Hallett's Estate* (1880) LR 13 Ch D 696, 712, per Jessel MR; see above, ch 2, n 111.
[46] Above pp 45, 59.

a result of D's non-performance. In such circumstances D's responsibility for C's reliance generates a duty on the part of D to perform
the contract. This is the basis for the 'damages are inadequate' test for
the availability of specific performance. Furthermore, if D does not
perform when he has a duty to perform, and specific performance is
no longer possible, D should be subject to disgorgement if he has
made a profit. As mentioned in chapter 2, the possibility of disgorgement for breach of contract has only recently been explicitly recognised,[47] and the test for its availability is unclear; but it seems to be
consistent with this argument. Some examples of types of contract for
which specific performance or disgorgement may be appropriate
were mentioned in chapter 2.[48] A fiduciary relationship is a certain
type of contract for which it is always the case that there is a duty
actually to perform the contract, because only actual performance can
protect the principal in respect of his reliance on the fiduciary.
Specific performance is unlikely to be possible or attractive to the
claimant, but disgorgement should be available.

In the case of a trust, when the trustee agrees to look after property for the beneficiaries, this must generate a duty to perform and
not merely a responsibility for reliance because the property is there
to secure the claims of the beneficiaries. If the trustee were at liberty
to use or dispose of the property and then simply make up the missing amount as necessary to satisfy the claims of the beneficiaries when
they are due—which would be the position under the ordinary contract regime—there would be a greater risk that the claims would
never be satisfied at all. In this sense the reliance placed on the trustee
is uncompensatable. The argument applies generally for contracts that
are designed to reduce a risk of loss to the other contracting party.[49]

This point does not apply to all fiduciary relationships—not all
fiduciary relations concern the management of property. There is a
more general reason why disgorgement is appropriate for fiduciary
contracts in general (including trusts). A fiduciary contract provides
for F to act in some general way for the benefit of the P, for example
by managing his property or business. F's responsibility under the
agreement is to use his expertise and judgment to manage the property or business in the way that will best advance the interests of P.

[47] *Attorney-General v Blake* [2001] 1 AC 268.
[48] See above, ch 2, nn 35, 77.
[49] This argument does not actually depend on the beneficiary's having a property right.
See further P Jaffey, 'Disgorgement and "Licence Fee Damages" in Contract' (2004) 20
Journal of Contract Law 57.

By its nature, F's task is not open to precise specification. It will always be difficult to say exactly what F should do for the best in particular circumstances in respect of the management of P's property or business.[50] It is by virtue of this feature of the relationship that F is said to have a power or discretion, and P is described as dependent. Also because it is difficult to say how F should have acted and what the consequences would have been, it is liable to be very difficult to protect P purely through compensation, and F's responsibility for P's reliance on him generates a duty actually to perform the contract, which means to advance the interests of P. This is the fiduciary duty of loyalty. Consequently, disgorgement is an appropriate response.[51] As mentioned above, this rationale for disgorgement is consistent with the recent development in contract law to recognise disgorgement, and recognising that fiduciary relationships are contractual would assist in the development of the law of disgorgement in contract. Thus to go back to an issue mentioned earlier, whereas all contracts protect reliance, a fiduciary contract can be said to involve trust because of the vulnerability or dependency of the principal or beneficiary that arises from the fact that only actual performance of the contract will provide adequate protection.

The Fiduciary No-conflict Rule

The discussion above has not mentioned another distinguishing feature of a fiduciary relationship. This is that the liability to surrender a profit arises not only where F has committed a breach of his duty of loyalty, but where he has received a profit in a situation where there is a reasonable likelihood of a conflict between his duty of loyalty and his personal interest—the so-called 'no conflict rule'.[52] This is not, strictly speaking, disgorgement, because it is not based on a wrong by F. It is quite possible that F may act entirely consistently with his duty of loyalty and yet be in a position where there is a possibility of conflict of interest and receive a profit. He may as a matter of course have to investigate and consider on behalf of P opportunities for investment or business development that he could take instead for himself, and if the

---

[50] FH Easterbrook and DR Fischel, 'Contract and Fiduciary Duty' (1993) 36 *Journal of Law and Economics* 425.

[51] Specific performance of the duty is invariably not in issue, because if F has failed to perform his duty it is generally impossible to rectify this, even if P were happy to keep him on in the fiduciary position.

[52] eg, *Boardman v Phipps* [1967] 2 AC 46. Liability under the no-conflict rule can easily overlap with liability to account for property invalidly transferred from the trust in a case of misappropriation, or liability for wrongfully diverting opportunities away from the trust.

opportunity is for some reason inappropriate for P and F takes it for himself he may have profited from a position of conflict of interest while at the same time having acted consistently with his duty of loyalty.[53] The rationale for the no-conflict rule appears to be evidential: because of the difficulty of proving that F acted in breach of his duty of loyalty, he is required to surrender any profit he has made that might have been made through such a breach. By removing any incentive to make a profit from a position of conflict of interest the rule will also necessarily remove any incentive to make a profit through an actual though unprovable breach of the duty of loyalty.[54]

Because a fiduciary is held to a duty of loyalty to advance the interests of the principal and is subject to the no-conflict rule, it is sometimes said that altruism is a feature of fiduciary relationships. Sometimes a fiduciary may indeed have acted altruistically, as where a friend of the settlor agrees to act as trustee without payment. But nowadays most fiduciaries, including trustees, are professionals who are paid for their work. The duty of loyalty and other features of a fiduciary relationship do not make the fiduciary's position intrinsically altruistic. They result from the distinguishing feature of a fiduciary relationship, the fact that the fiduciary has to exercise discretion as to what is best for the principal because of the problem of defining his task in precise terms.

Similarly it is not helpful to say that fiduciaries are held to a higher standard of morality or that a fiduciary relationship is distinctive in having a moral basis. The strictly enforced duty of loyalty of a fiduciary is necessary to protect the principal because of the nature of the task that the fiduciary has undertaken. This is the difference between the fiduciary relationship and an ordinary contract; the difference is not in the basic moral principle underlying the law, which is simply the contractual principle that an agreement should be performed; the difference arises because the principle can have different effects in different circumstances.

---

[53] Thus it cannot be right to say that the no-conflict rule imposes a duty on the fiduciary 'not to place himself in a position of conflict of interest', which is how it is often formulated. The no-conflict rule establishes a primary right-liability relation, and this is the crucial point in explaining why it can be excluded by agreement despite a prohibition on excluding liability for breach of duty in the company law case of *Movietex v Bulfield* [1988] BCLC 104; see further Jaffey, *The Nature and Scope of Restitution*, above n 42, at 406–07.

[54] The no-conflict rule is often thought to be unfair because it is not dependent on any wrongdoing by the fiduciary. But it is not unfair provided that the fiduciary knew or ought to have known that the rule applied to him: see Jaffey, ibid, at 414–17. One might say that it is justified if it is reasonable to imply a contractual term to this effect.

The characterisation of the trustee as a fiduciary and the 'trusting' elements of the relationship between the trustee and the beneficiaries are only an elaboration of the contractual analysis of the trustee's duties. It is because fiduciary relationships developed in equity, with a distinct terminology and distinct rules, that they have not been recognised as contractual, and this was the case because a fiduciary relationship is a type of agreement that needs special treatment that the common law was unable to provide.

THE TRUST AND THE FUSION OF LAW AND EQUITY

Historically the trust developed as part of the law of equity. In a conventional sense the law of trusts is still part of the law of equity. On a traditional view, equity's significance is not just historical and conventional, and reducing the trust to a combination of property law and contract law, as argued above, necessarily omits a crucial element. The trust and the beneficiary's right was originally said to be based simply in the conscience of the Chancellor. But, as discussed in chapter 4, the concept of equity or conscience does not contribute anything to the law in terms of justification. The idea of equity or conscience as a ground for a decision at one time gave equity its strength—the scope and flexibility of its power to override the common law—but it also served to conceal the rationale for its rules, which may have been expedient at one time but should nowadays be understood as a serious weakness.[55] Continued reliance on equity or conscience as the basis for the trust conceals the need for a proper analysis in terms of genuine justificatory categories. The assumption that equity is not merely descriptive of the law of trusts in an historical or conventional sense, but is necessary to it in a justificatory sense, implying that equity is a justificatory category like contract or tort or property, or that the law of trusts depends on a divided system, is an example of the anti-fusion fallacy mentioned in chapter 4.[56]

This is not to deny that the courts of equity made significant contributions in terms of new concepts that are essential to the modern law of trusts. With respect to contract law, it devised the fiduciary relationship. With respect to property, it devised the concepts of the separation of control from benefit, the beneficiary's property right

[55] See above pp 113, 118.
[56] Above p 120.

under a trust, property rights in the abstract value of a fund, and protection for third parties through bona fide purchase.

With respect to the contractual dimension of the trust, and fiduciary relationships in general, the idea mentioned above that they are
based on 'trusting' in the ordinary sense, or that they are altruistic or
call for a higher standard of morality, seems to be influenced by the
idea that because the fiduciary relationship developed in equity it is
in some sense a matter of conscience. At the same time, fiduciary
relationships continue to be dissociated from their true basis in contract, with the risk of false differentiation. In particular, this has held
back the development of the law with respect to disgorgement in
contract.

Similarly a clear understanding of the property dimension of the
trust, consisting of the allocation of property rights or separation of
title, is still generally frustrated by the assumption that the separation
of control and benefit cannot be achieved without a divided system,
involving a tension or conflict between equitable and common law
claims to ownership, and of course this is encouraged by the conventional usage of the expressions 'legal title' and 'equitable title' or
'equitable interest' to refer to control and benefit respectively. For
this reason it would be helpful to abandon these labels in favour of
'beneficial interest' or 'beneficial title' and 'control title' or 'management title'. As mentioned in chapter 4, the association of the trust
with a divided system has misled some writers into thinking that substantive fusion of law and equity would eliminate the trust from the
law, apparently because this would mean that either the trustee, or
the beneficiary or beneficiaries collectively, would be the absolute
owner of the property, and either outcome would of course be
incompatible with a trust.[57] This is a form of the anti-fusion fallacy.[58]
As pointed out above, although the trustee is still sometimes
described as the legal owner, he is not really an owner at all; he
merely has one aspect of the rights of a true owner, namely, the
power to control the trust property and deal with the property with
respect to third parties, all the rights to benefit now being with the
beneficiaries. Conversely equity never asserted absolute ownership,
including control of the trust property, for the beneficiaries; to the
contrary, it was crucial to the development of the trust that equity did
not assert absolute ownership for the beneficiaries but recognised the

---

[57] See eg A Burrows, 'We Do This At Common Law But That In Equity' (2002) 22
Oxford Journal of Legal Studies 1; Pettit, above n 28, at 11.
[58] See above, p 120.

trustee's power to control the property and required it to be used for the benefit of the beneficiaries, as intended by the settlor. The trust simply involves a certain allocation of rights in property law, or a separation of title, not a divided system or the appearance of conflict between rival claims of ownership to property.

A particular example of confusion resulting from the association between equity and the trust arises from an ambiguity in the expression 'equitable interest'. In one sense it means a particular type of property right, namely a beneficiary's property right under a trust—a right to some part of the benefit of the trust fund controlled by a trustee for the benefit of the beneficiaries.[59] But it is also used to refer to a property right in land recognised by equity, for example an equitable easement or an equitable lease or a restrictive covenant typically an informally created property right. These are lesser property rights in land that derogate from the right of ownership of the owner of the land. Thus there are two quite different types of concept, but they are liable to be confused because of the use of the expression 'equitable interest' for both.[60] After substantive fusion, they are unlikely to be confused.

SUMMARY: THE NATURE OF THE TRUST

The express trust has two dimensions, a contract dimension and a property dimension. It is by virtue of his agreement to act as trustee that the trustee incurs a duty to manage the trust property and all the other duties affecting the administration by the trustee of the express trust. This is a matter of contract, in the broad sense that these duties arise from the fact that the trustee agreed to act as such. The relationship is also fiduciary, but this is just to say that it is a particular type of contractual relationship having the distinctive features of a fiduciary relationship. The contractual dimension affects only the trustee and the beneficiaries as parties with rights under the contract.[61]

---

[59] Or the compound of a property right and a contractual right under the trust, above p 138.

[60] eg, it seems that Lord Browne-Wilkinson, discussing the trust, confuses a trustee who holds trust property subject to beneficial rights with a landowner whose land is subject to an equitable easement, mortgage or restrictive covenant: *Westdeutsche Landesbank Girozentrale v Islington Borough Council* [1996] AC 669, 707. S Gardner, *An Introduction to the Law of Trusts* (Oxford, Clarendon Press, 2nd edn, 2003) 14, makes the distinction that a trustee must not have a personal interest, but this does not seem to capture the essence of the trust, which is the seperation of control and benefit.

[61] Together with third parties liable for interference or complicity.

The property dimension of the trust is the separation of the right to benefit from the trust property from the right to control it and deal with others with respect to it, which means that a beneficiary has a property right in the trust property that is capable of binding strangers as well as the trustee, either a right of beneficial ownership or a lesser property right. The trust property is outside the trustee's estate and is protected against his bankruptcy, and the beneficiary has a claim against recipients of the trust property transferred in breach of trust.

The creation of an express trust by the settlor involves legal acts having effect in contract and property law. The terms of the trust declared by the settlor are the terms of the agreement accepted by the trustee, which impose a duty on the trustee to carry out the terms of the trust, and give correlative rights to the beneficiaries. The transfer of the trust property on the terms declared causes the separation of title and the allocation of property rights to the beneficiaries, binding on the trustee and third parties. The important difference is that the contractual dimension is derived from the *agreement* of the trustee and the property dimension from the *transfer* by the owner as settlor.

Trusts textbooks often adopt a version of the following compact definition of a trust: it is an 'equitable duty binding a person (the trustee) to deal with property over which he has control (trust property), for the benefit of persons (beneficiaries) any one of whom may enforce the duty'.[62] In the light of the discussion above, this definition has a number of shortcomings.

One problem concerns the reference to equity. This is apt in an historical and conventional sense, but it is misleading if it is taken to imply that equity supplies a distinctive type of justification for the duty, or that the trust depends on a divided system. It contributes nothing to understanding, interpreting or developing trust law. Further, the definition omits any reference to a genuine justificatory category, and this is a crucial requirement for any adequate definition (and this omission tends to suggest that the reference to equity is mistakenly understood to serve this purpose). There is nothing to indicate that the trustee's duty is contractual in the sense discussed above, that is to say, that it arises from the trustee's having agreed to take on the position of trustee. Even more importantly, there is nothing to indicate that the beneficiaries have property rights in the trust fund. It is true to say that the trustee has a duty to deal with the property for the benefit of the beneficiary—this is the contractual duty—but

---

[62] Pettit, above n 28, at 27.

this does not amount to saying that the beneficiaries have property rights. Also, there is no suggestion of two different dimensions.

It would be better to define the trust as follows. A trust comprises (1) an allocation of property rights in respect of specified property, between the trustee, who has control of the property and the power to deal with it, and the beneficiary or beneficiaries, who have the rights to benefit from it; in conjunction with (2) a contractual duty owed to the beneficiaries by the trustee arising from his assumption of the trusteeship, to manage the property and distribute it on the terms of the trust. As discussed above, the allocation of property rights has the form of an *in rem* right–liability relation and the contractual relationship has the form of an *in personam* right–duty relation.

This is the definition of an express trust, and as mentioned above it is possible for the trust to exist in only the property dimension, that is to say as an allocation of property rights without any contractual duty. This is the situation discussed in chapter 6.

6

Invalid Transfers and Proprietary Claims

The Nature of the Claim to Recover an Invalid Transfer

This chapter deals in more depth with the property-based claim to recover an invalid transfer of property, which was introduced in chapter 3.[1] An invalid transfer is a transfer that was not made by way of a valid exercise of the owner's power of disposal by or on behalf of the owner, C. A putative exercise of the power may be vitiated by mistake or some other vitiating factor,[2] or the transfer may have been made without authority from the owner, as where it was made by an unauthorised stranger or by an agent or trustee acting beyond his authority. As discussed in chapter 3, the property may be a tangible thing or an intangible thing, including a contractual right, and the transfer could be a transfer of abstract value from one bank account to another. The claim is property-based, in the sense that it falls in the justificatory category of property law. The claim can be described as a restitutionary claim in the sense that the remedy is the recovery of the transfer, or as an unjust enrichment claim in the sense that the claim arises from the receipt of property by D that, in the absence of a claim, would leave him unjustly enriched. But it is not a restitutionary claim or unjust enrichment claim in the sense of falling in a supposed justificatory category of restitution or unjust enrichment rather than property.

The Effect of an Invalid Transfer

There is something paradoxical about the idea of an invalid transfer: if the transfer from C to D is invalid it appears that C retains ownership of the property, and so, it might appear, although the property has come into D's possession or control, there has been no change in

---

[1] Above p 93.

[2] The various vitiating factors are not discussed here: see P Jaffey, *The Nature and Scope of Restitution* (Oxford, Hart Publishing, 2000) ch 5.

the legal position with respect to property rights in the property and so no transfer in law at all. But even if a transfer is invalid, there is good reason why the mere fact of the change of possession and control should itself alter the legal position, by transferring from C to D one element of ownership, namely the power to deal with the property as its owner. The effect of this is that third parties, and D himself, are entitled to rely on D being the owner of the property, and in this way the law provides protection to third parties dealing with D as bona fide purchasers, and to D himself with respect to his own consumption and disposal of the property.[3] Furthermore, where there is a transfer of property in the form of a contractual right as an object of property, or a transfer of abstract value from an account of C's to an account of D's, the power to deal with the property means the authority to act as the creditor or account-holder, and this is necessarily with D as the contractual creditor, so the transfer necessarily involves a transfer of this aspect of ownership.

Thus there is good reason why in principle an invalid transfer should give rise to a separation of title, the control title moving from C to D with the property, and the right to the benefit of the property remaining with C. In other words, an invalid transfer should in principle give rise to the property dimension of the trust. In the case of an express trust, the separation of title arises because this was the intention of the settlor when, as the owner of the property, he made the transfer to the trustee, in order to enable the trustee to hold the property and allocate it in accordance with the trust. In the case of an invalid transfer, the reason for the separation of title is that it is the appropriate response to an invalid transfer, that is to say, it is the remedial relation that should arise in response to the causative event of an invalid transfer, according to the monist principle, and in the light of the hardship argument that takes account of the interests of D and third parties.[4]

Because D has not agreed to act as a trustee there can be no contractual dimension of the trust, and D cannot be subject to a contractual or fiduciary duty to manage or preserve the property. However, as discussed in chapter 7, if D knows or ought to know that the transfer was invalid, he can incur a duty to C not to dispose of or consume the property and can be liable to C for breach of this duty.

---

[3] This is relevant to the duty D may have with respect to the receipt of an invalid transfer, which is discussed in ch 7.

[4] Above p 43.

For the most part, I will disregard this aspect of D's position in this chapter.

This is the approach to an invalid transfer taken in equity. Conventionally the control title is of course referred to as a legal title and the beneficial ownership as equitable title. C's claim is generally referred to as an 'equitable proprietary claim', or sometimes as a claim under a constructive trust.[5] But, as discussed previously, one should not be deceived by the traditional terminology of equity into thinking that the claim is in any way dependent on a divided system of law and equity, or on distinct bodies of law and equity, or on the idea of conscience or equity in the ordinary sense as the basis for a claim. This would be the anti-fusion fallacy discussed in chapter 4.[6] The equitable proprietary claim is simply a right of beneficial ownership of property that is held by someone else with the legal power of control over it as a result of an invalid transfer. (I will elaborate on this statement below.)

It follows that this approach is in principle appropriate for all invalid transfers, though it is actually found only in relation to those types of invalid transfer that have traditionally come within the jurisdiction of equity, which means mainly transfers made by C's trustee or fiduciary in breach of trust or fiduciary duty. Other types of invalid transfer, which were dealt with at common law, were not dealt with in this way because the common law did not have the concept of the trust or separation of title. The common law's response to an invalid transfer is much cruder, as considered later in the chapter. Substantive fusion of law and equity would allow the superior approach of equity to be adopted generally.

In the standard case in equity of a transfer by C's trustee or fiduciary in breach of duty, C's equitable proprietary claim is sometimes regarded as a claim arising from a wrong, but, although the trustee or fiduciary may act wrongfully vis-à-vis C,[7] it is not a wrong that generates the claim. The claim arises because the trustee or fiduciary acted beyond his power under the trust instrument or fiduciary

---

[5] The usage of 'constructive trust' is controversial, as considered below.

[6] Above p 120.

[7] Generally it is assumed that the trustee or fiduciary is subject to a strict liability duty, so that he necessarily acts wrongfully by making a transfer beyond his power, but it makes better sense to say that he acts wrongfully only where he acted unreasonably or without due care. In fact, although the trustee is said to be subject to a strict liability duty, the court has a statutory power to relieve the trustee of liability if he acted honestly and reasonably, so generally he will be liable only when he committed a genuine breach of duty: see s 61 Trustee Act 1925.

appointment, so that the transfer was invalid. As between the beneficiary C and D, the recipient of the transfer, the question whether
the trustee or fiduciary acted wrongfully towards the beneficiary C is
irrelevant. Why should it affect the position of the recipient, who did
not commit the wrong and was not complicit in it? Furthermore, in
accordance with the monist principle, the appropriate legal consequences of a wrong by the trustee against the beneficiary would be
to give the beneficiary a remedy against the trustee as the wrongdoer.

Proprietary and Personal Claims

The claim to recover an invalid transfer is a property-based claim, and
as mentioned in chapter 3 it is a distinct question whether it should
be a proprietary or personal claim.[8] It is actually found in both forms,
generally as a proprietary claim in equity and as a personal claim at
common law. It seems natural to assume that the claim to recover an
invalid transfer should always be proprietary. If there has been an
invalid transfer of property from C to D, it appears that C should
retain ownership of the property, or more particularly beneficial
ownership, and so have a proprietary claim, and this appears to follow from the monist principle. But if the property transferred is lost
or becomes unidentifiable in D's estate, it might appear (if the claim
is not lost altogether) that the claim should be merely a personal
claim. This might appear to account for the absence of a proprietary
claim at common law, though this is really more to do with the
absence of the concepts necessary for the recognition of a proprietary
claim, namely the trust and separation of title. In fact, if there is a
claim at all it should indeed always be a proprietary claim, in accordance with the monist principle. I will come back to this issue, which
is of great practical importance.

TRACING AND THE OBJECT OF THE PROPRIETARY CLAIM

Tracing is generally regarded as an arcane and technical area of law,
but it raises important theoretical problems concerning the nature of
property and property rights, and for this reason it deserves quite
detailed treatment.

[8] Above p 95.

The Problem with the Transactional Theory of Tracing

Consider an ordinary case of an invalid transfer of an asset from C to D. I will assume that the equitable approach discussed above is applicable, so legal or control title passes to D but C retains the beneficial ownership and has a proprietary claim. Say the asset is destroyed. C's claim must lapse. This is the exigibility condition concerning property rights.[9] Similarly if the asset is transferred to a third party, there can no longer be a proprietary claim against D in respect of it, though there may be a claim against the third party. However, it is well established that, if the asset is exchanged for a different asset, C has a proprietary claim in respect of the so-called 'exchange product'.[10] This is the exchange product rule of tracing. It appears that C's property right jumps from the original asset to the exchange product.[11] The usual understanding of tracing is based on the idea that it consists in the transmission of a property right from one asset to another, triggered by a particular transaction. This understanding is generally described as the transactional theory of tracing. The problem in understanding the exchange product rule of tracing under the transactional theory is how to explain why a property right should be transmitted from one asset to another in this way.[12]

It is sometimes said that the answer lies in the 'power theory'.[13] According to this theory, C has a power to transfer his property right to a new asset in D's estate in certain circumstances, in particular if the original asset is lost from D's estate and replaced by another asset. But the theory offers no explanation of why C has such a power. If the justification of the power is to ensure that C still has a proprietary claim, notwithstanding the loss of the original asset, the question is why this is justified. This is the crucial issue about tracing, and the power theory does not address it. Furthermore, assuming it is justified for C's proprietary claim to be preserved in such circumstances, it is not apparent why it should not be transmitted automatically by virtue of the exchange without the need for the exercise of a power.

---

[9] See above p 89.

[10] See eg PH Pettit, *Equity and the Law of Trusts* (Oxford, OUP, 10th edn, 2006) 550.

[11] One might prefer to say that a new but equivalent property right is created and the original one extinguished, but nothing turns on this for present purposes.

[12] Some of these arguments are discussed in Jaffey, above n 2, at 294–96.

[13] See P Birks, 'Mixing and Tracing: Property and Restitution' (1992) 45 *Current Legal Problems* 69, 89; RB Grantham and CEF Rickett, *Enrichment and Restitution in New Zealand* (Oxford, Hart Publishing, 2000) 445ff. A version of the power theory seems to be alluded to by Lord Goff in *Lipkin Gorman v Karpnale* [1991] 2 AC 548, 573.

Thus it is doubtful whether the power theory adds anything to the understanding of tracing.[14]

Another suggestion is that the claim in respect of the original asset is extinguished, but a new claim arises in respect of the exchange product by virtue of the principle of unjust enrichment. The idea seems to be that the new claim is not property-based, but falls in a distinct justificatory category of unjust enrichment. It is true of course that if a proprietary claim ought to arise in the exchange product as a result of D's receipt of it, and no such claim actually arises, D is unjustly enriched. But this gives no indication of the justification of the claim when it does arise. It is the purely remedial notion of unjust enrichment rejected in chapter 3.[15] The argument is question-begging as far as justification is concerned: more particularly, it is an example of the remedy-as-justification fallacy. What is required to support such an argument is an explanation of what the principle of unjust enrichment is and how it generates a claim in these circumstances, and it appears that no plausible explanation is available.[16]

Yet another suggestion is that it is because D acted wrongfully in disposing of the original property that he becomes subject to a proprietary claim in respect of the exchange product. The claim in respect of the exchange product is a remedy for this wrong. D should not be able to deprive C of his proprietary claim by a wrongful act, so the remedy for the wrong should be a substitute proprietary claim. But this argument is also unsuccessful. First, as discussed further in chapter 7, D does not necessarily act wrongfully in disposing of the original property. If D does not know and has no reason to know that the property in question reached him through an invalid transfer, he does not act wrongfully by disposing of it,[17] but nevertheless the proprietary claim attaches to the exchange product. In any case, even if D does act wrongfully, a proprietary claim in respect of the exchange

---

[14] In any case, it is difficult to reconcile the power theory with the operation of the law of tracing. It is in the nature of a power that it must be deliberately exercised, and it is difficult to see how the claimant can be understood to have chosen to exercise a power to transmit his right of ownership to a substitute asset—in some cases, the power would have to be exercised before the claimant has any knowledge of the claim, and where there has been a series of exchanges, the power must be exercised retrospectively in relation to a substitute asset that has since been lost through a subsequent exchange. See LD Smith, *The Law of Tracing* (Oxford, Clarendon Press, OUP, 1997) 326.

[15] See further below p 219.

[16] The explanation would also have to account for the fact that the claim is proprietary: if the only concern is to remove D's enrichment there is no reason why this should be the case.

[17] See below p 190.

product is not an appropriate response to the wrong. D's wrong is a breach of his duty to C. In accordance with the monist principle, C should have a personal claim for compensation for loss caused by the wrongful disposal. The measure of compensation would be the value of the original property, and the value of the exchange product might be taken to be a reasonable proxy for this. But the remedy must be a matter affecting only C and D, not third parties, and there is no basis for a proprietary claim, which affects third parties as well. For a proprietary claim to arise from a wrong involves the dualist fallacy.[18]

In my view, none of these arguments can explain the law of tracing. The only plausible account of tracing is at odds with the transactional theory of tracing and has some significant implications for the ordinary rules of tracing.

The Proprietary Claim to Abstract Value

The basis for the law of tracing is simply that the beneficial owner C has a right to the exchange value of the property transferred. This is an element of the right of beneficial ownership derived from his original primary right of ownership.[19] One might take this to mean that C should have ownership of the exchange product as the standard exchange product rule holds, in accordance with the transactional theory of tracing. But this is not how it should be understood. If the original transfer was of a tangible thing, C may have a particular interest in recovering that specific thing, but once it is lost from D's estate, C's interest can only be in recovering its value from D. In principle, there is no reason to require D to surrender the exchange product itself, as opposed to its value in money. The reason for giving C ownership of the exchange product is that it is a means of securing to him its value, which is taken to represent the exchange value of the original asset transferred. In that case, why not say simply that C has a claim for the value of the asset transferred? The standard answer is that a proprietary claim is a claim of beneficial ownership (or some other property right) in respect of a specific asset, whereas a personal claim is a claim to abstract value or value detached from any specific asset; a claim in respect of 'the value of the transfer' is a claim for abstract value and so must be a personal claim, in the nature of a claim for a debt in the measure of the transfer. This would not explain the exchange product rule of tracing, because the effect of tracing is to preserve a proprietary claim in respect of a specific asset.

[18] See below p 173.
[19] See above p 88.

It may be true to say that the object of a right of *absolute* ownership must be a specific asset, because absolute ownership includes a
power of control and transfer that must relate to a specific asset. But
there is no reason in principle or logic why there cannot be a proprietary claim of *beneficial* ownership of abstract value, under a trust or
separation of title, in the following sense. D's estate is made up of specific assets—tangible things, contract rights as objects of property, and
maybe money as coins or banknotes—but it can be treated as a body
of wealth or abstract value, as if it were a fund. C can have a proprietary claim to a part of that abstract value, namely that part of the
abstract value that is derived from the invalid transfer—the 'surviving
value' of the transfer. This is the part of the value of the estate that
would not have been there but for the invalid transfer: thus the
surviving value is determined by a test of causation. This is a well-
defined part of D's estate, considered as a fund of abstract value. It can
in principle be ascertained and given to C by way of a money payment. Indeed if D is bankrupt the estate is converted into abstract
value in the form of money for the purpose of distribution to
claimants. It would also be possible to say whether a further transfer
of surviving value has been made to a third party, according to a test
of causation—ie, if the further transfer would not have occurred in
the absence of the original invalid transfer—for the purposes of establishing a claim against the third party in respect of surviving value in
the third party's estate.[20]

At the time of the invalid transfer the surviving value will be the
value of a specific asset transferred.[21] One might say that C retains
beneficial ownership of the specific asset, but it would be better to
say that C has beneficial ownership of the surviving value, which is
for the moment located in this specific asset. If this asset is destroyed
or reduced in value, the measure of the claim is reduced or the claim
eliminated, because the surviving value is lost.[22] Locating a thing or
asset may be relevant in this causative sense, to establish the measure
of the surviving value derived from the invalid transfer. But the surviving value may, as a result of events occurring after the transfer,
diverge from the value of the transfer or the specific asset transferred.
As the exchange product rule shows, surviving value may persist after

---

[20] The same type of argument is normally applied with respect to the ownership of tangible things or specific assets, as opposed to abstract value: see eg EL Sherwin, 'Constructive
Trusts in Bankruptcy' [1989] *University of Illinois Law Review* 297.

[21] Or a proportion of it, as considered below in connection with tracing into mixtures.

[22] But see below p 167.

the specific asset has been disposed of from the estate. Also, it may be that the surviving value cannot be located in the form of a specific asset, though it is known that the surviving value is in the estate as a whole—this is the situation addressed in terms of the 'swollen assets' principle considered below.

Sometimes a proprietary claim is equated with a right to specific restitution, meaning the return of a specific asset. In principle they are distinct, however. In theory C could have a claim for the specific restitution of an asset correlated with a duty on the part of D to return it, purely as a matter of contract or tort, the legal relation being *in personam*. For example, specific restitution would be appropriate as a means of securing a tangible thing of special personal value to C, which D had contracted to sell to C or had appropriated from C. Such a right of specific restitution of an asset is not the same thing as a proprietary claim in respect of it. In particular, if D is insolvent, the right to specific restitution based on such a duty in contract or tort should lapse. One reason for confusion between the two is that traditionally where equity has found that C has a right to specific restitution of an asset it has also given him the beneficial ownership of it.[23]

For present purposes, the interesting point is that it is often assumed that a proprietary claim must be in respect of a tangible thing that can be physically removed from D's estate, or if not a tangible thing at least a specific asset like a debt that can be isolated and transferred,[24] and this may be because of the assumption that a proprietary claim is equivalent to a claim for specific restitution of an asset. To the contrary, a claim for specific restitution of an asset invalidly transferred is justifiable only where the surviving value of the transfer in D's estate has not diminished and so the value of the asset does not exceed the surviving value in the estate. In general, a proprietary claim will be satisfied by way of a claim for money.

There is no plausible explanation of tracing in terms of the traditional transactional theory, which conceives of it in terms of the transmission of a property right from one specific asset to another. In the tracing literature there is some discussion of the causational theory of tracing as an alternative to the transactional theory, which

---

[23] See below p 249.

[24] See eg R Goode, 'Ownership and Obligation in Commercial Transactions' (1987) 103 *Law Quarterly Review* 433, 439; R Goode, 'Proprietary Restitutionary Claims' in WR Cornish et al (eds), *Restitution: Past, Present and Future* (Oxford, Hart Publishing, 1998) 65.

might be understood to refer to the approach suggested above. However, it appears that generally the causational theory is understood to hold that the proprietary claim is a property right in a specific asset, which jumps from one asset to another according to a causation test rather than a transactional test.[25] The crucial point about tracing is that it can only be explained in terms of a proprietary claim to abstract value. Causation is relevant in determining the measure of abstract value derived from the invalid transfer, and the disposal or consumption of an asset may be causally related to the receipt of another asset with which it has no transactional link.

Some other Difficulties with the Transactional Theory of Tracing

There are other aspects of the law of tracing that make more sense if they are interpreted in terms of a proprietary right to abstract value. Say D receives an asset from C through an invalid transfer and makes a shrewd investment with it. Through his own effort and expertise, he manages to exchange the original asset for another asset worth considerably more. It is difficult to see why C should be the beneficial owner of this more valuable asset, leaving D with no benefit from his work of investment. This would be appropriate where the original asset was held by D under an express trust, and D was acting as a trustee for C and investing C's beneficial property on his behalf. But, in the present situation, surely C should be entitled only to the value of the original transfer, together with a claim in respect of unauthorised use.[26] According to the conventional view presupposed by the transactional theory, C cannot have a proprietary claim to the abstract value of the transfer, and this is why he is given ownership of the exchange product. As a general rule the value of the exchange product is likely to be a reasonable proxy for the value of the original transfer, but in this particular case the standard exchange product rule is inappropriate, and for a satisfactory outcome it is necessary to recognise a proprietary claim to abstract value.

A similar issue arose in *Foskett v McKeown*.[27] Say that money invalidly transferred from C to D is used by D to pay the premiums on a life insurance policy on D's life, and then when D dies C claims

---

[25] S Evans, 'Rethinking Tracing and the Law of Restitution' (1999) 115 *Law Quarterly Review* 469.

[26] Above p 99; leaving aside any claim based on D's wrongdoing. See further Jaffey, above n 2, at 311.

[27] [2001] 1 AC 102. Arguably this is a case where the property is used to buy services and there are no traceable proceeds at all, so if there is a claim it must have a different basis: see P Jaffey, 'Tracing, Property, and Unjust Enrichment' [2000] *Trust Law International* 194.

the proceeds of the policy, which greatly exceed the value of the transfer. C should surely have a proprietary claim to the value of the transfer, rather than all the proceeds. According to the House of Lords in *Foskett v McKeown* (although the facts were slightly different) C should be entitled to the proceeds of the policy, though the Court of Appeal had held that C should recover only the amount of money transferred.[28] According to the argument above the Court of Appeal's decision is preferable.

Another problematic example for the transactional theory of tracing is the conundrum of 'geometrical expansion'. Say that the original asset transferred to D is exchanged by D for another asset from a third party, but the third party is not a bona fide purchaser. Then, according to the transactional approach, C owns both the original asset, which is now in the hands of the third party, and also the exchange product in the hands of D. The process could be repeated again and again, with respect to the original asset and the exchange product, and as a result C's original ownership of a single asset invalidly transferred could spawn ownership of many different assets, together worth far more than C's original asset. In fact the position appears to be that C does not have claims to all these assets; he can trace into only one asset. This suggests that the property right is not transmitted at the time of the transaction and is somehow in suspense until some later time when C specifies which asset he asserts a claim to, possibly when the matter is disposed of in court.[29]

This approach may often reach an acceptable outcome. The problem is that there must surely be at any time a determinate property right that depends on the circumstances at that time and the events preceding it, and if, as the transactional theory holds, it subsists in a specific asset and is transmitted from one asset to another, it is very difficult to account for the legal position in this type of case. According to the abstract value theory, the issue is whether and to what extent there is surviving value of the original transfer in D's or a third party's estate, according to a causation test. There is always a subsisting, determinate property right, though not in a specific asset. Surviving value cannot be duplicated or multiplied, though it can be divided up and distributed to different people. Its location is in principle a matter of causation.

---

[28] [1998] Ch 265.
[29] Possibly this suggests that there is a power, though there is no indication of its basis: cf above p 159.

Tracing and Change of Position

The discussion above has been concerned with C's standpoint. From C's standpoint, if he cannot recover the original specific asset, he should be able to recover its value—he should be able to treat the transfer as a transfer of abstract value that adds to the abstract value of D's estate. Often he is only concerned with the transfer as a transfer of abstract value, because it was simply a transfer of money in some form. Looking at the position from D's standpoint, fair treatment of D also requires that the invalid transfer be treated as a transfer of abstract value. Say there is an invalid transfer of an asset from C to D—say a sum of cash—and this remains untouched in D's estate, but D, having received the transfer, and being under the impression that he is richer by this amount, incurs an expense that he would not otherwise have incurred, say by making a payment out of his current account. If C still has a proprietary claim of beneficial ownership of the cash transferred, D is now worse off than if he had never received the transfer, and this is surely unfair to him. He should be protected by a reduction of the claim to the extent of his expenditure, and this is because he should be able to treat the receipt as an accretion to the abstract value of his estate. This is an application of the hardship argument that takes account of the interests of D in avoiding an overly burdensome remedy.

A version of this rule has been recognised in the form of the change of position rule.[30] However, the recognition of the change of position rule has been in the context of the common law claim to recover an invalid transfer considered later, which is a personal claim against D for the value of the invalid transfer. Change of position is treated as a partial defence to the claim for the value of the transfer, which reduces the measure of recovery. It has seemed awkward to apply the rule in response to a proprietary claim, because of the assumption that a proprietary claim is a claim of ownership of a specific asset, which is indivisible or discrete, and incapable of being

---

[30] *Lipkin Gorman v Karpnale* [1991] 2 AC 548. Two versions of the change of position defence have been distinguished in the literature: see eg A Burrows, *The Law of Restitution* (London, Butterworths, 2nd edn, 2002) 510. On one view, it is purely a matter of causation, which corresponds to the approach in the text. On the other view, it requires reliance by D. There is no basis for this condition if change of position is concerned with defining surviving value or protecting D against excess recovery. But where there has been reliance by D, there may be a separate basis for giving him protection, arising from the property law principle protecting reasonable reliance discussed above p 87; see also below p 255.

reduced in part in any straightforward way.[31] But once it is understood that the proprietary claim is or can be a claim in respect of abstract value this problem disappears.

Also, because change of position has been understood as a defence to a personal claim against D the point has been missed that change of position is also necessary to protect creditors of D. It is not just D's interest that is at stake: it is also unfair to D's creditors if the effect of C's proprietary claim is to reduce the value of the estate available to creditors below its value at the time of the invalid transfer from C to D. The effect of this would be that some of the value of the estate available to satisfy the claims of creditors at the time of the invalid transfer is in effect redistributed away from these creditors in favour of C's proprietary claim, and there is surely no justification for this. Thus change of position should be understood as a rule that limits the value of the proprietary claim. It is really the corollary of the exchange product rule, because it is based on treating the transfer as a transfer of abstract value for the benefit of D, and the exchange product rule does the same thing for the benefit of C.

In the case mentioned above at the start of the discussion of tracing,[32] where the original asset is consumed or disposed of without generating an exchange product, the reason why the claim is lost is, strictly speaking, change of position, meaning loss of abstract value, not the loss of the specific asset in itself. If D consumed or disposed of the specific asset received, but would have consumed or disposed of property of the same value even if he had not received the invalid transfer, then there remains surviving value of the invalid transfer in his estate. Although the proprietary claim still depends on its being exigible against an object of property, the object is not the asset itself but abstract value, namely the causally-defined surviving value in D's estate.

In general, the proprietary claim to abstract surviving value, like separation of title,[33] provides a means of accommodating the interests of the claimant C with third parties with whom the recipient D may deal or have dealt, namely creditors and indirect transferees.

---

[31] See eg the discussion in P Birks, 'Overview: Tracing, Claiming and Defences' in Birks, ed, *Laundering and Tracing* (Oxford, Clarendon Press, 1995), and RC Nolan, 'Change of Position' in Birks, ibid.

[32] Above p 159.

[33] Above p 156.

The 'Swollen Assets' Theory and the Nature of the Proprietary Claim

A version of this abstract value approach to tracing has sometimes been considered under the name of the 'swollen assets' theory of tracing.[34] This has not generally been considered in connection with the rationale for the exchange product rule, but in connection with a different type of case. This is where there has been an invalid transfer from C to D, and it is known that the proceeds of the invalid transfer remain in the estate as surviving value—there has been no change of position, though the point is not usually put in this way—but it is impossible to identify a specific asset as the traceable proceeds by exchange, direct or indirect, of the specific asset originally transferred, because it is not known what transfers were made within D's estate as a result of the receipt. According to the argument above, in such a case C should have a proprietary claim to the surviving value as abstract value in D's estate.[35]

The swollen assets approach has generally been rejected.[36] It is assumed that the proprietary claim cannot really be a claim in respect of abstract value, and so (if it is not a claim of beneficial ownership of a specific asset)[37] it must be a charge against the estate—ie, a floating charge over all D's assets—securing D's personal liability to pay back the value of the invalid transfer.[38] This is not the analysis above, and such a claim would indeed be unfair to D and D's creditors, because the charge would secure to C the value of the invalid transfer even if the actual surviving value in the estate had fallen below this—in other words, it would deny D and his creditors the protection of the change of position rule.

The form of the proprietary claim suggested above is neither a claim of beneficial ownership of a specific asset, nor a floating charge against the estate for the value of the invalid transfer. One might say that it is a floating charge against D's estate to secure D's liability for surviving value. But it is not best described as a charge at all, because this implies that the property right secures a separate liability. The proprietary claim is really a distinct form of property right. It is like a floating charge inasmuch as the object of the property right is the

---

[34] See eg DA Oesterle, 'Deficiencies of the Restitutionary Right to Trace Misappropriated Property in Equity and in UCCC §9-306' (1983) 68 *Cornell Law Review* 172.

[35] There is some support for the swollen assets theory in *Space Investments Ltd v Canadian Imperial Bank of Commerce (Bahamas) Ltd* [1986] 1 WLR 1072, 1074, per Lord Templeman.

[36] *Re Goldcorp Exchange* [1994] 2 All ER 806; Smith, above n 14, at 310–11.

[37] Or a charge over a specific asset.

[38] As in *Foskett v McKeown*, considered above at n 27.

estate as a trust fund or body of abstract value, but the content of the claim is not the right to satisfaction of a debt but the beneficial ownership of the surviving value of the invalid transfer.

Tracing into Mixtures

The discussion of tracing above has been confined to the exchange product rule, which is concerned with specific assets. The other main type of tracing rule concerns mixtures. A mixture involves a fungible, meaning something consisting of equivalent and interchangeable units. This could be water or oil or cereal, but the most common example is money in the form of cash or a bank balance. Commonly tracing cases involve a money transfer from C that is paid into an account of D's with an existing balance of D's money, and this is treated as a mixture of C's and D's money. The usual rule here is the *pari passu* or proportionate share rule.[39] The account is an asset to which D has legal or control title, and beneficial ownership of the asset is shared between C and D in the proportions that they contributed to it. If money is withdrawn from the account and dissipated, the loss is borne by C and D in proportion to their contributions, and if money is withdrawn and invested the investment is owned by C and D in the same proportions, which means that C benefits from an increase in value. Again this approach is based on the assumption that the proprietary claim must subsist in a specific asset—the contractual right to the balance on the account—though here beneficial ownership of the asset is shared.

Under the *pari passu* rule, C has to bear a share of losses from the mixture, but why should this be the case? If the invalid transfer from C is paid into an account of D's and then money is withdrawn from D's account and dissipated, C's proprietary claim should be reduced only if this constitutes a change of position. This is the case if the withdrawal was caused by the receipt of the invalid transfer, that is to say, if it would not have been made in the absence of the invalid transfer to D. If the withdrawal would have been made anyway, it should be treated as a withdrawal of D's money, leaving C's claim unaffected. If there is a withdrawal that was caused by the invalid transfer, and the money withdrawn is invested and the investment loses value, there is a change of position that reduces the value of C's claim.[40] But if money is withdrawn and invested in an asset that

---

[39] Pettit, above n 10, at 560; *Re Diplock's Estate* [1948] Ch 465.
[40] Some support for this comes from *Re Tilley's WT* [1967] Ch 1179.

appreciates in value, as discussed above in connection with *Foskett v McKeown* it is difficult to see why C should take the benefit from the increase in value, even if the investment would not otherwise have been made, though he should have a claim in respect of the unauthorised use of his money, ie an unauthorised use claim.[41]

Thus the important point about mixtures is that they are not really a different type of case for the purposes of tracing. Under the abstract value approach to tracing above, D's estate is always treated as a mixture of wealth or abstract value as a fungible, and the appropriate tracing rule is always the causation or change of position approach.

The origin of the *pari passu* rule for mixtures appears to lie in a different type of situation where it is more appropriate.[42] Say that D receives invalid transfers from C1 and C2 and these are mixed in D's account. This might be the case if D is a solicitor or broker acting for two clients. If a withdrawal is made and the money dissipated, it makes sense here to use the *pari passu* rule as between C1 and C2, if there is no reason to think that D is intending to draw on money from one party rather than another. It seems that this type of case has been equated with the case of a mixture of C's money with D's, at least where D is an innocent recipient rather than a wrongdoer.[43]

The *pari passu* rule is not applied when D has acted wrongfully by failing to keep the money received separate from his own money, when he knew or ought to have known that the transfer was invalid.[44] Here, instead of a principle of shared risk, the risk of loss is imposed entirely on the wrongdoer. If D withdraws money and it is dissipated, it is assumed in favour of C that his own money was left in the account.[45] But if D withdraws money and invests it and the money left in the account is subsequently dissipated, or the invest-

---

[41] Above p 99.

[42] See Pettit, above n 10, at 560.

[43] In cases of this sort involving money from two or more different sources, a problem arises when there is a series of deposits and withdrawals from the account. The appropriate approach in principle is the approach used in some US courts, according to which a withdrawal is treated as a mixture in the same proportions as the account at that time, the proportions in the account being recalculated after each deposit and withdrawal. The English courts traditionally use the 'first in, first out' rule, or rule in *Clayton's case* (1816) 1 Mer 572. This takes account to some extent of the idea that earlier deposits contribute less to the final balance, but in an excessive and capricious way. Where the rule in *Clayton's case* has seemed unjust the English courts have used the '*pari passu ex post facto*' approach, which takes the final balance of the account and divides it proportionately among contributors to the account over the period: *Barlow Clowes International v Vaughan* [1992] 4 All ER 22. This may also give unfair weight to earlier deposits.

[44] ie, where D is a wrongdoer in the sense discussed in ch 7.

[45] *Re Hallet* (1880) 13 Ch D 696.

ment appreciates, it is assumed that it was C's money that was withdrawn and invested.[46]

This approach is very difficult to reconcile with the transactional theory of tracing. Just as in the example of geometric expansion discussed above, although it is assumed that C's claim must be a property right in a specific asset, it is impossible to say at any time which asset the right subsists in, because it depends on what happens subsequently. One could say instead that C is entitled to a charge over the mixture, including any investments made from withdrawals from the original mixture,[47] but as considered above this may operate unfairly because it fails to take account of change of position.

Furthermore, it should be irrelevant to the proprietary claim whether D is a wrongdoer. C should recover surviving value from D's estate; if D withdraws money from the account and dissipates it, and this reduces surviving value under a causation test, then the measure of C's proprietary claim should be reduced, even if D knows that the transfer was invalid and so acts wrongfully. This may seem unfair: why should D be able to reduce the measure of C's proprietary claim against him through a wrongful act? The answer is that the wrong does not alter the position as between C and D, since D is liable to pay compensation for any loss in surviving value wrongfully caused.[48] This is the appropriate remedy for the wrong, in accordance with the monist principle.[49] Whether the claim is personal or proprietary is significant only as between C and D's creditors. If D is bankrupt, although the proprietary claim to surviving value will be unaffected, C will not be able to recover the full amount of the compensation claim, since this is a personal claim. By contrast, if the risk of any loss from the account is imposed on D, even if on a causation test it is a loss of surviving value, as the wrongdoer rule provides, C is unfairly favoured at the expense of D's creditors with a proprietary claim whose measure exceeds the actual amount of surviving value in the estate.[50]

---

[46] *Re Oatway* [1903] 2 Ch 356. If the mixture increases in value, it appears that C may instead take a proportionate share, as in *Foskett v McKeown*.

[47] *Re Oatway* [1903] 2 Ch 356.

[48] This type of wrong is considered in ch 7.

[49] See above p 161.

[50] The approach for wrongdoers has something in common with the causation approach proposed above, namely that the risk is not shared, but imposed on one party. The approach for wrongdoers corresponds to the causation approach where, under a causation test, the loss of traceable value is not a loss of surviving value.

'Priority' and Contract and Tort Claims

A proprietary claim is a claim of beneficial ownership of the abstract value in D's estate, arising from an invalid transfer to D that contributed abstract value to D's estate. It is a type of property right in D's estate. A personal claim is not a property right in D's estate or any asset in D's estate; it is a claim against D which has to be satisfied out of the property available to D, namely his estate, in competition with other such claims. In D's bankruptcy the basic principle is that D's beneficial estate, meaning the wealth or abstract value realised from the assets in the estate, excluding abstract value beneficially owned by C by virtue of a proprietary claim, is allocated among his creditors— ie, claimants with a personal claim—in proportion, so that each creditor receives an amount in proportion to the value of his claim, irrespective of the type of claim.[51] In equity, the property-based claim to recover an invalid transfer of property is a proprietary claim, but at common law it has always been a personal claim, as discussed below.

Traditionally a proprietary claim has been understood as a claim in respect of a tangible thing or specific asset. This is the basis of the transactional theory of tracing discussed above. Sometimes, as mentioned above, it may be thought that the proprietary claim is equivalent to a right of specific restitution of a specific asset; that is to say, that the reason why C has a proprietary claim is that he can identify a tangible thing or specific asset that he is entitled to have set aside and withdrawn from D's estate. But in fact the proprietary claim is a right of beneficial ownership of abstract surviving value, not necessarily of a specific asset. As discussed above, this is clear from the law of tracing, and it is also justified in principle. In favour of C it is right to recognise the object of the claim as abstract value in order to protect C's interest in the abstract value of his property, and in favour of D and D's creditors it is right to do the same in order to protect them in respect of change of position. There is no reason to doubt that abstract value can be an object of property, as discussed in chapter 3.[52]

---

[51] This quite different rule is also referred to as the *pari passu* rule. The basic principle is overridden in certain respects by statute so that certain types of claim are satisfied first, but it is not necessary to consider this.

[52] Above p 84.

One might put this point differently, as follows. Say there is an invalid transfer of abstract value from C to D, which gives rise to a claim against D to recover the transfer. C clearly has a claim against D for the value of the transfer (subject to reduction for change of position). But C's position vis-à-vis D is exactly the same as C's position vis-à-vis D2, to whom there is a transfer of abstract value via D, that is to say, a transfer of surviving value in D's estate, according to a causation test.[53] This is just the same as saying that C retains beneficial ownership of the abstract value transferred. The argument applies to all transfers, since any transfer can be treated as a transfer of abstract value.

The general availability of a proprietary claim follows from the monist principle. The primary right of ownership is *in rem*, in the sense of being binding on all the world, and the transfer is invalid not only as against the recipient D, but as against all the world as well, and accordingly the remedial right to abstract value is also in principle *in rem*. By contrast, a wrong committed by D against C has legal effect, as a wrong, only as between C and D. In general, in accordance with the monist principle a wrong cannot generate a proprietary claim.[54]

Claims in contract or tort are never claims to recover an invalid transfer of property, and should not be proprietary. A claim in contract can be a claim to recover a payment made under the contract—for example, if C paid in advance for goods or services that are never provided, C may have a claim to recover the payment.[55] But this claim is personal, because the transfer was valid: it was a transfer pursuant to a valid exercise of C's power to dispose of his wealth, and it is no less a valid transfer where C is entitled to be repaid because the contract is not performed.[56] It is sometimes said that the contractor C has assumed the risk of D's bankruptcy. But it would be better to say that there was a valid exercise of the power of transfer, and that this carries with it the risk of bankruptcy whether C adverted to the risk or not.

A tort by D against C does not usually involve a transfer from C to D, but it can do where D's wrong is the wrongful acquisition of

---

[53] It would normally be said that a claim arises against D2 only if there is a transfer to D2 of traceable proceeds of the invalid transfer, and as discussed above the established rules of tracing are not based on the causation approach. But, as argued above, there is no rational basis for tracing other than that in principle it identifies surviving value, causally determined.

[54] Above p 161.

[55] Below p 213.

[56] It would hardly need to be pointed out that there is an important contrast with the case of a transfer under a void contract, if it were not that in the theory of unjust enrichment the two are often assimilated under the concept of failure of consideration: see below p 223.

property from C. Here there will generally be an invalid transfer to D, but this will be because the transfer was not effected by a valid exercise of the power of transfer, not because of the wrong itself, and the invalid transfer will generate a property-based proprietary claim. In tort there will be a personal claim against D for compensation, the measure of which is the value of the transfer, as an alternative to the property-based claim.[57] (This could in principle be a claim for specific restitution of the transfer rather than pecuniary compensation, but this is still a personal claim not a proprietary claim and C's claim for specific restitution should lapse in the event of D's bankruptcy.) Dagan suggests that a tort claimant is in the same position as a claimant seeking to recover an invalid transfer of property, because both cases show the same two relevant features[58]: first, C has conferred a benefit on D involuntarily, and secondly, there remains a benefit in D's estate. In the case of the tort, according to Dagan the benefit remaining in D's estate is the sum that D should pay C in compensation for the tort. But in the tort case there has been no transfer of property from C to D, in the form of abstract value or otherwise, such as to augment D's estate. The supposed benefit accruing to D's estate is not the result of the tort, but of the failure to pay compensation for it.

It is sometimes asked why claimants who assert a proprietary claim should have priority over contract and tort creditors. The implication is that it is unfair that the proprietary claimant does not share in the loss resulting from the shortfall in D's estate. It might also seem to be at odds with the basic *pari passu* rule of allocation in bankruptcy.[59] But, although it is often a convenient usage, it is misleading to say that the proprietary claimant has 'priority' over the contract and tort creditors. The assumption is that the proprietary claimant is in competition with the creditors for satisfaction of their respective claims with respect to some part of D's estate that, in the absence of the proprietary claim, would be available to satisfy the claims of creditors. But, whereas contract and tort claims are claims against D, exigible against D's beneficial estate, the proprietary claim is a right of beneficial ownership of some part of the property under D's control—his legal or control estate—which means that it is not part of D's beneficial estate at all, but the proprietary claimant's beneficial estate. Subject to the argument discussed next, the mere fact that

---

[57] See below p 236 n 94.
[58] H Dagan, *The Law and Ethics of Restitution* (Cambridge, CUP, 2004) 320.
[59] Ibid, 318–21.

property is under D's control should not justify treating it as available to satisfy D's debts. Only D's beneficial estate should be available for this purpose. This point may be obscured by the fact that the beneficial estate is a matter of abstract value, which does not necessarily correspond to particular assets in D's estate that can be separated out from the rest.

The Apparent Wealth Argument

There is a possible objection to the argument that D's creditors are entitled to be satisfied only out of D's beneficial estate and not out of D's whole legal or control estate. I will call this objection the 'apparent wealth argument'.[60] Creditors inevitably rely on their judgment of the wealth of the debtor D in making a decision to lend to him, or to give him credit in a transaction, or to refrain from calling in a debt. The receipt of an invalid transfer by D will contribute to his apparent wealth, since the apparent wealth will depend on D's legal or control estate. However, if D is subject to a proprietary claim in respect of the property transferred, his beneficial estate—the actual wealth available to satisfy his creditors—has not increased. If D then goes bankrupt, a creditor will get a lower recovery than he would have done if D's actual beneficial estate wealth had been as it appeared to the creditor. Arguably a creditor should receive protection in respect of his reliance on D's apparent wealth, including the value of the invalid transfer, just as D, as a direct recipient of the invalid transfer, is himself protected by change of position if he relies on an increase in his own apparent wealth in incurring expenditure.

A proprietary claim has indeed been denied on this basis. In *Westdeutsche Landesbank Girozentrale v Islington BC*,[61] the House of Lords rejected an argument for a proprietary rather than a personal claim to reverse an invalid transfer (a payment under a void contract) on the ground that a proprietary claim would have the effect that 'assets which apparently belong to one person in fact belong to another', which would amount to creating 'off balance sheet' liabilities that are unfair to creditors.[62]

The apparent wealth argument does not distinguish between different types of invalid transfer, unless one tries to assess in different cases the extent to which creditors are prejudiced by the invalid transfer, taking into account, say, the size of the transfer, and its effect

---

[60] See also Jaffey, above n 2, at 285.
[61] [1996] AC 669.
[62] At 705, per Lord Browne-Wilkinson.

on D's apparent wealth. The argument suggests that proprietary claims should never be recognised, though the court in *Westdeutsche* did not suggest that the well-established cases of proprietary claims should be reconsidered, or make any suggestion about how the invalid transfer in *Westdeutsche* could be distinguished from them. In fact a better position would surely be to disregard the apparent wealth argument, on the ground that, as a general rule, a particular invalid transfer is likely to contribute only marginally to the apparent wealth of the recipient, and to have only a marginal effect on any decision by a creditor to grant or not to withdraw credit.

Tracing as Redistribution in Favour of the Proprietary Claimant

It is sometimes said that when the court recognises and enforces a proprietary claim this may entail a diversion or redistribution of D's estate away from his creditors in favour of the proprietary claimant C. One argument is that even if it would be quite fair to recognise C's proprietary claim in respect of the original asset transferred, recognising a proprietary claim in respect of traceable proceeds of the original asset is unfair because it amounts to a redistribution of property rights, since the exchange product, which would otherwise contribute to the estate available to creditors, is appropriated to satisfy the proprietary claim.[63] On this view it is a proprietary claim in respect of traceable proceeds rather than a proprietary claim as such that is unfair to the creditors.

The problem with this argument is that it is based on the transactional understanding of tracing. Under the transactional theory it may be true to say that the exchange product is an asset that would, but for the tracing rule, have entered D's beneficial estate and contributed to the value available to satisfy creditors' debts. This suggests that C is being unfairly favoured, especially given the difficulty of explaining exactly what the rationale of tracing is in a way that accounts for the transactional approach. But under the causational or abstract value approach to tracing it is clear that a proprietary claim based on tracing is justified. C has a claim to abstract value in the estate, and this is value derived from the invalid transfer. The tracing rules simply determine what the measure of this surviving value is, and (subject to the apparent wealth argument) they do not prejudice D's creditors, since the value of the estate available to satisfy their claims is just as it would have been if the invalid transfer had not been

---

[63] Dagan, above n 58 at 303–04.

received. In fact if C were not allowed a proprietary claim, D's creditors would unfairly benefit from the invalid transfer, just as if there had been an invalid transfer directly from C to the creditor and C were denied any claim to recover it. It may be that C's proprietary claim is satisfied by way of a transfer to C of a specific asset that was in D's estate before the invalid transfer, and this may give the impression of a redistribution in favour of C. But both C and the creditors of D are interested in D's estate as a body of abstract value, and the object of C's beneficial ownership is only abstract value in D's estate that was derived from the invalid transfer. Thus there is no redistribution of property rights in D's estate in favour of C.

However, it is true that, because they reflect the transactional theory, the current tracing rules do not always work fairly in accordance with this approach. For example, if C is allowed a claim to an exchange product notwithstanding that the surviving value in the estate falls short of the value of the exchange product, then the creditors are unfairly prejudiced. Conversely, if C is denied a proprietary claim because he cannot identify a specific asset as the object of his proprietary claim, even though there has been no change of position, then the creditors benefit unfairly at C's expense. These rules do entail a redistribution of property rights.

The 'US Remedial Constructive Trust'

Where there is an invalid transfer from C to D and C acquires an equitable proprietary claim, the claim should be understood as a remedial right of beneficial ownership of abstract value in D's estate, which has arisen from C's original primary right of ownership of the property. The invalid transfer is an event that, by virtue of the primary right of ownership, triggers this remedial right. This is an application of the monist principle.[64] The remedial relation here—the property dimension of the trust—is sometimes described as a constructive trust, though there is some debate over the usage of this expression. Some would say that in this position there is a resulting trust not a constructive trust, and I will return to this issue in chapter 9. For the moment I will refer to this as a constructive trust. In English law, the constructive trust in this situation is conventionally understood in this way as a right of beneficial ownership, though, in accordance with the transactional theory of tracing, the object of beneficial ownership is thought to be not abstract value but a specific

---

[64] Above p 40.

asset, or a share of a specific asset, which may be the original asset transferred or its traceable product.

In the United States, the position is often understood in a very different way, in accordance with what I will refer to as the 'US remedial constructive trust'.[65] On this approach it is thought that, after the invalid transfer to D, C has no property right in the asset transferred or in any other asset or in D's estate. When the matter subsequently comes to court and C claims that he should be entitled to recover the asset transferred, or some substitute asset under the law of tracing, the court may make a declaration to this effect and an order of constructive trust. The court order vests in C a right of beneficial ownership of the asset under a trust, and the asset is then transferred to him. If the court does not make the order of constructive trust, C is left with a personal claim for the value of the invalid transfer in competition with D's other creditors. It is also said that the court has a discretion whether or not to make the order of constructive trust. Before the remedial constructive trust order is made, C has some sort of right against D, though it is difficult to say what it is. It might be described as an inchoate right capable of materialising into a proprietary or personal claim.

Various factors may have been influential in the development of this understanding of a proprietary claim. One factor may be an understandable scepticism about tracing conceived in terms of the transactional theory as the transmission of a property right from one asset to another, which may have led, in the absence of any recognition of the possibility of a proprietary claim to abstract value, to the view that there is really no subsisting property right at all. Thus it is sometimes said that the constructive trust is a legal fiction.[66] But, more importantly, there would be no room for this understanding to have developed if it were not for the assumption of a dualist approach to remedies, including the possibility of discretionary remedialism. It is assumed that the constructive trust is not a remedial relation that arises directly from the invalid transfer, by virtue of the nature of the primary right of ownership, in accordance with the monist principle; instead, there is a new justificatory issue that arises independently of the primary relation and requires a quite separate body of rules, or more particularly a discretion, to determine what sort of remedy

---

[65] For an example of this approach see *In re Omegas Group Inc* 16 F.3d 1443 (6th Cir. 1994). For criticism of this case, see A Kull, 'Restitution in Bankruptcy: Reclamation and Constructive Trust' (1998) 72 *American Bankruptcy Law Journal* 265.

[66] See Dagan, above n 58, ch 9; *Omegas*, above n 65, at 1449.

should arise, and in particular whether it should be proprietary or personal. The US remedial constructive trust is, in other words, an example of the dualist fallacy.

The US remedial constructive trust is also in tune with scepticism about property as a justificatory category in private law. Property sceptics reject any talk of a primary right of ownership that generates the proprietary claim. The proprietary claim is understood as a free-standing remedy.[67] Thus it is thought that, where a proprietary claim is awarded, there is a redistribution of D's estate away from D's other creditors in favour of C, which may undermine the ordinary rules for distribution among creditors in bankruptcy.[68] And it follows that the real issue is how to divide up D's estate, and whether to elevate some claims above others, and this is really a matter for bankruptcy regulation. If this issue is not openly and directly addressed in this way, then the proprietary claim is just a rhetorical device or a fiction that conceals the true issues.

One factor that might be thought relevant on this understanding is whether D acted wrongfully—whether the invalid transfer to D was induced by a fraud or other wrong by D, as opposed to resulting from, say, an unprompted mistake by C that vitiated the transfer.[69] It might be thought that in such a case C is deserving of special treatment. But, as mentioned above, a proprietary claim for C against D is never the appropriate remedial response to a wrong by D against C, because the wrong is the breach of a duty owed by D to C, and in accordance with the monist principle such a primary relation will generate a remedial relation binding D alone and not the world in general.

Sometimes it is said that the US remedial constructive trust serves to remedy unjust enrichment.[70] This might be understood to imply that there is a principle of unjust enrichment that can provide a rational basis for determining when a proprietary claim should be awarded. This is ironic because, whereas the proprietary claim can be perfectly adequately explained in terms of the law of property as a justificatory category, together with the monist principle, the category of unjust enrichment that is supposed to make up for the shortcomings of the law of property is open to all the criticisms that are mistakenly directed at property law.[71]

---

[67] See above p 56.
[68] Dagan, above n 58, at 305.
[69] *Omegas*, above n 65, at 1451; Sherwin, above n 20, at 301.
[70] eg, *Omegas*, above n 65, and Sherwin, above n 20.
[71] See further chs 8 and 9.

The US remedial constructive trust has rightly been rejected in England.[72] It is generally said that in English law the constructive trust is an 'institutional trust' not a remedy. But, although pervasive, this is a very unhelpful way of making the contrast. To say that in English law the constructive trust is institutional presumably means that, like an express trust, it entails subsisting property rights. It differs from the express trust in that it is confined to the property dimension and lacks a contractual dimension imposing a duty of management and distribution on D as a trustee (though if D knows of the invalidity of the transfer he can incur a duty not to dispose of surviving value, as discussed in chapter 7). But the equitable proprietary claim or constructive trust is institutional in this sense and at the same time remedial. It is a remedial relation or set of relations that arises to protect and fulfil C's primary right of ownership of property in response to the invalid transfer, in accordance with the monist principle. The supposed contrast between an institution and a remedy seems to be based on the assumption that there are no subsisting remedial rights arising from the primary relation, which reflects the dualist fallacy. Certainly it is unfortunate that a reference to the 'remedial constructive trust' is liable to be understood to refer to something in the nature of what is referred to above as the US remedial constructive trust.

COMMON LAW CLAIMS

Common Law and Equity

I have discussed the claim arising from an invalid transfer, and in principle the arguments apply to any invalid transfer of property. But only where the law of equity is applied and the equitable proprietary claim is available does the law approximate to this approach. The main cases where the law of equity has traditionally been applied are where the transfer was made by a trustee in breach of trust or by a fiduciary

---

[72] *Re Polly Peck (no 2)* [1998] 3 All ER 812, per Nourse LJ 830–31; S Gardner, 'Remedial Constructive Trusts: the Element of Discretion' in P Birks (ed), *The Frontiers of Liability* (Oxford, OUP, 1994) vol 2; P Birks, 'Proprietary Rights as Remedies' in Birks, ibid. It is ironic that the strongest criticism of the US remedial constructive trust and discretionary remedialism has come from supporters of the theory of unjust enrichment, because many of the objections to the US remedial constructive trust also apply to the theory of unjust enrichment.

in breach of fiduciary duty.[73] Generally other types of invalid transfer, such as transfers vitiated by mistake or duress, or made under a void contract, or transfers taking effect through appropriation or the finding of lost property, were dealt with at common law. At common law, there are distinct regimes for money and goods.

Money Claims at Common Law

The Nature of the Claim

For money, the claim to recover an invalid payment was historically known as the claim for money had and received and is now generally known as common law restitution.[74] The most important difference between the common law claim and the equitable proprietary claim is that the common law claim is a personal claim, in the nature of a debt for the value of the transfer. At one time the claim was described as 'quasi-contractual' and said to be based on implied contract. This is the fiction of implied contract: the claim is clearly not in the justificatory category of contract. As mentioned in chapter 1, the classification of the claim as contractual or quasi-contractual was influenced by the remedy-as-justification fallacy: the form of remedy required was equivalent to the payment of a contractual debt and so the claim was assimilated to contract.[75] The modern characterisation of the claim as an unjust enrichment or restitutionary claim also appears to reflect the remedy-as-justification fallacy. The remedy is to recover a benefit received, and it is thought that the justification lies in the character of the remedy, as discussed generally in chapter 8. The only plausible justificatory category for the claim is property. It arises from a primary right of ownership of the money, by virtue of the fact that there was no valid transfer. This point may have been obscured by the fact that the claim is personal,[76] and possibly also by the misapprehension that money in its various forms, particular in the form of debt, is not an object of property.[77]

In accordance with the monist principle, if a claim arises to reverse an invalid transfer it should be proprietary, as argued above. There is no plausible reason why claims that arise to reverse an invalid payment in the circumstances conventionally governed by the common

---

[73] A fiduciary relationship is still said to be a condition for an equitable proprietary tracing claim: see eg Pettit, above n 10, at 556.

[74] *Lipkin Gorman v Karpnale* [1991] 2 AC 548.

[75] Above p 17.

[76] Above p 97.

[77] See above p 84.

law should not be proprietary. It is sometimes thought that in the case of a transfer in breach of trust, the equitable proprietary claim arises only because C originally had beneficial ownership under a trust, and that the proprietary claim arises because this beneficial ownership survives the invalid transfer. This implies that the equitable proprietary claim should be available where the primary right was a right of beneficial ownership under a trust, but not where it was a right of absolute ownership, as in the ordinary case of invalid money payments. But the reason why there is a proprietary claim is not that there was a pre-existing trust; it is that separation of title is the appropriate response to the invalidity of the transfer.[78] The reason why the common law does not award a proprietary claim is simply that it has never had the necessary conceptual tools in the form of the law of trusts and separation of title.

The problem at common law is that there is, as it were, only one title to play with. Two approaches to dealing with invalid transfers are possible on this basis. One is to say that title does not pass and the claim arises from C's retention of title. This is the approach taken with respect to goods, as considered below. With respect to money payments, generally title does pass. Title to money generally passes with possession or control, even if the transfer is invalid, because it is crucial that the person in possession or control should be able to give good title to the money, so that it can function as currency. But whereas in equity the title that passes for this purpose is only a legal or control title, at common law the single title passes.[79] It is because the invalid transfer is understood in this way that, in the absence of separation of title, there is no room for a proprietary claim to recover money, and the claim has traditionally been a personal claim in the nature of a debt.[80] Furthermore, money is a fungible that forms a mixture with other money, and this means that it is untraceable unless a claim to abstract value is recognised, and again this is possible only if there is a separation of title.

[78] Above p 156.

[79] The recipient's title is sometimes described as a new rather than a derived title because it did not pass to him by way of a valid transfer: see eg D Fox, 'The Transfer of Legal Title to Money' [1996] RLR 60, 62. As argued above, the passing of legal or control title should not depend on the validity of the transfer. At common law, with no separation of title, the title is not purely a control title but relates to absolute ownership. But beneficial ownership should not be acquired without a valid transfer except in favour of a bona fide purchaser.

[80] It is sometimes said that that the transfer is valid and the claim arises not from invalidity of the transfer but from its vitiation. As discussed in ch 3, this is a misunderstanding of what is meant by invalidity and why it generates a claim: see above, p 97.

Overlap of the Claims in Law and Equity

In recent times there have, not surprisingly, been attempts by claimants to extend the availability of the equitable proprietary claim to cases traditionally treated at common law, in order to secure a proprietary claim. The attempt was successful in *Chase Manhattan v Israel-British Bank*,[81] a case involving a mistaken payment, where the judge contrived to characterise the claim as arising from a breach of fiduciary duty in order to hold that a proprietary claim was available. More recently, by contrast, in *Westdeutsche Landesbank Girozentrale v Islington BC*,[82] which concerned a payment made under a void contract, the House of Lords rejected the argument and confined the claimant to a personal claim. The main reason seems to have been the apparent wealth argument discussed above. But, even if the apparent wealth argument is convincing, it provides no basis for distinguishing between different types of invalid transfer. There is no apparent reason why it should be significant that the claim arose from a transfer of wealth held under the control of a trustee or fiduciary, or that it was originally dealt with by the Chancery courts rather than the common law courts, and the court offered none.[83] In principle a proprietary claim should always be available in respect of an invalid transfer, irrespective of whether there was an express trust or fiduciary relationship, and irrespective of whether the case would originally have been dealt with at law or in equity.

As discussed above, US law has adopted the idea of the US remedial constructive trust. Because the constructive trust is regarded as a freestanding remedy it has provided the means of dissociating the proprietary claim from any need for a pre-existing trust or fiduciary relationship, so that the proprietary claim is not confined to the traditional equity jurisdiction but is in principle available generally as a response to invalid transfers, for example mistaken and fraudulent transfers, transfers under duress, and unauthorised transfers and takings by strangers as well as transfers in breach of trust or fiduciary duty.[84] Unfortunately, as the discussion above showed, this approach

---

[81] [1981] Ch 105.

[82] [1996] AC 669.

[83] Lord Browne-Wilkinson did accept at 716 that a proprietary claim would be available in respect of stolen money, which would traditionally generate a common law personal claim. The implication seems to be that the wrongdoing justifies a proprietary claim, but this is mistaken as discussed above: see p 161. It is the invalidity of the transfer that justifies the proprietary claim.

[84] As discussed in *Omegas*, above n 65.

has come at the cost of scepticism about whether a proprietary claim should be available at all.

In some circumstances, the common law claim has advantages over the equitable proprietary claim. In the well-known case of *Lipkin Gorman v Karpnale*,[85] a solicitor used sums of the firm's money for gambling and the action was by the firm C against the casino as the recipient D.[86] This seems to fall squarely into the traditional scope of the equitable proprietary claim, and the proceedings were initially pursued on that basis. But in the end the claim was made at common law. For present purposes the reason was that it was impossible to trace into a specific asset in D's estate for the purposes of the equitable proprietary claim.[87] In other words, the problem was the failure to recognise the possibility of a proprietary claim to abstract value or 'swollen assets'. In the end, C was allowed a personal claim at common law for the value of the transfer to D.

The measure of the claim in *Lipkin Gorman* was the value paid over less a reduction in respect of change of position. Change of position was recognised as a defence that reduces the prima facie measure of the claim, but the claim can also be expressed as a claim for surviving value in D's estate,[88] though the claim is personal not proprietary. Thus one might say that, in a sense, the common law has recognised the abstract value or causation-based approach to tracing, including a version of the swollen assets theory, in contrast to equity's insistence on a transactional theory based on claims in respect of specific assets not abstract value, and this is why the common law provided a claim in *Lipkin Gorman* where equity did not.

Goods Claims

Whereas for invalid transfers of money at common law the general approach is that title passes, the claim arising in respect of an invalid transfer of goods is based on C's retention of title. One might think then that the claim would be understood as a property-based, proprietary claim to recover the goods. However, there is no such category in the traditional common law (as opposed to equity). Instead the claim is conventionally understood as arising in tort, in the form

---

[85] [1991] 2 AC 548.

[86] The money was actually client money but this does not affect the discussion.

[87] The other problem was the knowledge condition for a knowing receipt claim in equity, which is discussed in ch 7.

[88] See P Birks, 'Change of Position: the Nature of the Defence and its Relationship to Other Restitutionary Defences' in MP McInnes (ed), *Restitution: Developments in Unjust Enrichment* (LBC Information Services, 1996).

of the wrong of 'interfering with title', or, more helpfully, taking, detaining or disposing of C's property. This is the tort of conversion.[89] The standard remedy is compensation for the wrong, though for a long time 'specific restitution' of the goods has been available as an alternative remedy for the wrong. But this does not amount to a proprietary claim, though it is argued that the effect of a proprietary claim can sometimes be contrived.[90]

It is fair to say that a recipient commits a wrong if he disposes of property received or consumes it when he knows or ought to know that he received it through an invalid transfer. This type of wrong is considered in chapter 7. As discussed in chapter 3,[91] a claim arising from such a wrong is in principle quite distinct from the property-based claim that arises from the receipt of an invalid transfer. The claim based on the wrong presupposes the claim to recover the invalid transfer. But the law of conversion has to do the work of both the receipt-based claim to recover an invalid transfer and the claim in respect of a wrongful disposal, and so conflates them.[92] Insofar as the tort claim does service as a claim to recover the surviving value of an invalid transfer, the tort is really fictional. Unfortunately, whereas the implied contract fiction in the law of invalid money payments has been exposed and repudiated, the tort fiction remains firmly in place to deal with invalid transfers of goods.[93] The correct approach, of distinguishing between the property-based primary liability claim that arises from receipt, and the tort claim arising from a genuinely wrongful disposal, is, in a disguised way, taken by equity. I will return to these issues in chapter 7.

THE DEVELOPMENT OF AN INTEGRATED REGIME

As argued in chapter 1, a mistaken justificatory classification can cause incoherence. The law concerning the recovery of invalid transfers is

---

[89] See eg S Deakin, A Johnston and B Markesinis, *Tort Law* (Oxford, OUP, 5th edn, 2003) 438.

[90] By saying that D's trustee in bankruptcy is liable in conversion if he does not return the property: R Goode, 'The Right to Trace and its Impact in Commercial Transactions' (1976) 92 *Law Quarterly Review* 360 and 528, 564. If the claim is based on a wrong, in accordance with the monist principle it should not be proprietary, and the measure should be not surviving value but loss of surviving value.

[91] Above p 106.

[92] See below p 206. The common law restitutionary claim also conflates the two types of claim, as discussed in ch 7.

[93] Thus this type of claim is not generally covered in the restitution and unjust enrichment books.

blighted by incoherence in the form of false differentiation resulting from classificatory errors. The claim to recover an invalid transfer is a property-based claim. There should be a single framework and a common set of concepts for such claims. In the traditional common law the claim was characterised as either a quasi-contractual claim in respect of money transfers, or a claim in tort in respect of transfers of goods. In equity, the claim can be understood as a property-based claim. Equity also has the advantage of separation of title and the proprietary claim. This developed out of the express trust, and even nowadays the availability of the proprietary claim is confined to transfers in breach of trust or fiduciary duty. But in principle the claim to recover an invalid transfer should always be proprietary, and this follows from the monist principle. It should not depend on whether there was a pre-existing trust; and it should not depend on the historical accident of whether the claim falls in the traditional jurisdiction of equity.

The argument for the general availability of proprietary claims also depends on the recognition that the object of a proprietary claim is the abstract surviving value of an invalid transfer. This is contrary to the conventional assumption that a proprietary claim is in respect of a specific asset, and the transactional theory of tracing, which is based on this assumption, but it is the only way to explain the law of tracing, and it also follows from the need to accommodate the conflicting interests of the claimant and the creditors of the defendant-recipient.

Sound analogical reasoning should lead to the development of a category of property-based claims to recover invalid transfers, and it should involve substantive fusion of the common law and equitable regimes. Sometimes, instead, there have been moves to expand the equitable proprietary claim and the common law claims so that they overlap and provide alternatives.[94] The anti-fusion fallacy may lead to the misconception that substantive fusion would destroy the trust and the proprietary claim because it would eliminate the distinction between legal and equitable title.[95] To promote fusion, it would be helpful to emphasise the functional significance of legal title and equitable title as opposed to their traditional association with the division between law and equity. A regime along the lines suggested would draw more from equity than the common law, but it would

---

[94] A good example of a sound pro-fusion approach in this context is the judgment of Denning J in *Nelson v Larholt* [1948] 1 KB 339.

[95] Above p 151.

draw support from the common law's development of change of position, understood as a tracing rule that defines abstract surviving value.

A more recent obstacle to the development of a rationale scheme has been the emergence in recent times of a law of restitution or unjust enrichment, understood as a justificatory category. This is a spurious justificatory category and its recognition interferes with the proper recognition of property-based claims. The problem of unjust enrichment is considered further in chapter 8.

7

Wrongful Disposals

PROPERTY CLAIMS AND TORT CLAIMS

As discussed in chapter 3, a coherent regime for dealing with invalid transfers of property should have two distinct types of claim. The first is the property-based restitutionary claim to recover the invalid transfer, which was discussed in chapter 6. The second is the claim in tort for compensation for breach of the duty incurred by the recipient D, on or after the receipt of the invalid transfer, not to dispose of or consume the property invalidly transferred or its surviving value. This chapter is concerned with the tort claim, and in particular with differentiating it from the property-based claim.

THE KNOWING RECEIPT CLAIM

The Knowing Receipt Claim as a Restitutionary Claim

The knowing receipt claim was developed in equity and arises, like the equitable proprietary claim considered in chapter 6, in connection with transfers of property in breach of trust or fiduciary duty. As discussed in chapter 6, the significance of the breach of trust or fiduciary duty is that the transfer is invalid. The knowing receipt claim is nowadays generally understood to be a restitutionary claim like the equitable proprietary claim. Generally the measure of the claim is the value of the transfer, and its object appears to be the return to C of the value of the property transferred on the basis that the transfer was invalid.[1] On the analysis suggested in chapter 6, this would mean that it is a property-based claim, though it is often said to be based on unjust enrichment and the description of it as a restitutionary claim is generally taken to imply this.

There are two important differences between the equitable proprietary claim and the knowing receipt claim. First, the knowing

---

[1] *BCCI v Akindele* [2001] Ch 437. This is the standard view in the restitution textbooks.

receipt claim is personal rather than proprietary. Secondly, it is a condition of the knowing receipt claim that D knew that the transfer was invalid, or more broadly that the circumstances were such that he ought to have known this, ie that he had 'constructive knowledge'. There is some controversy on the issue of constructive knowledge, which I will come back to below. For convenience, for the moment I will simply say that knowledge is required. If D acquires knowledge of the invalidity of the transfer after receipt, the measure of the claim is the surviving value at this time rather than the original value of the transfer.

The knowledge requirement presents a problem for the interpretation of knowing receipt as a restitutionary claim to recover an invalid transfer. If the claim is based on the invalidity of the transfer and D's receipt of it, it is difficult to see any justification for the knowledge requirement. The claim should arise from the receipt of the invalid transfer and from the continuing presence in D's estate of the property or its surviving value. For this reason it has been contended that the knowledge requirement should be abandoned.[2] One response to this has been that such a 'strict liability' condition would be unfair to recipients.[3] But this objection misses the point. If the claim for knowing receipt is indeed properly understood as a restitutionary claim to recover the invalid transfer, then it should, in the nature of the claim, arise from receipt. Any unfairness can be avoided by protection for change of position to limit the claim to the surviving value of the transfer.

Even nowadays it is sometimes said that the knowledge requirement arises from equity's concern with 'conscience'. As discussed in chapter 4, it seems that this originally referred to the conscience of the Chancellor, meaning that the Chancellor could apply his sense of right and wrong and was not bound by the rules of the common law, but it has also led to the view that in equity a defendant's liability depends on *his* conscience having been affected in some way, which implies a requirement of knowledge. But the reference to 'conscience' merely obscures the basis in principle for D's liability. This characteristic failing of equity was referred to earlier.[4] In any case, it does not overcome the objection that a knowledge requirement is not appropriate for a restitutionary claim to reverse an invalid transfer.

---

[2] eg, P Birks, *Restitution—The Future* (Annandale, Federation Press, 1992) 26ff.
[3] *BCCI v Akindele*, above n 1, at 456 per Nourse LJ.
[4] Above pp 113, 118.

The Knowing Receipt Claim as a Composite Claim

There is a more principled way of explaining the knowledge requirement, which suggests that the restitutionary analysis is misconceived.[5]
The knowledge requirement suggests that D must have done or failed
to do something in the light of his knowledge of the invalid transfer:
in other words, that the claim is based on a breach of duty or wrong
by D. More particularly, the claim should be understood not as a
restitutionary or property-based claim like the equitable proprietary
claim, but, as anticipated above, as a claim based on a breach by D of
his duty not to dispose of or consume the property invalidly transferred or its surviving value.[6] When D discovers that the property
was transferred to him invalidly, he becomes subject to such a duty
to C and, if he commits a breach of the duty, he is liable to compensate C for the resulting loss. This explains the knowledge requirement. In the absence of knowledge, although D should be liable to a
claim to recover the property transferred or its surviving value, there
is no reason why he should incur a duty that restricts the way he can
deal with property that is ostensibly part of his estate. This would be
a strict liability duty that he could not necessarily follow and that he
could breach without fault. (I will come back to this point later.) This
interpretation also explains why the claim is personal. A claim for
compensation for breach of duty is a personal claim, since, in accordance with the monist principle, the remedial liability should bind
only the person subject to the primary duty.[7]

An immediate objection to this analysis of knowing receipt concerns the measure of liability. The remedy for knowing receipt is the
account of profits, and the measure is the value of the property
received by D, or its surviving value at the time when D acquired
knowledge of the invalidity if this is after receipt, whereas the
implication of the suggested approach is that the measure of liability
should be the *loss* of surviving value resulting from D's wrongful disposal or consumption. However, although it is not ordinarily
expressed in this way, the standard measure of the knowing receipt
claim is actually equivalent to the sum of the actual surviving value
in the estate and any loss of surviving value since the time when D

---

[5] See P Jaffey, 'The Nature of Knowing Receipt' [2001] *Trust Law International* 151.

[6] It is sometimes said that the claim for knowing receipt is analogous to the claim for conversion. This might be understood to be equivalent to the statement in the text save that, as
considered below, the law of conversion also combines the property-based claim and the
wrong-based claim.

[7] Above pp 161, 173.

acquired the necessary knowledge. In other words, the standard measure is the measure of the equitable proprietary claim plus the true—
ie, the compensatory—measure of the claim for breach of duty. One
might say that the knowing receipt claim as it currently operates is a
composite claim, combining the equitable proprietary claim and a
claim for compensation for loss of surviving value, but taking the
form of a personal restitutionary claim. This composite claim may
often be a convenient formulation. If there is no advantage in the circumstances in establishing a proprietary rather than a personal claim,
there is often no need to distinguish between the property-based
claim to recover surviving value and the compensatory claim. But
some particular problems arising from the failure to distinguish
between the two types of claim are considered below; and in principle the two types of claim should be distinguished from each other,
because they come from different justificatory categories and perform
different functions, though of course the name 'knowing receipt'
would not be apt for the wrong-based compensation claim on its
own. (Nor would it be appropriate, of course, for a receipt-based
restitutionary claim.)

If the knowing receipt claim were (contrary to the argument
above) truly a restitutionary claim to recover an invalid transfer—and
was accordingly a strict liability claim—it would in fact be redundant,
because there is already a restitutionary claim in the form of the
equitable proprietary claim. The usual assumption here seems to be
that there should be a personal as well as a proprietary restitutionary
claim. But if there is a proprietary claim there is in principle no need
for a personal claim (and the claim to recover an invalid transfer
should be proprietary not personal, as discussed in chapter 6).[8] It is
true that this point is not easy to appreciate as the law stands, because
of the preconception, which is behind the transactional theory of
tracing, that a proprietary claim must always have as its object a specific asset and not abstract value. This implies that sometimes there
may be no proprietary claim, because no specific asset is traceable
from the invalid transfer, even though there is abstract surviving
value. This may give the impression that there is a need for a personal
claim in respect of abstract surviving value to supplement the proprietary claim in respect of a traceable specific asset. But the problem
here is the misconception that abstract value cannot be the object of
a proprietary claim, which is assumed in the current body of tracing

[8] Above pp 161, 172.

rules under the transactional theory. As discussed in chapter 6, the answer is to reject the transactional theory and reinterpret or modify the tracing rules, not to have a separate personal restitutionary claim for abstract surviving value. Indeed it is clear from the recognition and operation of the personal restitutionary claim at common law that it is perfectly possible in practice to trace abstract surviving value, in the sense that it can be identified and measured.[9]

Some Problems arising from the Composite Claim

There are a number of particular problems that arise from the composite form of the knowing receipt claim. One problem is overlap between the knowing receipt claim and the equitable proprietary claim. The knowing receipt claim cannot in principle be used to secure double or excess recovery where there is also an equitable proprietary claim to surviving value. But what exactly is excess recovery? This is obscure on the conventional understanding of the knowing receipt claim, but in the light of the argument above it is clear that, if there is also an equitable proprietary claim for surviving value, the measure of knowing receipt should be limited to the loss of surviving value, which is the true compensatory measure of recovery.

Another problem is that, on the conventional understanding, although the recipient D incurs no liability in respect of any loss of surviving value before he knows of the invalidity of the transfer, once he does have this knowledge he can be liable for any such loss, even a loss caused by 'act of god'. There is an inconsistency here, because if the reason why the claim is based on D's knowledge of the invalidity of the transfer is that it depends on his being subject to a duty in respect of the property received, then he should not be liable, even once he has such knowledge, in respect of losses that were not caused by his breach of duty. The error arises because D is said to be accountable for the trust property once he has knowledge, without any consideration of the significance of his knowledge or its relation to the basis of the claim.

Another reason why it is important in principle to distinguish between the two types of case is to do with the fault of the claimant C. C might be at fault if, for example, the invalid transfer was a transfer by C's fiduciary in breach of duty to C, and the fiduciary had a history of dishonesty and incompetence and was appointed by C without any inquiries into his past. C's property-based restitutionary

---

[9] See the comment on *Lipkin Gorman*, above p 184.

claim should not be affected by the fact that he was in some way at fault in making the invalid transfer or allowing it to be made. C's fault provides no reason for allowing D to keep property belonging beneficially to C (and the same applies if the claim is a personal claim to surviving value).[10] However, insofar as C is seeking compensation for loss of surviving value rather than the recovery of actual surviving value, the claim is based on D's wrong, and here D's liability should be reduced to some degree where C was also at fault,[11] in accordance with the principle of contributory negligence. It is feasible to apply the principle once C's claim in respect of loss of surviving value is separated off from the restitutionary claim and recognised as a tort claim.

The Origin of the Composite Claim

It is understandable how the knowing receipt claim has come to have this composite form that combines the property-based restitutionary claim and the wrong-based claim for compensation. The liability of the recipient in knowing receipt is said to be based on constructive trusteeship,[12] by analogy with the trusteeship of the trustee of an express trust. As discussed in chapter 5, an express trust has two dimensions, in property and (in the extended sense discussed) in contract. As a matter of property law, a trustee of an express trust can be subject to a proprietary claim in respect of trust property, and as a matter of contract he can be subject to a personal claim for breach of his duty to manage and distribute trust property. The trustee is also sometimes said to be accountable for trust property,[13] and this makes him liable to account for the value of the property entrusted to him, whether it has been lost or not. This formulation is unhelpful because it tends to conceal the distinction between the two dimensions and the two types of claim.

A recipient of trust property invalidly transferred is subject to a proprietary claim in respect of the trust property or surviving value, and, if he knows it was invalidly transferred, he also has a duty not to

---

[10] This is taken for granted with respect to the equitable proprietary claim, and it is also the position for personal claims to recover an invalid transfer: *Kelly v Solari* (1841) 9 M&W 54.

[11] One might argue that, even where the owner cannot be said to have been at fault, he should bear some part of the risk of loss resulting from a transfer made by a fiduciary if he appointed him.

[12] PH Pettit, *Equity and the Law of Trusts* (Oxford, OUP, 10th edn, 2006) 151; *Barnes v Addy* (1874) 9 Ch App 244.

[13] Ibid.

dispose of or consume the property or its surviving value. His position is analogous to that of an express trustee, save that his duty is in tort and not contract, and it is less onerous than the true trustee's duty of management and distribution. The recipient's liability for knowing receipt 'as a constructive trustee' is also understood as a liability to account. It is equivalent to the unhelpful formulation of the claim against the express trustee in terms of a liability to account, and this is why it obscures the distinction between the property-based claim and the tort claim. One reason why it has always been formulated in this way is that equity has never explicitly recognised anything in the nature of a tortious duty.

KNOWLEDGE, CONSTRUCTIVE KNOWLEDGE AND THE DUTY OF REASONABLE CARE

The Subjective and Objective Concepts of a Duty and the Role of Constructive Knowledge

I have said that a recipient D of an invalid transfer of property incurs a duty not to consume or dispose of the property only if he knows of the invalidity of the transfer, and that this is the explanation of the knowledge requirement for the knowing receipt claim. This formulation appears to reflect the subjective concept of a duty. According to the subjective concept, the duty is a genuine prescription or requirement of action for D personally, and D is at fault if he breaches the duty.[14] This means that it depends not only on what D is capable of doing, given his own personal characteristics, but on whether D knows of the facts by virtue of which (if he is aware of them) the duty arises.

But the subjective approach seems to encounter the problem that D can avoid incurring a duty by avoiding any situation or course of action that might bring to his attention facts that would give rise to a duty—by burying his head in the sand. In the law of knowing receipt this possibility is avoided by the constructive knowledge condition mentioned above, by which D can be held liable even though he did not actually know that the transfer was invalid, if in the circumstances he ought to have realised it or to have made inquiries that would have revealed it. However, the constructive knowledge condition appears to be at odds with the subjective concept of duty. If D's knowledge is a condition of his being subject to a duty, why is it sufficient for

---

[14] Above p 23.

him to have constructive knowledge, which is knowledge that he does not actually have? And if actual knowledge is not required, why does it matter whether he ought to have acquired it, and what is the basis for saying that he ought to have acquired it?

Some commentators prefer the objective concept of a duty, according to which the duty depends only on the actual circumstances, not on whether they are known to D, or on D's personal characteristics. On the objective approach it seems that a duty should in principle arise from the invalid transfer itself, irrespective of whether D knows about it. This avoids the problem mentioned above that D can avoid incurring a duty by burying his head in the sand, but it is a strict liability duty according to which D can commit a wrong without fault, and it is not apparent why there is a knowledge condition for the claim in knowing receipt. A possible answer is to say that, although D can be subject to a duty and breach it without knowing of the relevant facts, his ignorance gives him an excuse that relieves him of liability.[15] This seems to make sense of the constructive knowledge condition as well, on the basis that ignorance must be reasonable for it to count as an excuse, and it is not reasonable where D ought to have known the true position. But, first, it seems very doubtful whether ignorance of the facts, whether reasonable or not, can properly be understood as an excuse. Generally someone is said to have an excuse when he acted wrongfully but the circumstances were such that he is not culpable and should not be blamed, or not to the full extent, for example because he was provoked or manipulated by someone exercising undue influence over him. This hardly seems to be appropriate where D acted entirely justifiably on the basis of the facts known to him. It seems more like the case where D acts in self-defence or to prevent a greater harm and so does not act wrongfully at all. Furthermore, the effect of an excuse is generally thought to be to negate criminal liability—to make punishment inappropriate—and, because D has still acted wrongfully, not to negate the civil liability that arises from the wrong; and yet in the case of knowing receipt it is of course civil liability that is in issue.[16]

---

[15] eg, J Gardner, 'Wrongs and Faults' in AP Simester (ed), *Appraising Strict Liability* (Oxford, OUP 2005) 21–22. According to S Gardner, *An Introduction to the Law of Trusts* (Oxford, Clarendon Press, 2nd edn, 2003) 24, D has a duty irrespective of knowledge but does not breach the duty unless he has the necessary knowledge.

[16] Thus excuse is generally contrasted with justification in connection with the criminal law. See eg L Alexander, 'The Philosophy of Criminal Law' in J Coleman and S Shapiro (eds), *The Oxford Handbook of Jurisprudence & Philosophy of Law* (Oxford, OUP, 2002). There is a considerable literature on the issue of mistaken justification.

Thus neither of the above approaches seems entirely satisfactory. In fact the way the problem has been presented above is misleading. The particular duty, the duty not to consume or dispose of property invalidly transferred, should not be considered in isolation. It is actually a concrete duty arising in particular circumstances by virtue of a more abstract duty to take reasonable care to avoid causing loss of property to others. The effect of D's knowledge of an invalid transfer is not really to trigger a duty or to expose a hidden duty, but to reveal how D's behaviour will affect the interest of C that is protected by the duty of reasonable care, and thereby to determine what the duty requires of D in the circumstances. This is why the concrete duty not to consume or dispose of property is subject to a condition of knowledge of the transfer and its invalidity.

This also explains the role of constructive knowledge. The duty of reasonable care may involve, in the first place, a duty to monitor the circumstances and consider whether there has been an invalid transfer, and to make appropriate inquiries to establish whether there has been an invalid transfer. It is said that the duty not to consume or dispose of property arises with constructive knowledge, but strictly speaking D does not have such a duty unless he knows that the transfer was invalid; in other cases, it is more accurate to say that D is in breach of the duty of reasonable care because he has failed to take steps required by the duty, such as monitoring his receipts or making reasonable inquiries, which would have revealed an invalid transfer and led to a duty not to consume or dispose of the property transferred. But to say that there is a condition of actual or constructive knowledge is a convenient formulation that in practice has the same effect.

Two Ways to Understand the Standard of Reasonable Care

Thus the knowledge condition and its extension to constructive knowledge arise from the fact that the duty not to consume or dispose of the property received is generated by a duty of reasonable care. The standard of care—how much is demanded of D—depends on balancing the interests of owners of property and the recipients of invalid transfers of property. The higher the standard, the greater the burden placed on recipients, in the form of a responsibility for monitoring and investigating their receipts, and the greater the protection given to owners of property in connection with invalid transfers.

This leaves open whether D's duty is subjective or objective. In my view, a genuine duty of reasonable care must be subjective and fault-based, as discussed earlier.[17] It should reflect the position as it appears to D, which depends on D's competence to understand and interpret the circumstances and events, and it should take account of D's ability to respond to them. The standard position in negligence in tort law, to the contrary, is that there is an objective standard of care, which takes no account of individual strengths and weaknesses,[18] although there is persistent controversy about whether this ought to be the case.[19] As suggested in chapter 1,[20] if there is an objective standard, this really means that, rather than a genuine duty of reasonable care, there is a primary liability relation that allocates the risk of loss by reference to the standard of reasonable care. If D falls short of the standard, he is liable for a resulting loss, but he has not breached a duty to reach the standard.

For knowing receipt, the issue is whether, for the purposes of the knowledge condition, knowledge should be understood as subjective or objective, that is to say whether it refers to D's actual knowledge, or to the knowledge that a reasonable person in D's circumstances would have. If D is held liable in knowing receipt on the ground that a reasonable person in D's position would have known of the invalid transfer, though D himself, being unusually obtuse, did not know of it, or on the ground that a reasonable person making due inquiries would have discovered it, though D would not, then the test is based on objective knowledge and the standard of care is objective. The knowledge condition itself does not imply that D's duty is subjective, unless one can say that it refers to subjective rather than objective knowledge, and this is often unclear or immaterial.

Should there be a genuine duty of reasonable care, with a subjective standard, or a primary liability relation with an objective standard?[21] It is often thought that an objective standard of care is unfair to D, because it means that he may be required to reach a standard he is incapable of—it means there is a strict liability duty. In my view, it is indeed unfair (if it even makes sense) to hold D to be a wrongdoer by reference to an objective standard of care. But it is not nec-

---

[17] Above p 23.

[18] T Weir, *Introduction to Tort Law*, (Oxford, Clarendon Law Series, OUP, 2nd edn, 2006) 61.

[19] See eg S Deakin, A Johnston and B Markesinis, *Tort Law* (Oxford, OUP, 5th edn, 2003) 172–74.

[20] Above p 25.

[21] There could be a primary liability with a subjective standard. Also, it is possible and it could be quite appropriate to have both types of primary relation operating in parallel.

essarily unfair to have a primary liability relation with an objective standard, at least if it is reasonable to expect D to know when this is the case, and to avoid an activity regulated in this way or to insure himself or bear the risk. The advantage of a primary liability with an objective standard is predictability, since it means that the standard of care others can rely on (in the sense of being compensated with respect to it) is uniform. But it seems doubtful whether there should be an objective standard for ordinary consumers with respect to invalid transfers, though it may be appropriate for commercial and financial bodies which can treat the receipt of an invalid transfer as an ordinary business risk.[22]

The Test for Knowing Receipt

Until recently, it has been customary to assess D's liability in knowing receipt in terms of the so-called *Baden Delvaux* scale or classification of levels of knowledge.[23] This is a scale running from actual knowledge of the breach of trust, through cases where this knowledge can be inferred from known facts, or is suggested by suspicious or anomalous circumstances, to the case where, though there is nothing amiss on the surface, the breach of trust would be revealed by inquiries that are deemed reasonable in the circumstances.[24] This seems to be principally an oblique way of stating the level or burden of the standard of care, running from a low to a high level. This approach led to a series of cases that attempted to stipulate precise points on the scale as the condition of liability in knowing receipt, but the law on this issue was never fully settled.[25]

---

[22] It is important to have a genuine duty where C's interests are not easily compensatable in money, as where personal injury is in issue, but this is not generally an issue with respect to invalid transfers. The danger with respect to a duty (even if the standard is subjective) is that it may operate unfairly in the absence of recognition of the hardship rule against excessive liability for compensation: above p 44.

[23] *Baden Delvaux v Société Générale* [1993] 1 WLR 509, 575–76, per Gibson J: '(i) actual knowledge; (ii) wilfully shutting one's eyes to the obvious; (iii) wilfully and recklessly failing to make such inquiries as an honest and reasonable man would make; (iv) knowledge of circumstances which would indicate the facts to an honest and reasonable man; (v) knowledge of circumstances which will put an honest and reasonable man on inquiry'.

[24] If there is a primary liability relation, there could be a further position not represented on the *Baden Delvaux* scale according to which D is automatically liable for any loss in surviving value. As considered below, with respect to goods at common law, and money at common law before change of position was recognised, D is at risk in this way. In both cases this resulted from the historical mischaracterisation of the claim, not from any argument of policy or principle to support it: see P Jaffey, *The Nature and Scope of Restitution* (Oxford, Hart Publishing, 2000) 325–27.

[25] As discussed in *BCCI v Akindele* [2001] Ch 437.

Discussion of the *Baden Delvaux* scale does not generally distinguish explicitly between the question whether the standard of care, or the condition of knowledge or constructive knowledge, is objective or subjective, and the question of the level or burden of the standard of care, though on the original formulation of the scale it is clearly objective.[26] It is worth briefly considering the law of knowing or dishonest assistance, which has taken these matters further.

A claim in knowing or dishonest assistance arises against an accessory who has acted wrongfully in assisting a fiduciary or trustee in the commission of a breach of trust or fiduciary duty, generally involving an invalid transfer. It was traditionally treated as a matter of constructive trusteeship, in the same way as knowing receipt,[27] but is now increasingly recognised as a tort.[28] In the leading case of *Royal Brunei Airlines v Tan*,[29] a contrast was drawn between 'negligence' and 'fault' as possible conditions for liability, and it was held that the claim for knowing assistance was based on fault, or, more particularly, 'dishonesty'. This is the issue of the level or burden of the standard of care, or, in other words, the extent of the duty of inquiry or constructive knowledge. The contrast between fault and negligence might suggest that a fault–based liability cannot be expressed in terms of a duty of reasonable care at all. But the fault position is just a certain low level of the standard of care: it means that his duty of care does not require D to take any action unless circumstances come to his attention that show that he is or may well be assisting in a breach of trust or fiduciary duty, whereas the negligence approach imposes a higher standard of care that may require D to make inquiries where nothing is apparently amiss.

The second issue, which is treated separately in *Tan*, is whether the standard of care is subjective or objective in the sense discussed above. In *Tan* it was held to be subjective,[30] although there was no discussion of why this should be. The traditional idea that claims in equity are based on 'conscience' might support this view, but since knowing assistance is increasingly understood as a tort, one might have expected the ordinary objective standard in tort law to have

---

[26] Above n 23.

[27] *Barnes v Addy* (1874) 9 Ch App 244.

[28] See eg *Abou-Rahmah v Abacha* [2006] EWCA Civ 1492; L Hoffmann, 'The Redundancy of Knowing Assistance' in P Birks, *The Frontiers of Liability* (Oxford, OUP, 1994) vol 1, 27.

[29] [1995] 2 AC 378.

[30] At 389. At the same time Lord Nicholls describes the standard as objective in the different sense considered below.

been considered. Also liability for knowing assistance was previously assessed according to the *Baden Delvaux* scale, which as mentioned above seems to be formulated according to an objective standard. If the standard were objective, the claim could still be fault-based, in the sense of objective knowledge or fault. What the level or burden of the standard of care should be is a different question from whether it should be objective or subjective.

A third issue was referred to in *Tan*. This is the question whether the level of the standard of care should vary with D's own moral standards, which would mean that a morally scrupulous defendant would be held to a higher standard of care than a rogue. In *Tan* it was said that it should not vary in this respect, and this seems obviously correct. However, there is room for confusion here because this point was made by saying that the standard of honesty is 'objective',[31] though as mentioned above it was held that in the usual sense, which is quite distinct, it is subjective.[32]

The Unconscionability Test for Knowing Receipt

These issues have not been explored as fully in the law of knowing receipt. More recently the courts have taken a different approach to knowing receipt. In *BCCI v Akindele*[33] the court attempted to find an approach that would accommodate the conflicting decisions on the required level of knowledge for knowing receipt under the *Baden Delvaux* scale. Its suggestion was that liability for knowing receipt does not depend on whether the recipient D's state of knowledge meets a certain fixed point on a scale but whether the circumstances are 'such as to make it unconscionable for him to retain the benefit of the receipt'.[34] The recognition that there may be no fixed level of knowledge for all cases is consistent with the argument above, because a duty of reasonable care can make different demands in different circumstances, but, on the face of it, an unconscionability test

---

[31] At 389.

[32] This sense of objectivity may be more important in criminal law and seems to have been imported from criminal law along with the concept of dishonesty. There seems no need to introduce the concept of dishonesty at all. Subsequently in *Twinsectra v Yardley* [2002] 2 AC 164 the House of Lords appeared to hold that D had to be aware that his conduct breached the standard of care. This is not the same as saying that the burden varies with the defendant's moral standards, though it means that D avoids liability when he has no understanding of what is required of him. In *Barlow Clowes v Eurotrust International* [2005] UKPC 37 this interpretation was rejected by the Privy Council.

[33] [2001] Ch 437.

[34] Ibid, at 455.

makes little sense. One problem is that it is expressed in the language of a restitutionary claim, and whether D is entitled to retain the benefit of a transfer of property, or whether to the contrary C should have a restitutionary claim to recover it, can sensibly only depend on whether the transfer was invalid, not on whether D acted unconscionably. In effect, the proposition must be not that the claim arises on the basis of unconscionability, but that it is unconscionable not to satisfy the claim by providing a remedy. This goes without saying; it may be wrongful not to satisfy a clear claim, but this says nothing about why the claim arises.[35] However, the reference to unconscionability can be understood to move the law towards recognising that the knowledge requirement for the knowing receipt claim arises from a wrong or breach of duty by D, since 'unconscionability' is really just a heavy-handed way of referring to wrongfulness or a type of wrongfulness. Possibly also it suggests that the standard of care should be subjective.[36] Unfortunately this approach does not begin to explain the basis or content of the duty, or the role of constructive knowledge. A court that invokes 'unconsionability' should attempt to explain what the duty in question is. As with the use of 'conscience', this is a characteristic failing of equity.[37]

The underlying problem lies in the division between law and equity, which has meant that the issues have been addressed purely in terms of the equitable concepts of conscience, constructive knowledge, and liability to account, without any reference to a duty not to cause loss or a principle of reasonable care or a standard of care in tort. Formulating the law in terms of these concepts does not overcome all the difficulties that arise in particular cases, but it at least identifies the appropriate framework for addressing them.

A Positive Duty to Act?

I have described the duty that D incurs when he knows of the invalidity of a transfer as a duty not to consume or dispose of the property received. But why does he not simply have a duty to return the property? C is entitled to recover the property, and one might think that this right to the return of the property must be correlated with a duty to return it. But, as discussed in chapter 3, C's right of recovery is actually a power correlated with a liability on the part of D, not a duty

---

[35] See below p 258.
[36] Cf *Re Montagu's ST* [1987] Ch 264.
[37] Above pp 113, 118.

to return the property.[38] Unless this is recognised, it is impossible to see the distinction between the property-based claim and the tort claim.[39] Although C is entitled to the return of the property (and this is so irrespective of D's state of knowledge), it is unreasonable for D to have a duty to return it in the ordinary course (even once he knows that the transfer was invalid), because such a duty might be extremely burdensome. For example, the property might be a large and cumbersome tangible thing that is expensive to handle and transport. There is no reason why D should have to bear this cost, as opposed to simply refraining from consuming or disposing of the property.

This might be taken to reflect a general rule that tort law does not recognise positive duties.[40] But it is not clear that the concrete duty that D incurs when he knows of the invalidity of a transfer cannot sometimes be a positive duty, rather than merely a negative duty to refrain from disposing of the property or consuming it. Although D may not generally have a duty of return, it is reasonable for him to have a duty to take the positive step of notifying C that he believes a transfer to be invalid, or to make a payment of money or a execute a document of conveyance to C to satisfy a clear liability. Furthermore, possibly D may have a duty to take certain precautions to reduce the risk of loss of the property pending its return or collection, for example by depositing money in a bank, or placing a valuable item in a secure place, although he surely would not have anything like a trustee's duty of investment.[41] Elsewhere I have described D's duty as a 'duty of preservation',[42] which suggests a slightly more demanding duty than a purely negative duty not to consume or dispose of property.

In general, it appears that the position in tort is not that there is anything objectionable in principle about a duty of positive action, but that, according to the criteria that determine whether a duty should arise, a duty of positive action is likely to be justified only in very limited circumstances, because the burden involved is greater and often more open-ended.[43] A well-known example of a positive

---

[38] Above p 94.

[39] Above p 105.

[40] SA Smith, 'Justifying the Law of Unjust Enrichment' (2001) 79 *Texas Law Review* 2177, 2194. Smith suggests that D's duty is simply a duty of non-interference.

[41] See eg *National Bank of New Zealand v Waitaki International* [1997] NZLR 724, affm [1999] 2 NZLR 211.

[42] Jaffey, above n 24, at 234–35.

[43] See Jaffey, ibid, at 309. Furthermore, where D has a duty of reasonable care in the conduct of an activity, it may be very difficult to make any distinction at all between positive and negative action.

duty is the duty owed by a landowner to his neighbours to take steps to prevent harm emanating from the land, for example to put out fires. It seems that a duty is justified here because, although it is a duty of positive action, it is confined to the defined and limited sphere of the landowner's management of his land, and the cost to the landowner of suppressing the fire at source is likely to be far less than the cost imposed on neighbours through fire damage and fire-fighting if the fire is allowed to spread.[44] The position of someone who is liable to receive an invalid transfer has something in common with the landowner's position, in that some precautions at low cost to him may save property-owners from greater loss, and a positive duty of inquiry may be justifiable on the same basis.[45]

THE COMMON LAW CLAIMS

A satisfactory regime for invalid transfers requires a restitutionary property-based claim and a wrong-based compensation claim oper-ating together, and equity has managed to develop a regime along these lines, though the distinction between the two claims is not properly recognised and understood. As discussed in chapter 6,[46] the common law tries to manage with only one claim, and this can give rise to difficulties. There are separate regimes for money and for goods.

Money Claims

The claim to recover an invalid payment of money, as discussed in chapter 6, was traditionally known as the claim for money had and received, and is now generally referred to as the common law claim for restitution. It is a personal claim, though as discussed in chapter 6 this type of claim should in principle be proprietary.[47] There is no second claim in tort as the analysis above requires.

Until quite recently, the claim was always for the value of the pay-ment, without any reduction for change of position. This meant that, where there had in fact been a change of position, and the surviving

---

[44] eg, *Stovin v Wise* [1996] AC 923; *Goldman v Hargrave* [1967] 1 AC 645.

[45] The 'duty of inquiry' may be not a genuine duty but a formula for defining the con-structive knowledge condition for liability under a primary liability relation, though defined in terms of a standard of care involving position action.

[46] Above p 182.

[47] Above p 172.

value had fallen below the value of the payment, the measure of the claim exceeded what was actually justified for a property-based restitutionary claim. In such a case, to the extent that the measure of recovery exceeded the actual surviving value, the claim in effect incorporated recovery of compensation for loss of surviving value. Where this was not justifiable on the basis that it had been caused by D's wrongdoing, the claim was unjust.[48]

Nowadays D can invoke change of position,[49] so C is generally rightly confined to the claim for actual surviving value. (As mentioned in chapter 6,[50] because of the origin of the claim, and because it is not proprietary, change of position is understood to operate not by limiting the surviving value as the object or measure of the claim, but by way of a defence in part to a claim for the value of the original payment.) However, say that D knows that the payment is invalid but still spends money that he would not otherwise have spent, maybe thinking or hoping that C does not know and will not discover that the invalid payment has taken place. On the suggested scheme involving two distinct claims, here C's restitutionary claim should be reduced by the amount of the expenditure even though it was incurred wrongfully, and C should in its place have a claim for compensation for loss caused by D's wrongdoing. Instead, under the current law it is said that the change of position defence is subject to the condition that D not be in bad faith, and here he is in bad faith because he knows that the transfer was invalid. The restitutionary claim is allowed for a measure of *deemed* surviving value that exceeds the *actual* surviving value and encompasses compensation for loss of surviving value wrongfully caused by D. For most purposes this has the same effect and leads to the right outcome, although it is artificial because, like the knowing receipt claim, it is in effect a composite claim that conceals the difference between two different types of claim with their different rationales, and there are certain issues that cannot be adequately dealt with in this way.[51]

---

[48] Subject to the point made above n 24.

[49] *Lipkin Gorman v Karpnale* [1991] 2 AC 548.

[50] Above p 166.

[51] As mentioned above, n 2, some writers have argued that the knowing receipt claim should be reformulated as a restitutionary claim, and if this were to happen the claim would presumably be subject to change of position. But again it would be necessary for change of position to be subject to a knowledge condition, and this would mean that the claim would no longer be genuinely a restitutionary claim for actual surviving value, causatively defined, but a claim for a deemed measure of surviving value, including the value actually lost. The wrong-based claim would be in effect reintroduced in a disguised form, and this is bound to happen whenever the tort claim is mischaracterised as a restitutionary claim.

First, this approach works only because at common law the restitutionary claim is not proprietary. If it were proprietary, as it ought
to be, in accordance with the monist principle,[52] it would be necessary to identify true surviving value as the object of the proprietary
claim. Deemed surviving value, actually representing compensation
for loss, cannot be the object of the proprietary claim. Secondly, there
is the issue of contributory negligence, which was mentioned
above.[53] If C was at fault in making the invalid transfer or allowing it
to happen, although this should not affect a claim to actual surviving
value, in principle it should be taken into account as a matter of
contributory negligence with respect to a claim for compensation for
surviving value wrongfully disposed of or consumed. This again
requires the two claims to be distinguished. There is some support for
reducing the measure of recovery to take account of contributory
negligence in the context of the common law restitutionary money
claim,[54] but there is stronger authority against, although the issue has
been confused by the failure to distinguish between the genuinely
restitutionary element and the compensatory element of the claim.[55]
Another problem is that the current formulation leaves it open to the
courts to hold that the recipient D has not acted wrongfully, but then
also deny him the defence of change of position on the ground of his
bad faith. But where the claim against D is in respect of lost surviving value (not surviving value still in his estate), the only sound basis
for a claim is that he has acted wrongfully; there is in principle no distinct issue that could be at stake in this situation in the question of bad
faith.[56]

Goods Claims

The other regime at common law is the law of conversion, governing invalid transfers of goods. Again, as discussed in chapter 6, the law

---

[52] Above p 173.

[53] Above p 192.

[54] See eg *National Bank of New Zealand v Waitaki International* [1997] NZLR 724, affm
[1999] 2 NZLR 211.

[55] As in *Dextra Bank & Trust v Bank of Jamaica* [2002] 1 All ER (Comm) 193.

[56] In *Abou-Rahmah v Abacha* [2006] EWCA Civ 1492, a claim was denied in knowing
assistance but then the defence of change of position to a claim for restitution at common
law was also denied on the basis of absence of good faith. This also involves the anti-fusion
fallacy, above p 120. In equity, similarly, the same condition of actual and constructive
knowledge should apply for bona fide purchase and knowing receipt, since in both cases the
issue is whether D has incurred a duty not to dispose of or consume the property received.
This is the traditional position: *Belmont Finance Corp v Williams Furniture Ltd (No 2)* [1980] 1
All ER 393; but it was denied in *Re Montagu's ST* [1987] Ch 264.

operates with only one type of claim, but here it takes the form of a claim in tort, not a restitutionary claim arising from the receipt and retention of property invalidly transferred. In reality, conversion, though recognised and formulated as a tort, is again a composite claim that performs the functions of both the tort claim for compensation for wrongful consumption or disposal of the property and the property-based claim to recover an invalid transfer of property. In some circumstances, the true basis of the claim is that D has property invalidly transferred from C or its surviving value, and in other circumstances it is that D has wrongfully disposed of it; sometimes the two bases account for different elements of the claim. Inevitably the law of conversion performs the two distinct functions awkwardly and unsatisfactorily, as has sometimes been pointed out.[57] More particularly, one can identify a number of practical problems, some of them similar to those affecting the common law money claim.

First, the claim in conversion is, like the money claim, generally understood as a personal claim,[58] and although this is appropriate insofar as the claim is genuinely based on a wrongful disposal or consumption of the property, insofar as it functions as a claim to recover the invalid transfer it should in principle be a proprietary claim.[59] It is of course understandable that the claim is personal since it is understood to be a claim based on a wrong. For money claims, the conventional reason why the claim is personal is that title has passed.[60] In the law of conversion, it is said that title has been retained, but the claim is not a proprietary claim to enforce it.[61] Only once it is appreciated that the claim is sometimes based on the invalidity of the transfer—the retention of title—and not on a wrong will the justification for a proprietary claim in those circumstances be apparent. (As discussed in chapter 6,[62] what is really required is the general recognition of two types of title with different functions.)

Secondly, there is the issue of the measure of damages for conversion. In the case of a claim to recover an invalid transfer of property, the measure of recovery should be the value of the property in D's

[57] Weir, above n 18, at 166–67. At one time the common law did have a distinct claim along the lines of the property-based claim to recover an invalid transfer: this was the now-defunct claim in detinue. See further Jaffey, above n 24, at 325–27.

[58] The standard form of remedy is compensation; there is a discretion to award specific restitution; see Weir, above n 18.

[59] See above p 172.

[60] Above p 182.

[61] Above p 184.

[62] Above p 182.

hands.[63] ('Damages' is an inappropriate expression for what is really the measure of restitution, but this is the function that the claim in conversion is performing here.) In the case of the claim for compensation for wrongful consumption or disposal the measure should also be, in the first place, the value of the property lost. But where D has acted wrongfully, he should also be liable for C's consequential losses (subject to remoteness), for example losses resulting from C's being unable to use the property in his business.[64]

Thirdly, also in connection with the measure of damages, unlike torts in general a claim in conversion is not subject to contributory negligence,[65] and this is presumably because it is appreciated that it often performs the function of returning invalidly-transferred property or its value to C. If C's property or its surviving value is in D's hands, there is no reason to deny full recovery on the ground that C was in some way at fault in allowing the invalid transfer to take place.[66] But if C's claim is for compensation for loss of surviving value caused by D's wrong, it is right that D's liability should be reduced if C was at fault in making the invalid transfer or allowing it to take place.[67]

But the most serious problem in the law of conversion arises from the need to characterise it as a strict liability tort, that is to say, a tort based on a strict liability duty, which can be breached without fault.[68] In my view, this amounts to a fiction, and it certainly leads to injustice in some circumstances. Say D is in possession of C's goods as a result of an invalid transfer. C should in principle have a claim, arising from his primary right of ownership, to recover the property or its surviving value, based not on a wrong, but on the invalid transfer. A court should be able to recognise such a claim simply by virtue of the monist principle. Instead the common law allows only a claim in respect of a supposed wrongful act by D. But what if the property is just sitting in D's hands, and D does not dispose of it or consume it, or otherwise do anything at odds with C's right of ownership? This appears to be a problem for the law so long as the claim is conceived

---

[63] Weir, above n 18, at 171.

[64] See Jaffey, above n 5.

[65] By virtue of the Torts (Interference with Goods) Act 1977, s.11(1).

[66] This is accepted in the case law on the recovery of invalid money payments at common law, and appears never to have been doubted with respect to the equitable proprietary claim. Above n 10.

[67] Above p 205.

[68] Above p 26.

of as being based on a breach of duty.[69] And what if at this point D dies or goes bankrupt, and C's claim against D's estate depends on showing a subsisting claim at the time of death or bankruptcy? In such cases, if the basis of the claim is understood to be a wrong, it is necessary to say that D has acted wrongfully merely by receiving the property and doing nothing with it, although he may know nothing about the transfer, and it may have been completely beyond his control.

Similarly, take the case where D receives property through an invalid transfer and then sells it on. There should in principle be a property-based claim in respect of the surviving value of the original transfer, ie the proceeds of sale, as happens in equity, as discussed in chapter 6. The approach at common law is to say that the sale was wrongful, as an act of conversion, and the claim attaches to the sale proceeds as the proceeds of a wrong. This will generally achieve the right outcome, although it seems to imply that the basis of the claim is disgorgement,[70] which is quite misconceived: the basis of the claim is not the quasi-punitive principle that D should not be allowed to profit through his wrongdoing, but C's right to the surviving value of property invalidly transferred. The problem is that where D does not know and has no reason to know of the invalidity of the transfer, it is still necessary to describe him as a wrongdoer in order to allow C a claim to the proceeds of sale.

The characterisation of D as a wrongdoer in order to contrive the right outcome in these cases causes injustice in some other cases. For example, if D receives the invalid transfer as a bona fide purchaser, he should have the protection of the bona fide purchase defence, at least in some circumstances,[71] but this possibility is ruled out by the fact that D is understood to be a wrongdoer.[72] Similarly, if D receives an invalid transfer of goods as a donee and disposes of them, he should have the benefit of change of position, but again this is excluded by his characterisation as a wrongdoer.[73]

All these various problems in the law of conversion can be avoided only by distinguishing between the two types of claim, the property-based claim that arises from the invalid transfer, and the claim arising from the wrongful disposal or consumption of the property.

---

[69] Weir, above n 18, at 166–67.
[70] See A Burrows, *The Law of Restitution* (London, Butterworths, 2nd edn, 2002) 464.
[71] If only for the sake of consistency with cases historically dealt with in equity.
[72] See eg *Hollins v Fowler* (1875) LR 7 HL 757, 764, per Blackburn J.
[73] Above p 204.

Some commentators describe tort as a remedial category, particularly in relation to property.[74] Conversion is taken to be the standard illustration of this remedial role. It is a true in a rough sense to say that tort protects property rights, but, as discussed in chapter 3,[75] it is misleading, where careful analysis is required, to say that tort law generates remedial rights from primary rights in property law. If this is what is meant, it is a systematic example of the dualist fallacy. Both property law and tort law have primary and remedial rights. A primary right in property generates a claim to recover an invalid transfer of property or its surviving value; the primary right in tort is correlated with the duty of reasonable care and in particular circumstances the duty not to consume or dispose of property, and generates a claim for compensation for wrongful disposal or consumption. The true difference between property and tort is not that one is a primary category and the other a remedial category, but that the two categories are different justificatory categories founded on different underlying principles.

FUSION

There is a striking contrast between the regimes for money and goods at common law. For goods, the law has adopted a purely tort-based analysis, and for money a purely restitutionary or receipt-based analysis. The underlying issues are the same, however, and for both there should really be a regime with two claims, a property-based restitutionary claim in respect of actual surviving value, and a tort claim for compensation for loss of surviving value. The reason for the different treatment lies in the old exhaustive division between contract and tort in the common law. Money claims were treated by way of a fiction as a quasi-contractual debt for the value received, which came later to be described as a restitutionary claim, and goods claims were treated as a matter of tort, and even now are not covered in the restitution textbooks. In connection with both money and goods, there has been, in different ways, a false assimilation of the two distinct types of claim. At the same time the quite different treatment of the same issues with respect to money and goods is a case of false differentiation.

[74] Above p 104.
[75] Above p 106.

Equity has come closer to establishing a regime with two distinct types of claim, in the form of the equitable proprietary claim and the knowing receipt claim, although the knowing receipt claim is actually a composite claim combining a compensatory tort element and a restitutionary element. The problem in equity is that it lacks the concepts of tort law, including the simple concept of a duty to avoid harm, and more particularly the duty of reasonable care, which would deal more appropriately with the issues that equity currently wrestles with in the law of knowing receipt in terms of liability to account and constructive knowledge. As discussed in chapter 7 in connection with the claim to recover an invalid transfer, it seems feasible that the law can develop a single coherent regime out of these different bodies of law. The substantive fusion of law and equity would contribute to this, since the common law and equity have available between them all the necessary concepts for such a regime. Resistance to fusion, based on the idea that law and equity give effect to different basic principles, or are concerned with different types of subject matter, reflects the anti-fusion fallacy discussed earlier.[76]

---

[76] Above p 120.

8

Restitution and the Unjust Enrichment Fallacy

There are various types of claim that arise from the receipt of a benefit or enrichment,[1] in the sense that the receipt is a necessary element of the claim.[2] Historically, these various benefit-based claims were found in different and unrelated parts of the law, but, as I have already mentioned,[3] in modern times it has been strongly argued that they should be brought together and recognised as a single category of law, governed by a common framework, and having an equivalent status and role in the common law to the long-established categories of contract and tort.[4] This is the theory of unjust enrichment, and it has been very influential in recent years. It is now widely accepted in the academic literature and increasingly in the courts that there is a category of unjust enrichment claims that should be addressed according to a uniform three-stage test:[5] (1) the defendant has received an enrichment; (2) the enrichment is at the expense of the claimant; (3) the enrichment is unjust. Much attention has been directed at

---

[1] I will not distinguish between 'benefit' and 'enrichment'. This reflects standard usage, which does not distinguish between persisting property or wealth and other benefit.

[2] In some cases the benefit is relevant to the measure of the claim, not a condition for it to arise.

[3] Above p 15.

[4] See eg A Burrows, 'Restitution: Where Do We Go From Here?' in *Understanding the Law of Obligations* (Oxford, Hart Publishing, 1998); D Laycock, 'The Scope and Significance of Restitution' (1989) 67 *Texas Law Review* 1277; EL Sherwin, 'Restitution and Equity' (2001) 79 *Texas Law Review*. This approach is generally assumed in the restitution textbooks.

[5] There are variants of this framework, which it is not necessary to discuss for present purposes. See eg P Birks, *An Introduction to the Law of Restitution* (Oxford, Clarendon Press, rev edn, 1989); A Burrows, *The Law of Restitution*, (London, Butterworths, 2nd edn, 2002); G Virgo, *The Principles of the Law of Restitution* (Oxford, OUP, 2nd edn, 2006); R Goff and G Jones, *The Law of Restitution* (London, Sweet & Maxwell, 7th edn, 2002). The cases might include *Lipkin Gorman v Karpnale* [1991] 2 AC 548; *Banque Financière de la Cité v Parc (Battersea)* [1999] 1 AC 221; *Portman Building Society v Hamlyn Taylor Neck* [1998] 4 All ER 202; *Cressman v Coys of Kensington* [2004] 1 WLR 2775.

identifying and expounding the law of 'unjust factors', which amount to different ways in which the third condition can be satisfied.

These various benefit-based claims were first brought together by characterising them in terms of the remedy of restitution, meaning a remedy by which the defendant D hands over to the claimant C the benefit received or its value or some part of it, and it is still more common to refer to the law of restitution than the law of unjust enrichment. This is presumably largely because of the traditional remedial orientation of the common law. The theory of unjust enrichment amounts to the claim that there is a justificatory category of unjust enrichment, governed by a general moral principle of unjust enrichment, and the crucial question is whether there really is a principle of unjust enrichment, or whether this is just an empty phrase that reflects the influence of the remedy-as-justification fallacy. It will be apparent from previous chapters that I take the latter view.[6] In my view, there is no 'principle of unjust enrichment' that could justify the theory of unjust enrichment. Of course this is not to deny that there are claims that arise from the receipt of a benefit, or that in this weak sense there are benefit-based or unjust enrichment claims.[7] The issue is whether, according to a sound system of classification by justification, these claims fall within a single category governed by a unifying underlying principle of unjust enrichment. It seems to me that, to the contrary, the receipt of a benefit is a type of event that is relevant to a claim by virtue of quite different principles in different contexts. In particular, it can be relevant to claims in contract and property.

It is worth addressing the theory of unjust enrichment at some length because of its ramifications for property law and property-based claims and also for contract law and private law as a whole. I will begin the chapter by outlining what appear to me to be the main types of claim that arise from the receipt of a benefit, classified by reference to justification, some of which have been discussed earlier.

---

[6] There are a number of works critical of the theory of unjust enrichment, although the criticisms and the preferred approaches vary. These include P Jaffey, *The Nature and Scope of Restitution* (Oxford, Hart Publishing, 2000); J Dietrich, *Restitution A New Perspective* (Annandale, Federation Press, 1998), and S Hedley, *Restitution—Its Division and Ordering* (London, Sweet & Maxwell, 2001), and *A Critical Introduction to Restitution* (London, Butterworths, 2001); IM Jackman, *The Varieties of Restitution* (Sydney, The Federation Press, 1998).

[7] This might be called the 'weak' theory of unjust enrichment: see P Jaffey, 'Two Theories of Unjust Enrichment' in JW Neyers, M McInnes and SGA Pitel (eds), *Understanding Unjust Enrichment* (Portland, Hart Publishing, 2004).

BENEFIT-BASED CLAIMS CLASSIFIED BY JUSTIFICATORY CATEGORY

Property-based Claims

Claims to Recover Invalid Transfers

The most common sort of claim that might be described as an unjust enrichment claim is the claim to recover an invalid transfer of property, including intangible property and money, which arises from the receipt by D of the invalid transfer. As discussed in previous chapters,[8] the claim to recover an invalid transfer is property-based, meaning that it arises from the claimant C's primary right of ownership in the justificatory category of private property. The claim should in principle be a proprietary claim as discussed in chapter 6, although it is also found as a personal claim, as in the case of the common law claim to recover a mistaken payment, which has been described as the standard or 'core' case of an unjust enrichment claim.[9] The rules on tracing and change of position ensure that the recipient D is liable only in respect of value surviving in his estate.

Claims for Reasonable Payment for Unauthorised Use

Another type of property-based claim was discussed in chapter 3[10]: the claim arising from the unauthorised use of property, where D has trespassed on C's land or used C's goods or intellectual property without permission. Here there is no transfer to D, and C's claim is not to recover a transfer but to be paid for the benefit obtained by D through the unauthorised use of the property. The measure is generally some fraction of the benefit received by D.

Contractual Reliance Claims

There are claims that arise from the non-performance of a contract that are sometimes thought to be unjust enrichment claims. First, where a contractor C makes a payment under the contract, and the contract, though valid, is not performed by the other party D, C is entitled to recover the payment.[11] Also, where C has carried out part

---

[8] Above pp 93, 155.

[9] See below p 238.

[10] Above p 99.

[11] The long-established position is that the claim is available only where there has been no performance at all, under the doctrine of complete failure of consideration: Burrows, above n 5, at 333. However, it is widely agreed that a claim to recover part of the payment

of the work due under a contract, and the contract has terminated, he may be allowed a claim for reasonable payment for what he has done (a quantum meruit).

One reason why these claims are thought not to be contractual may be simply that they are not for expectation damages, and the assumption may be that contractual claims are necessarily claims for expectation damages. But this is the remedy-as-justification fallacy: the form of the remedy cannot be assumed to indicate the basis of the claim. Another reason may be that, as discussed in chapter 2,[12] according to the conventional understanding of contract, a contract claim always arises from the breach of a duty to perform the contract, and these claims cannot be understood, consistently with the monist principle, as claims arising from such a breach of duty. Only a claim for specific performance to compel performance of the duty, or compensation for the lack of performance in the form of expectation damages, can be understood as arising in this way. Furthermore, these two types of claim often arise where the contract has terminated as a result of frustration, and here D clearly has not committed a breach of duty. Thus many commentators have inferred that these claims must instead be unjust enrichment or restitutionary claims arising from the receipt by D of the payment or the benefit of the work done under the contract.[13]

In my view, these two types of claim fall in the true justificatory category of contract. If a claim arises by virtue of the fact that an agreement was not completed as agreed, it is difficult to see how else it can be explained, even if it is not immediately apparent what the connection is between the claim and the underlying principle in contract law. A possible explanation of this connection was suggested in chapter 2.[14] It was suggested that contract law protects reliance on the agreement, so that each contracting party is responsible to the other in respect of the other's reliance on the agreement. This requires that D compensates C for reliance loss incurred through payments or expenditure, and pays C for work done in reliance on the agreement. This is not to say that benefit received by D is not relevant. If each

---

ought to be available where there has been part-performance and 'partial failure of consideration', and this is consistent with the reliance analysis suggested in the text.

[12] Above p 51.

[13] This is the standard view in the restitution and unjust enrichment textbooks: eg Burrows, above n 5, ch 10.

[14] Above p 48.

party is responsible for the other's reliance, it is reasonable to say that either party or both of them may have a prima facie reliance claim, and there is a resultant net reliance claim for one or other party that depends on the extent of loss and work done in reliance and the extent of benefit received by the two parties. There is a sort of balancing exercise that reflects the mutual responsibility for reliance in the contractual relationship.[15] C's claim is a contractual reliance claim, but if a benefit has been received by D it is relevant in determining the measure of the claim.[16]

It seems to be that this approach (which has only very briefly been outlined above) can in principle account for these two types of claim; though it is not orthodox, it seems to me the most plausible if not the only plausible way to account for them.[17] It is not necessary to accept this account, or the version of the reliance theory suggested in chapter 2, in order to conclude that these claims are reliance claims of some sort, or some other form of contract claim. A better contractual analysis may be available. Assuming it is right that these claims should be available in at least some circumstances, the issue in the end is whether they are contract claims or unjust enrichment claims, and to show that they are unjust enrichment claims it is necessary to establish that they arise from a principle of unjust enrichment. This problem will be considered below.

Claims for Reasonable Payment in Respect of Non-contractual Exchange

Usually a claim for payment for a benefit provided is a contractual claim, and C cannot recover payment for a benefit conferred on D unless D first agreed to pay.[18] This is justified in order to protect D's freedom to choose how to use his money in the light of his own

---

[15] Or an 'accounting' exercise, as described in *Cargill International v Bangladesh Sugar & Food Industries* [1996] 4 All ER 563, 568; *Tradigrain v State Trading Corp of India* [2005] EWHC 2206 (Comm) para 26.

[16] There are also cases where as a result of unforeseen circumstances one contracting party, D, has benefited from the contract in a way that is inconsistent with its terms, though not because of anything D has done, and without frustrating the contract. Then the argument in the text again explains a claim on the basis of the contract. In two recent examples of this type of case the claim was said to be an unjust enrichment claim: see *Roxborough v Rothmans of Pall Mall Australia* (2001) 208 CLR 516; and *Cressman v Coys of Kensington* [2004] 1 WLR 2775; P Jaffey, 'Failure of Consideration' (2003) 66 *Modern Law Review* 284.

[17] See further Jaffey, above n 6, ch 2.

[18] *Falcke v Scottish Imperial Insurance Co* (1886) 34 Ch D 234. The concept of officiousness is generally used to refer to benefits conferred deliberately but not pursuant to an agreement.

wealth and tastes. However, sometimes a claim for reasonable payment for a benefit conferred is allowed in the absence of an agreement. A good example is 'necessitous intervention' where C conferred a benefit on D by saving D or his property from harm in an emergency, typified by the case of maritime salvage.[19] Generally it appears that such a claim should depend on the receipt of a benefit by D (including the avoidance of harm), and it is often regarded as a form of unjust enrichment claim, though it is sometimes suggested that a claim arises or should arise where C spent time and money trying to save D from harm but was not in the end successful. This type of claim is not a claim to recover an invalid transfer of property, nor a claim for payment for the unauthorised use of property, nor a contractual claim or a tort claim. It appears to fall in a quite different justificatory category. In functional terms it seems to be best understood as a device for effecting exchanges where agreement is impossible or impracticable.[20]

Unjust Enrichment Claims as Primary Liability Claims

The various claims above are unjust enrichment claims in the sense that they arise from the receipt of a benefit,[21] but they do not form a justificatory category. As to modality, they are primary liability claims: they do not arise from a breach of duty. This is not to say that the category of unjust enrichment claims in this sense corresponds to the category of primary liability claims, since there are primary liability claims that are not unjust enrichment claims.

Restitution

The claims above are generally said to be claims for the remedy of restitution, but one can distinguish between various types of remedy. Sometimes the claim is to recover a transfer, which seems aptly described as 'restitution'. This might be a claim to recover an invalid transfer, or a contractual reliance claim to recover a valid payment under a contract. Sometimes the remedy is payment for work done in conferring a benefit, or payment for the unauthorised use of property.[22] This is not the same as recovering a transfer: the purpose and

---

[19] See Burrows, above n 5, at 309.

[20] See further Jaffey, above n 6, ch 3.

[21] On the contractual reliance explanation above, the receipt of a benefit is relevant to the measure of the claim.

[22] On the suggested contractual reliance analysis, benefit is weighed into account in a balancing exercise to determine the measure of recovery for a reliance claim.

effect of this remedy is not to restore the property transferred or its value, but to provide payment in exchange for the benefit or the work done in providing it. (I will come back to this important distinction below.) The theory of unjust enrichment has obscured the distinctions between these different types of remedy.

Disgorgement

Disgorgement, in the sense explained in chapter 2,[23] is different again. Disgorgement strips the defendant of a profit on the basis of the principle that a wrongdoer should not be allowed to profit through a wrong. It is not the recovery of a transfer, nor payment for a benefit. In particular cases the effect may be the same but the rationale is different. Disgorgement is not a remedy in the strict sense at all: it is a non-remedial response. It arises from a wrong by D, but it does not rectify the wrong for the benefit of C[24]; it promotes the public interest in compliance with the law. This is one reason why there is controversy in the form of the 'procedural objection' over disgorgement and some inconsistency in the legal treatment of it.[25] Sometimes disgorgement is described as the removal of an unjust enrichment—this is a natural usage. Again, the effect of the theory of unjust enrichment has been to conceal the differences between disgorgement and the claims and remedies discussed above.

IS THERE A PRINCIPLE OF UNJUST ENRICHMENT?

What is meant by a Principle of Unjust Enrichment?

The various claims outlined above (or most of them) are said by many proponents of the theory of unjust enrichment to be based on the principle of unjust enrichment; if the theory of unjust enrichment is right, there must be such a principle. The issue is whether these claims are best explained, as argued above, as distinct types of claim based on property or contract or some other such category (or as a type of response to a breach of duty in the case of disgorgement), or whether there is indeed a general principle of unjust enrichment that accounts for them. It is a curious feature of the literature on the theory of unjust enrichment that it is difficult to find a statement of the

---

[23] Above p 57.

[24] Although disgorgement presupposes a benefit received by D, the receipt of the benefit was not a condition of C's claim, which arose from the wrong.

[25] Above p 62.

principle of unjust enrichment, though many writers and judges have invoked it.[26] There is certainly no canonical version of it.

Some writers may believe that it is so obvious that there is such a principle that no defence is called for—the 'elephant in the room' argument, as I have heard it put. Take the claim to recover a mistaken payment, which is often thought to be a standard and uncontrovertible case of an unjust enrichment claim.[27] It is clear that there must be a claim to recover at least some types of mistaken payment, and such a claim clearly arises from the receipt of a benefit (and it is not a contract claim or a tort claim); it follows, one might think, that there must be a principle of unjust enrichment to account for it. Possibly some writers would think that to doubt the existence of a principle of unjust enrichment is to doubt whether there should be a claim in this type of case. But of course the issue is not whether there should be a claim in this or other uncontroversial cases. It is about how to explain the claim in terms of an underlying principle, which other claims are analogous to it, and how to deal with other cases that are controversial. As discussed in previous chapters,[28] the claim to recover a mistaken payment is really a property-based claim.

A possible formulation of the principle of unjust enrichment is that a claim should arise in respect of a benefit received where justice requires. This does not amount to a principle at all. It gives no indication of any type of reason or justification that might guide a determination that a benefit is unjust, or, in other words, any basis for saying, even in the broadest terms, why or when a claim should arise from the receipt of a benefit. What is required for the purposes of the theory of unjust enrichment is a principle that is capable of supporting a justificatory category, which means a distinctive type of justification for a body of rules that can generate a primary relation.

Historically the most common objection to the theory of unjust enrichment has been that the principle of unjust enrichment is too uncertain or open-ended to have any practical role in the law.[29] This is not quite the same as saying there is no such principle at all, because genuine principles may be to some degree uncertain or open-ended.

---

[26] eg, the idea of a principle of unjust enrichment is defended, but without any statement of the principle, in K Barker, 'Theorising Unjust Enrichment Law' (2006) 26 *Oxford Journal of Legal Studies* 609.

[27] This is Birks's 'core case' of unjust enrichment, as discussed below.

[28] Above pp 97, 181.

[29] See WS Holdsworth, 'Unjustifiable Enrichment' (1939) 55 *Law Quarterly Review* 37; *Baylis v The Bishop of London* [1913] 1 Ch 127, 140, per Hamilton LJ.

It is unpersuasive to object that a principle is too uncertain to be readily applied, in the abstract, directly to a particular set of facts, since this is not the function of a general underlying principle; its function is provide the basis for a framework and a body of rules that can be applied to particular facts. In the case of unjust enrichment, it might be said, the three-stage framework and unjust factors give concrete effect to the abstract principle of unjust enrichment. But if there is no genuine principle of unjust enrichment at all, such a framework does not have any rationale and it misplaces claims and distorts the law, and this problem cannot be avoided by setting out the law in terms of the framework in ever more intricate detail, as much of the modern literature on restitution and unjust enrichment attempts to do.

An argument for the recognition of a new category in the common law calls for an account of the nature and function of the category and the system of classification on which it is based. Proponents of the theory of unjust enrichment, in particular Birks, have indeed placed great emphasis on classification. But the problem of formulating a principle of unjust enrichment has not been helped by the debate on classification in the literature. First, as considered later in the chapter, Birks himself has denied the need for any principle as the basis for the category of unjust enrichment, though this is not the usual view. Secondly, opponents of the theory, instead of calling for an explanation of the particular nature and function of the supposed category of unjust enrichment, have tended to express scepticism about classification in general, suggesting that it is futile to argue over issues of classification since they are irrelevant to legal argument. This seems to reflect the misconception, referred to in chapter 1,[30] that all classification is purely conventional. As a result, the focus has often been on the value of classification in general, not on the nature of the category of unjust enrichment and the general principle that underlies it.[31]

A Remedial Principle

The principle of unjust enrichment is sometimes expressed simply as the principle that unjust enrichments should be undone or

---

[30] See ch 1, above p 13.

[31] See eg P Birks, 'Unjust Enrichment—A Reply to Mr Hedley' (1985) 5 *Legal Studies* 67; 'Rights, Wrongs and Remedies (2000) 20 *Oxford Journal of Legal Studies* 1; 'Equity in the Modern Law: an Exercise in Taxonomy' (1996) 26 *Western Australia Law Review* 1; cf S Hedley, 'The Taxonomic Approach to Restitution' in A Hudson (ed), *New Perspectives on Property Law, Obligations and Restitution* (London, Cavendish, 2004).

reversed.[32] This is a purely remedial principle, that is to say a principle that generates a remedial relation out of a primary relation. Compare the principle that D should compensate C if D has committed a wrong against him, discussed in chapter 2. This is also a remedial principle.[33] It presupposes that there is a right-duty primary relation, without giving any indication of the content of the relation. It says nothing about the primary relation, about when or why an act of D's is wrongful, and so provides no basis for saying when or why a claim arises. Similarly, the principle that an unjust enrichment should be undone or reversed says nothing about when or why a claim should arise, because it says nothing about when a benefit is 'unjust'. It does not specify what the primary relation is, though it is implicit that it is a primary right-liability relation.

Consistently with this idea of a remedial principle, some commentators regard restitution or unjust enrichment as an essentially remedial category of law, meaning that it is a body of law that determines when a certain remedy should be available to protect a primary right arising in some other category of law, such as contract or property.[34] (Some commentators take the same view of tort, as discussed earlier.)[35] The problem with this is that, as discussed in chapter 2,[36] in principle a remedial relation follows directly from the primary relation in accordance with the monist principle. Just as the right to compensation for a wrong follows directly from a primary duty not to cause harm, so the claim for restitution in respect of a benefit arises directly from a primary right-liability relation. There is no room for a principle of unjust enrichment to operate in this way,[37] and the idea that it does is an example of the dualist fallacy.

More commonly, the remedial principle is treated as if it provided the basis for a justificatory category, analogous to contract or tort or property.[38] This is to commit the remedy-as-justification fallacy. As discussed already, this is a natural error to make in trying to make sense of a category of claims historically defined by reference to the

---

[32] See eg Burrows, above n 5, at 1.

[33] Above p 65.

[34] See eg D Friedmann, 'The Protection of Entitlements via the Law of Restitution—Expectancies and Privacy' (2005) 121 *Law Quarterly Review* 400.

[35] Above p 104.

[36] Above p 39.

[37] Above p 98.

[38] See eg Burrows, above n 5, at 1. This seems to be the standard position in the restitution textbooks, and also in some contract and tort textbooks.

nature of the remedy,[39] particularly where the claims do not arise from a breach of duty but from a primary right-liability relation.

A similar formulation of the principle of unjust enrichment, open to the same objection, is that the principle of unjust enrichment is the principle that invalid transfers should be recovered or reversed. Generally proponents of the theory of unjust enrichment equate the reversal of invalid transfers with the undoing of enrichments in general. This is presumably because the theory of unjust enrichment focuses on the receipt of a benefit as the basis for a claim, and so tends to treat it as an irrelevant or secondary matter whether the benefit reached D by way of an invalid transfer of money or property from C or by way of work done by C in providing a benefit. In effect all benefits are taken to result from transfers. On this understanding this formulation is equivalent to the previous one. In fact an invalid transfer properly refers to an invalid transfer of property, and a claim to recover an invalid transfer of property is a property-based claim. Interpreted in this way to mean that invalid transfers of property should be reversed, the principle of unjust enrichment is just the monist principle as applied to property-based claims to recover invalid transfers.

Gordley provides another variation of the remedial principle of unjust enrichment. On his approach, the principle of unjust enrichment is that D is unjustly enriched at C's expense where D has received a benefit from resources in respect of which C has the exclusive right to benefit.[40] Again this is concerned only with the remedial question of establishing a claim given the primary right, which is the exclusive right to benefit from resources. The supposed principle says nothing about when or why anyone has an exclusive right to particular resources. In fact, the determination of which resources should be the subject of exclusive rights and who should be entitled to them is a matter of property law, and once these difficult issues are settled in property law, claims to recover invalid transfers of resources and claims for reasonable payment for the unauthorised use of resources follow in accordance with the monist principle, without any need for a principle of unjust enrichment.

---

[39] This sometimes appears very explicitly, as where it is said that to describe an enrichment as 'unjust' is just to say that it is 'reversible': Birks, above n 5, at 19.

[40] J Gordley, *Foundations of Private Law* (Oxford, OUP, 2006) 423–26.

Unjust Enrichment and the Disgorgement Principle

When D has acquired a benefit through a wrong and is subject to disgorgement the basis for it is sometimes said to be the principle of unjust enrichment. But the disgorgement principle, the principle that a wrongdoer should not profit through his wrongdoing, cannot account for the various claims outlined above. These claims arise from the receipt of a benefit and are primary liability claims. They do not arise from a wrong at all, and they cannot be based on the principle that a wrongdoer should not be allowed to profit through his wrongdoing. Furthermore, the disgorgement principle cannot be behind a justificatory category at all. It justifies a response to a wrong, but it does not say anything about what should count as a wrong. Disgorgement is independent of the basis for the duty in question, and it cuts across different justificatory categories.

'Unjust Factors'

It is often said that unjust enrichment claims are triggered by 'unjust factors'.[41] These appear to be understood as factors that trigger the operation of the supposed principle of unjust enrichment in different types of situation, so the law of particular unjust factors must be understood to give concrete effect, in particular types of situation, to the abstract principle of unjust enrichment. Thus one might expect that the nature of the principle would be discernible from a consideration of the unjust factors. But take a claim to recover a mistaken payment, based on the unjust factor of mistake, often taken, as I have said, to be the standard example of an unjust enrichment claim. It was argued in chapter 3 that the significance of the mistake is in vitiating the exercise by C of his power of transfer as owner of the property, so as to generate a property-based claim.[42] If the mistake has some other legal effect in connection with a different type of justification for a claim, it is not apparent what this is—it is not apparent from any discussion of the claim in the unjust enrichment literature—and simply to refer to mistake as an unjust factor does not reveal what the principle behind the claim is.

Some of the other 'unjust factors' are also vitiating factors—for example, duress or undue influence. Another possible unjust factor is 'lack of authority', which might be said to be the unjust factor that applies where a transfer of property is made without the authority of

---

[41] This approach was developed by Birks, above n 5.
[42] Above p 97.

the owner, by an agent or trustee acting outside his authority or by a stranger.[43] The significance of vitiating factors and lack of authority, though not some other unjust factors, can be readily understood in relation to the property-based claim to recover an invalid transfer, since they are different factors or sets of circumstances that preclude the valid exercise of the owner's power of transfer. But it is not apparent what other general principle might account for these, or still less for all of the unjust factors.

'Failure of Condition'

There is another supposed unjust factor that has loomed large in the literature, which is not a vitiating factor (or lack of authority). This is the unjust factor that is thought to trigger a claim in the case where C confers a benefit for a certain purpose, or subject to a certain condition, or on a certain basis, and it turns out that the purpose or condition or basis fails—that is to say, it is not fulfilled or turns out not to be the case.[44] For convenience I will use 'failure of condition' to cover all of these variants.[45] The unjust factor of failure of condition is understood to operate mainly if not exclusively in a contractual context. It is said to be the unjust factor that generates the non-standard contract claims mentioned above, the claim to recover a payment made under a contract, and the claim for reasonable payment for work done under a contract when the contract terminates early. It is said that when C makes a payment or renders performance under a contract he does so on the condition that D will reciprocate by performing his side of the agreement, and when D does not do so as a result of early termination of the contract by frustration or breach there is an unjust factor of failure of condition.[46]

But, leaving aside for the moment the connection between 'failure of condition' and the supposed principle of unjust enrichment, when a payment is made or work is done pursuant to a valid contract, it is made and received subject to the terms of the contract. There is no room to say that the payment is made or the work is done subject to a condition or on a basis outside the contract. Furthermore, it must

---

[43] There is sometimes said to be an unjust factor of 'ignorance' corresponding roughly to 'lack of authority': see Burrows, above n 5, ch 4. The particular problems with this unjust factor are explained in Jaffey, above n 6, at 161.

[44] See eg Burrows, above n 5, at 324–26; Birks, above, n 5, at 224; Virgo, above n 5, at 304–05.

[45] Some but not all such cases may also involve mistake.

[46] Thus 'failure of consideration' in contract is interpreted to mean 'failure of condition'.

surely be a matter for contract law to determine what claims arise by virtue of the non-performance of the contract. The reason why it has seemed necessary to invoke the idea of a non-contractual claim arising from the non-performance of the contract is the problem mentioned above, that on a conventional view contract law can account only for claims arising from the breach of a contractual duty of performance, which means only claims for expectation damages and claims for specific performance.[47]

Failure of condition is also said to operate in the absence of a valid contract, though still in a contractual context. For example, where C does work for D at D's request it is said that C may have a claim in unjust enrichment for reasonable payment even though there is no contract, possibly because the terms on which the work was to be done were too uncertain for a contract to arise. Also, sometimes C begins work while negotiations for a contract with D are still underway, and then when negotiations fall through and no formal contract is signed C may have a claim for reasonable payment for what he has done, and it appears that this claim cannot be contractual because no contract was ever concluded. In these cases it is said that the claim is an unjust enrichment claim based on the fact that C did work for D on the condition that he would be paid.[48] However, it is generally accepted that for the condition to be binding on D it must have been accepted by him—presumably because it would be unjust for C to be able to impose such a condition unilaterally on D—and this acceptance is found in the fact that the work was done under some sort of vague or tentative agreement, though apparently not amounting to a contract.[49] This suggests that these claims are actually contractual in nature, in the sense that they are based on the principle that agreements should be performed, and fall in the true justificatory category of contract. It may be true that the claims are inconsistent with conventional-justificatory category of contract, in connection with the requirements of certainty or consideration or as to the types of remedy that are available or other matters, which is why the courts have looked elsewhere to find a rationale for a claim. But if the claims are justified, and the justification lies in the agreement between the parties, this is a case of false differentiation and the law of contract is

---

[47] Though unfortunately this idea has recently received support from the Australian High Court in the case of *Roxborough v Rothmans of Pall Mall Austriala* (2001) 208 CLR 516; see Jaffey, above n 16.

[48] Burrows, above n 5, at 372ff.

[49] eg, Burrows, above n 5, at 326, 408.

defective and needs to be developed to recognise the claims. The crucial question is, in the end, whether the rationale of the claim is to give effect to an agreement of some sort between the parties, in accordance with the principle that agreements should be kept, or, if not, what the basic principle is that does in fact justify the claim. The failure of condition approach does not reveal what this principle might be.

It is even apparently argued that something in the nature of failure of condition is behind *all* unjust enrichment claims.[50] But it is unclear what general principle this might reflect, if it is not really the principle behind the enforcement of agreements, and of course this would not provide the basis for a new justificatory category, and neither could it explain many claims that arise from the receipt of a benefit.[51] Although there is a considerable body of literature on failure of condition, it does not appear to be directed at this crucial question.

'No Legal Basis'

In the unjust enrichment literature the unjust factor approach has been contrasted with the 'no legal basis' or 'no juristic factor' approach, according to which a claim arises in respect of a benefit conferred by C on D if there is no legal basis or juristic factor to justify its retention by D.[52] (It appears that, on one view, the failure of condition approach, understood to apply to all unjust enrichment claims, amounts to this no legal basis approach.) One might think that these two rival approaches represent different versions or interpretations of a basic principle of unjust enrichment, but in fact neither approach offers a formulation of an underlying principle at all, and this makes it difficult to see what the real issue at stake between them is. Both approaches simply avoid—indeed they conceal—the crucial question of the nature of the principle of unjust enrichment.

An 'Organising Principle' of Unjust Enrichment

Some commentators have taken what may appear to them to be the cautious or noncommittal view that to recognise a law of unjust enrichment is only to accept what is indisputable, that there are claims that arise from the receipt of a benefit, without making any

---

[50] P Birks, *Unjust Enrichment* (Oxford, OUP, 2nd edn, 2005) pt 3.

[51] eg, the claims arising from transfers without authority or duress or mistake.

[52] This is said to be the civil law approach and it appears also to be the preferred approach in Canadian law: see LD Smith, 'The Province of the Law of Restitution' (1992) 71 *Canadian Bar Review* 672.

assumption about the possible basis for such claims—without in other words implying that there is a principle of unjust enrichment of the sort required to support a justificatory category of unjust enrichment. This seems to be behind the idea of an 'organising principle' of unjust enrichment, or a 'descriptive principle' as opposed to a 'normative principle'.[53] It seems to be thought that this position is neutral with respect to the interpretation and development of the law. Possibly the three-stage framework mentioned above is consistent with this approach. But what is the purpose and effect of the classification? The problem is that writers who follow this approach generally proceed to expound the law and interpret and criticise it in a way that makes sense only if the various claims arising from the receipt of a benefit do in fact form a justificatory category of unjust enrichment: in applying a standard framework to them and treating them as distinct from contract, tort and property-based claims, they presuppose that the law should be developed by analogical reasoning on the assumption that the claims are governed by a common principle.

A 'Supplementary' Principle of Unjust Enrichment

It is also sometimes said that, even if there is no distinct field of law defined in terms of an underlying principle of unjust enrichment, nevertheless there is a principle of unjust enrichment that acts as a supplementary or ancillary principle, helping to determine whether a claim should arise in contract or property or some other justificatory category.[54] But where the receipt of a benefit is relevant to a claim, this is not by virtue of a single principle of unjust enrichment that is imported into different areas as a supplementary or ancillary principle. The relevance of the benefit depends on the principle behind the relevant claim—the private property principle, for example, or the principle behind contract—and accordingly the benefit is relevant to the claim in different ways in different contexts. The significance of a justificatory category such as contract or property is that it is based on a certain general principle, and the relevance to claims within the

---

[53] Possible examples include G Virgo, above n 5, ch 3; H Dagan, *The Law and Ethics of Restitution* (Cambridge, CUP, 2004) ch 2; D Johnston and R Zimmermann, 'Unjustified Enrichment: Surveying the Landscape' in D Johnston and R Zimmermann (eds), *Unjustified Enrichment Key Issues in Comparative Perspective* (Cambridge, CUP, 2002) 3; E McKendrick, 'Taxonomy: Does it Matter?' in D Johnston and R Zimmermann, ibid, 628, 654.

[54] Possible examples include SM Waddams, 'The Relation of Unjust Enrichment to other Concepts' in EJH Schrage (ed), *Unjust Enrichment and the Law of Contract* (The Hague, Kluwer, 2001); RB Grantham and CEF Rickett, 'On the Subsidiarity of Unjust Enrichment' (2001) 117 *Law Quarterly Review* 273.

category of different types of fact or event, including the receipt of a
benefit, depends on this principle. The misapprehension here is that
different principles can be added together in some way to support a
mixed or hybrid claim.[55]

Is there a Principle?

In my view, no plausible version of the supposed principle of unjust
enrichment is to be found in the academic literature. Maybe there is
a principle of unjust enrichment that remains to be identified and
articulated, though this will seem very implausible to anyone who has
been persuaded that alternative explanations of most of the claims discussed in the restitution and unjust enrichment textbooks can be
found in contract law and property law. No doubt many adherents to
the theory of unjust enrichment will recoil from this conclusion.
Maybe this will spur them into considering what the principle of
unjust enrichment is; or if they conclude that there is no such principle, but that the theory of unjust enrichment is nevertheless sound,
it will fall to them to explain what sort of category unjust enrichment
is and how it supports the theory of unjust enrichment. In any case,
given the longstanding problems surrounding the theory of unjust
enrichment, they should be willing to give serious consideration to
alternative explanations in terms of contract and property.

SOME PROBLEMS OF INCOHERENCE

If there is no principle of unjust enrichment and no true justificatory
category of unjust enrichment, insofar as there is now a conventional-
justificatory category of unjust enrichment in English law,[56] it is a
spurious justificatory category. This means that when a court says that
a claim is based on unjust enrichment, although it identifies a conventional category of law, it does not disclose a genuine underlying
reason for the claim, even in broad terms[57]; even worse, an illusory
basis is offered that conceals this failing.

The recognition of a spurious category of unjust enrichment is
liable to cause incoherence, as discussed in chapter 1.[58] Some typical

---

[55] See above p 31.

[56] For which, as noted above, n 5, there is good authority.

[57] See eg *Vedatech Corp v Crystal Decisions* [2002] EWHC 818; *Cressman v Coys of
Kensington* [2004] 1 WLR 2775; and cf *Uren v First National Home Finance* [2005] EWHC
2529, where the claim was thrown out.

[58] Above p 16.

signs of incoherence were suggested: a lack of evident rationale for the rules of the category, and a tension between what seems important or relevant to a claim and the issues that the law actually raises. It seems to me that the developing modern law of unjust enrichment shows these signs, though this is a matter of impression. However, one can certainly point to possible examples of false differentiation and subversion, and false assimilation and fictions. The possibility of these types of incoherence arising from misclassification is recognised from the opposing standpoint by some proponents of the theory of unjust enrichment; indeed, the theory of unjust enrichment was thought to be the solution to the same problem of incoherence in the traditional common law. More recently, it has been argued that incoherence, in the form of fragmentation of the law of unjust enrichment, will result from any approach inconsistent with the theory of unjust enrichment that treats claims arising from the receipt of a benefit as property-based claims, or contractual claims, or claims in some other justificatory category.[59] As a defence of the theory of unjust enrichment, this is question-begging, because it simply assumes that there is a principle of unjust enrichment that can provide a common basis for a body of claims arising from the receipt of a benefit.

False Differentiation and other Forms of Incoherence in the Law of Contract

It was pointed out in chapter 4 that equity has sometimes developed doctrines that, although outside the common law of contract, are designed to give effect to agreements, and this has led to false differentiation. As the discussion above suggests, some so-called unjust enrichment claims based on failure of condition, such as the requested benefit claim and the 'pre-contractual' claim, also appear to be based on agreement and to involve false differentiation in the same way. As suggested above, the idea that these are claims based on unjust enrichment may have been due to the misconception that a contract claim must be a claim for expectation damages, and that it must be based on a wrong.[60] But coherence requires that, if their basis lies in the principle that agreements should be kept, these claims should be recognised through the development of the law of contract, as discussed in connection with equity.[61] It is inconsistent for a court to insist that it is not open to it to change well-established rules

---

[59] LD Smith, 'Unjust Enrichment, Property, and the Structure of Trusts' (2000) 116 *Law Quarterly Review* 412, 419; Dagan, above n 53, at 35.

[60] Above p 214,

[61] See above, p 119.

of contract in order to recognise a new claim based on agreement, and then to proceed to allow the claim under a different name. This is simply subversion of contract law.[62]

The same argument applies even more obviously to the claims mentioned above for the recovery of a payment under a contract or for reasonable payment for work done under a contract when the contract terminates early. If, as argued above, these are really contractual reliance claims, treating them as unjust enrichment claims again involves false differentiation and subversion of contract law. In particular, the unjust enrichment analysis is liable to subvert the law of contract by disturbing the contractual allocation of risk. Say C is to do work for D under a contract, and the contract specifies a fixed price. This means that C bears the risk that the costs of carrying out the work will differ from what he estimated when the contract was made, as a result of a change of circumstances or misjudgment. If the contract terminates before completion as a result of frustration or breach, and C makes a claim for reasonable payment for the work he has done so far, the measure of the claim should be in proportion to the price of the work under the contract; it should not be increased relative to the contractual price to reflect the fact that C's costs were greater than expected, or that the market rate for the work in question has gone up since the contract was made. This would be to undo the allocation of risk in the contract. If C is allowed such a claim, the effect is to relieve him of the consequences of a contract that has turned out to be a bad one for him.[63] This is again just the application of the monist principle, which carries over the contractual allocation of risk into the remedial relation.[64]

The objection of a supporter of the theory of unjust enrichment may be that unjust enrichment is a separate justificatory category and has equal standing with contract, and upsetting the contractual

[62] Above p 8. A similar case is where a contract is said to be unenforceable for failure to comply with the formality requirements, and then a claim is allowed anyway, and there is no underlying justification for such a claim apart from the principle that the agreement should be enforced: a good example in my view is *Pavey & Matthews v Paul* (1988) 162 CLR 221: see Jaffey, above n 6, at 114.

[63] See the famous *Boomer v Muir* 1933 24 P 2d 570; Burrows, above n 5, at 341. One might object that a party in breach of contract is a wrongdoer and should not be able to rely on the contractual allocation of risk. Generally non-performance of a contract is not characterised as a wrong, as discussed in ch 2, but this is surely a purely contractual matter.

[64] It is this that lies behind the established rule that C should never be able to claim more than the expectation measure of damages, for example where C makes a claim for his reliance loss in respect of expenditure incurred under the contract that exceeds the expectation measure: see eg *C&P Haulage v Middleton* [1983] 1 WLR 1461.

allocation of risk is simply the price that has to be paid for giving effect to the principle of unjust enrichment. Once again, whether this is plausible can be assessed only if the principle of unjust enrichment can be formulated, so that one can begin to consider how to deal with a clash between this principle and contract. It is commonly said, instead, that there is no conflict between contract and unjust enrichment because the unjust enrichment claim arises after the contract has terminated and so cannot be inconsistent with it or subvert it.[65] This argument is sensitive to the subversion argument, but it surely cannot be right. Most ordinary contract claims arise once the contract has terminated. Contract law does not cease to apply after termination: to the contrary, in accordance with the monist principle the remedial contractual relation arises directly from the primary relation to give effect to it as far as is possible in the circumstances. It is a case of the dualist fallacy to say that after termination the contract and contract law are irrelevant and the appropriate remedy is an entirely separate issue to be considered independently of the contract.

Sometimes proponents of the theory of unjust enrichment say instead that although the claim is an unjust enrichment claim, the contract price is relevant in measuring the benefit received by D for the purposes of determining the measure of the claim, because it is evidence of how D valued the benefit.[66] As a result, although the claim is not contractual, it will not disturb the contractual allocation of risk. But it is not clear why a genuine valuation of the benefit for the purposes of a non-contractual unjust enrichment claim should be governed or constrained by the terms of the contract. The actual value of the benefit is not necessarily the same as the value implicit in the terms of the contract. The adoption of this contractual limitation on the unjust enrichment claim really amounts to a tacit concession that the claim is essentially contractual.

The attempt to explain contractual claims in terms of unjust enrichment forces the law into the use of fictions. For example, it appears that there can be a claim for reasonable payment for work done by C under the contract, even though no benefit actually reached D. This is easily understood as a contractual reliance claim, but the attempt to explain it as an unjust enrichment claim involves

---

[65] eg, Burrows, above n 5, at 323.
[66] See Burrows, ibid, 346; A Skelton, *Restitution and Contract* (Oxford, Mansfield Press, 1998).

the fiction of deeming work done by C to be a benefit to D.[67] More generally, it is a fiction that contractual performance is made conditionally, as the failure of basis approach holds.[68] A contract may provide, explicitly or implicitly, that a payment under it is conditional, so that it is repayable in certain circumstances, but if so the claim for repayment is contractual. Generally a payment made under a contract is not conditional; it is an unconditional, outright payment, made under a contract that provides for a reciprocal performance. When a claim arises it is because the termination of the contract generates a claim by virtue of the rules of contract law (in my view, to protect reliance). Furthermore, where C has a claim for reasonable payment for work done under the contract, the work is said to have been done conditionally and so must be returned. But again it is a fiction to treat work as something that can be transferred and then returned in the way that property can. (I will come back to this fiction again.) These fictions are contrived, like other fictions, to force the claim into a framework that is at odds with its true justification. They are signs of a spurious justificatory category.

False Differentiation in the Law of Property

The relationship between property and unjust enrichment is even more problematic, because there is more controversy and confusion about the nature of property and about whether it is a justificatory category at all. With respect to the recovery of invalid transfers, as discussed in chapter 6 historically there were claims in equity and in quasi-contract and tort at common law. This meant (quite apart from the problems that affected these approaches individually) that there was false differentiation because issues that were fundamentally the same were treated in these different ways in different contexts. It also became obvious in due course that formulating these claims in these various ways obscures their basis in principle, certainly in the case of the fictional implied contract, but also where the claims were treated as a matter of equity and tort.[69] The theory of unjust enrichment was thought to be the solution to these problems. It would fill the theoretical vacuum with a fundamental principle and a justificatory

---

[67] This is the problem traditionally associated with *Planché v Colburn* (1831) 8 Bing 14; Birks, above n 5, at 126.

[68] The fiction led to a clear inconsistency in *Roxborough v Rothmans of Pall Mall Austriala* (2001) 208 CLR 516, as discussed in Jaffey, above n 6.

[69] Above p 185.

category of unjust enrichment, and eliminate the false differentiation between claims of the same sort.[70] But it is property as a justificatory category that was missing, not unjust enrichment or restitution. One problem in characterising these claims as property-based may have been the misconception that abstract value or money cannot be the object of property rights; another problem may have been the misconception that the personal restitutionary claim at common law cannot be property-based. These points were considered in chapter 3.[71]

Proponents of the theory of unjust enrichment vary in their under-standing of property. One view seems to be that there is no such thing as a 'property-based' claim, and that all claims in the nature of the claim to recover an invalid transfer are unjust enrichment claims. But mostly it seems to be accepted that there are property-based claims, and there-fore that there is an important distinction in the law of invalid transfers between property-based claims and unjust enrichment claims.[72] The problem on this understanding is to discern exactly what the distinc-tion is. With respect to the law of equity and the equitable proprietary claim, sometimes it is thought that a claim in respect of the original asset transferred is a property-based claim, but a claim in respect of a substitute asset under the transactional theory of tracing must be an unjust enrichment claim.[73] This argument was considered and rejected in chapter 6,[74] and it was pointed out that the argument was based on a misunderstanding of tracing and a failure to appreciate that the object of the equitable proprietary claim is abstract value.[75] With respect to the common law restitutionary claim, it is sometimes said that, if title passes, the claim cannot be a property-based claim and must be an unjust enrichment claim, whereas if title does not pass the claim can be a property-based claim.[76] Again this argument was rejected in chapters

---

[70] I have expressed this in my terminology, but I understand it to reflect the aims and understanding of many supporters of the theory of unjust enrichment.

[71] Above p 93.

[72] See eg Burrows, above n 5, at 60; D Fox, 'Legal Title as a Ground of Restitutionary Liability' [2000] *Restitution Law Review* 465; WJ Swadling, 'A Claim in Restitution' [1996] *Lloyds Maritime and Commercial Law Quarterly* 63. The discussion appears to me to conflate the distinctions between personal and proprietary and property-based and restitution or unjust enrichment conceived as the justificatory basis for a claim.

[73] eg, LD Smith, *The Law of Tracing* (Oxford, Clarendon Press, OUP, 1997) 300.

[74] Above p 159.

[75] The question whether an equitable proprietary claim is a claim in property law or unjust enrichment was thought to arise in *Macmillan v Bishopsgate* [1995] 3 All ER 747.

[76] Above p 97.

3 and 6.[77] The extensive debate in the literature on the supposed distinction between unjust enrichment claims and property-based claims is inconclusive and increasingly intricate, and on the view taken here this is not surprising because there is really no distinction to be found.

In the law of invalid transfers, there is more than one source of false differentiation. There is historically the division between law and equity and at common law between the conventional treatment of money and goods, and nowadays there is the false differentiation resulting from the division between property and unjust enrichment as justificatory categories. False differentiation arises in connection with various issues considered in earlier chapters, such as the measure of recovery, change of position, tracing, bona fide purchase, and on the question whether the claim should be personal or proprietary. If a coherent law of invalid transfers is to develop, it is crucial that property should be recognised as a justificatory category. Two important steps to achieving this are the substantive fusion of law and equity and the rejection of the theory of unjust enrichment, as discussed in chapter 6.[78]

A similar problem arises in connection with unauthorised use claims in respect of intellectual property as mentioned in chapter 3.[79] It is sometimes suggested that where D has exploited C's reputation for commercial purposes, D has been unjustly enriched and should be required to pay a reasonable licence fee to C.[80] Such a claim may in the end be justified, but it makes sense only as a claim in respect of the unauthorised use of property, on the basis that C owns his reputation as a form of intellectual property, not as a claim based on a supposed principle of unjust enrichment. Recognising a claim under the label of unjust enrichment evades and conceals the crucial question, which is whether reputation is indeed an object of property, and arguably it thereby subverts an existing rule of property law, that new forms of intellectual property are recognised only by statute.[81]

---

[77] With respect to the common law, *Lipkin Gorman v Karpnale* is often said to be the case that marked the formal recognition of the principle of unjust enrichment: see P Birks 'The English Recognition of Unjust Enrichment' [1991] *Lloyds Maritime and Commercial Law Quarterly* 330. But some commentators consider that it involves a property-based claim: see Swadling, above n 72.

[78] Above p 185.

[79] Above p 109.

[80] This is discussed in H Carty, 'Advertising, Publicity and English Law' (2004) 3 *Intellectual Property Quarterly* 209.

[81] Above p 85.

False Assimilation of Transfer and Exchange

In connection with benefits conferred by C on D, as pointed out above there is a distinction between a transfer from C to D and the conferral of a benefit on D by the supply of work or labour by C. A transfer relates to a thing that is separate from C and D and is capable of moving from C to D and back again: in other words, a transfer relates to an object of property. This is the separability condition for objects of property discussed in chapter 3.[82] By contrast, work or labour is not a thing existing separately from a person; it is not capable of being an object of property, which can be owned or transferred and recovered. It can only be expended by C in the conferral of a benefit on D. If C has a claim in respect of the benefit conferred through the labour, it is not a claim to recover a transfer, but a claim for reasonable payment for work done. The claim serves to complete an exchange of work or benefit for payment, not to recover a transfer. The same is true of a claim for payment for the unauthorised use of property. This is an exchange of payment for use, not the recovery of property transferred.

Because it focuses on the receipt of a benefit and the legal position after the receipt, the theory of unjust enrichment tends to disregard the position before that and so it tends to treat all claims in respect of a benefit as claims to recover a transfer.[83] By conflating the recovery of transfers and payment for work done in conferring a benefit, the theory of unjust enrichment in effect treats labour as property. This is apparent in Gordley's formulation of the principle of unjust enrichment, which was mentioned above.[84] According to Gordley, unjust enrichment is enrichment derived by D from resources to which C has the exclusive right. This seems to be simply a statement of a primary right of ownership, expressed from a remedial point of view in terms of a claim arising from it. It amounts to treating unjust enrichment as the remedial part of property law.[85] But Gordley takes the view that 'resources' include labour—in fact the controversial cases he discusses all relate to labour—so the provision of labour is treated

---

[82] Above p 82.

[83] Historically, these remedies were usually distinct: at common law money had and received to recover a money transfer, *quantum meruit* or *quantum valebat* for payment for goods or services.

[84] Gordley, above n 40-, at 423–26.

[85] Cf unjust enrichment as 'reversing invalid transfers', above p 221.

as a transfer that can be reversed. Thus there is a false assimilation of property-based and non-property-based claims.[86]

As a result of this false assimilation, the unjust enrichment literature treats the difference between transfers of property and supposed transfers of labour or use-value as merely a factual or evidential matter concerning ease of measurement, the value of a supposed transfer of labour or use-value being more difficult to measure that the value of a transfer of property.[87] As I said above, this is a fiction, and the artificial problems created by it have obscured and distorted the issues in the literature on this issue.[88]

False Assimilation in 'Restitution for Wrongs'

Some unjust enrichment writers recognise a category of 'restitution for wrongs',[89] where C has a claim to recover a benefit that D has obtained through a wrong against C. Most examples given of restitution for a wrong are cases of disgorgement, but the category is also commonly taken to include the use claim, where C has a claim for reasonable payment for the unauthorised use by D of C's property. These are often regarded as two types or measures of restitutionary or benefit-based remedy arising from a wrong: in the case of disgorgement, C recovers the full measure of the benefit, whereas in the case of the use claim C recovers a proportion of the benefit.[90] The expression 'restitutionary damages' is often used to refer to the reasonable payment remedy.[91] But, as discussed in chapter 3,[92] the use claim and disgorgement are completely different from each other. They are certainly not merely different versions or measures of a certain type of remedy for a wrong.[93] Disgorgement is not a remedy at all in the strict sense, because it is not designed to correct the wrong for the

---

[86] In particular, the basis of a claim by C against D in respect of work done to the benefit of D in the absence of a contract—referred to above, p 215, as a claim in respect of non-contractual exchange—is on Gordley's approach a claim to recover a transfer of labour.

[87] eg, Burrows, above n 5, at 16; P Birks, 'In Defence of Free Acceptance' in A Burrows (ed), *Essays on the Law of Restitution* (Oxford, Clarendon Press, 1991) 129.

[88] See also above, at n 20.

[89] Widely adopted from Birks, above n 5, at 313.

[90] See eg Burrows, above n 5; J Edelman, *Gain-Based Damages* (Oxford, Hart Publishing, 2002) ch 3.

[91] See above p 99.

[92] Above p 101.

[93] Historically they had different forms. The use claim took the form of a claim for damages, in modern times described as restitutionary damages, and in land law 'mesne' damages; disgorgement was an account of profits or constructive trust in equity or exemplary damages at common law.

benefit of C. The availability of disgorgement and the availability of the use claim are separate issues that in recent years have been compressed into a single debate on the question which types of wrong should attract a remedy of 'restitution for wrongs', and this has obstructed understanding of both of them.[94] The debate has also become associated with controversy over unjust enrichment and property, partly because of the link between the use claim and trespass, but also because disgorgement is sometimes effected by way of a constructive trust, as discussed further in chapter 9.

BIRKS'S CLASSIFICATION OF UNJUST ENRICHMENT AND PRIVATE LAW

Birks's Scheme of Classification and his Concept of Unjust Enrichment

The theory of unjust enrichment depends on showing that there is a justificatory category of unjust enrichment, based on a general principle of unjust enrichment. Most proponents of the theory refer expressly to such a principle, though it may not be articulated. But the most prominent modern advocate of the theory of unjust enrichment is Birks, and he appears to adopt a quite different approach: it appears that he does not rely on such a principle at all.[95] This is a striking difference between Birks and other proponents of the theory, though it has attracted surprisingly little attention.

Birks developed an influential scheme of classification of 'causative events', meaning events that create or alter legal rights or relations.[96] In chapter 1 and later chapters I have generally taken the elements of a legal classification to be 'claims' rather than causative events. For most purposes it does not seem important which approach is preferred. Some causative events generate a claim out of a primary relation: such a causative event is a cause of action, for example a tort or breach of contract. Some causative events establish or alter a primary relation, for example the making of a contract, or a change of circumstances that gives rise to a duty of care in tort. Generally using

---

[94] There is also the case where a wrong by D causes a transfer from C to D and C makes a claim to recover the transfer based on the wrong. This is a case where a personal claim for specific restitution is the means of effecting compensation for a wrong. Sometimes this is described as a claim for 'restitutionary damages': eg Edelman, above n 90, at 66. This is unhelpful because this type of case is distinct from both the use claim and disgorgement. This type of case is sometimes discussed in connection with the old doctrine of 'waiver of tort', as to which see further Jaffey, above n 6, at 367–73.

[95] Birks, above n 5, at 22–25; Birks, above n 50.

[96] Birks, above n 5, ch II; Birks, above n 50.

claims or causative events as the elements of the classification are equivalent ways of making the same distinctions concerning categories or departments of the law.[97]

One problem with Birks's scheme is that the element to be classified is confused with the criterion of classification. In presenting his scheme as a classification of causative events, Birks seems to suggest that this reveals the criterion of the classification as opposed to the elements to be classified. (It must be a classification *of* causative events, not a classification *by* causative event.) Thus it is not clear how causative events are being classified.[98] I have referred to various types of classification, including classification by reference to justification, remedy and modality. These types of classification were formulated with respect to claims but can equally be applied to causative events. For example, classifying by reference to the type of justification, one would have a contract category of causative events, which would include offers, acceptances, breaches of contract and frustrating events: these are events defined in terms of their significance under the rules of contract law. Similarly the tort category of causative events would include breaches of a duty of care, tortious harms, waivers of a duty of care, and events that generate or change the content of a duty of care in tort.[99] Also, at least with respect to events that are causes of action, one can classify in terms of the remedy that will be available: a cause of action may give rise to a claim for compensation, or a claim for specific performance or an injunction, etc.

One could also have a classification of causative events by reference to modality. Modalities were explained in chapter 1 in terms of legal relations—right-duty relations, power-liability relations, etc, but they can also be expressed in terms of events, because there is a certain type of event that has legal effect by virtue of a certain modality of legal relation. For example, if an event is a breach of duty or a wrong it is an event that has significance by virtue of a right-duty relation. Similarly the exercise of a power is an event occurring by virtue of a power-liability relation. Thus a classification that has a

---

[97] Above p 2.

[98] There are two dimensions in the Birks classification, the second of which is classification by types of response. 'Causative event' seems to be used to refer to both the element of the classification and the criterion of the first dimension of the classification. With respect to the second dimension, if 'response' refers to a court-ordered measure or the right to it, it seems to make sense to classify causative events by response only with respect to causative events that are causes of action, ie causative events that generate claims.

[99] Cf above p 196.

category of breaches of duty or wrongs, and a category of exercises of a power, is a classification of causative events by modality.

The main types of causative event identified by Birks in his scheme are Consents, Wrongs and Unjust Enrichments. The question is, what sort of classification is this? There does not seem to be any explicit statement of the criterion behind this classification—whether it is supposed to be a classification by justification, or by modality or by some other criterion. Some commentators equate Consents and Wrongs with contract and tort, implying (as I understand these categories) that Birks's classification is a classification by justificatory category. But there are indications that the classification is better understood as a classification by modality. 'Wrong' is obviously open to this interpretation; and a breach of contract, which is an event in the justificatory category of contract, is for Birks in the category of Wrongs, not the category of Consents. Also, for Birks not only offers and acceptances, but transfers of property and the making of wills are examples of Consents, though the last two are not concerned with making and enforcing agreements and cannot be understood as matters of contract; what unites these examples of Consents is that they are examples of exercises of a legal power, or in other words they all arise out of power-liability relations. This interpretation of the classification as a classification by reference to modality gains support from the fact that Birks does not at any point invoke general principles to explain any of the categories.

For present purposes, what is particularly noteworthy is the absence of any reference to a general principle, or any consideration of the nature of the justification for a claim, in connection with the category of Unjust Enrichments in Birks's scheme.[100] Birks defines the category by reference to what he describes as the 'core case' of unjust enrichment—the case that he takes to be an indisputable example. This is the case of a mistaken payment, where C has a claim to recover a sum mistakenly paid to the D (which I have explained above as a property-based claim). Birks defines his category of unjust enrichment as comprising all cases that are 'materially identical' to this core case.[101] This is not sufficient to define a category, however, because there are many different criteria according to which other cases might be taken to be identical to or different from this core case. Birks identifies the following three defining features from which to

---

[100] In other work he deprecates the idea of an underlying principle of unjust enrichment as the basis of a category of law: above n-, at 22–25.

[101] Birks, above n 50, at 3.

generalise from the core case to the category of unjust enrichment[102]: first, that D received a benefit; secondly, that the benefit was received 'at C's expense'[103]; and, thirdly, that there is a reason why it would be unjust for D to retain the benefit. These form the standard three-stage framework for unjust enrichment.[104]

The procedure of constructing a framework for a category by analogy from a core case looks like an exercise in analogical reasoning to form a justificatory category. But the procedure makes no explicit reference to a principle or type of justification. As discussed above, the 'unjust' requirement does not supply a principle or justification: to the contrary the effect is explicitly to leave open the nature of the justification. Thus the category simply brings together all claims that arise from the receipt of a benefit,[105] and it leaves open whether this is a genuine or a spurious justificatory category. It certainly does not establish that it is a genuine justificatory category. As suggested above, it may be that Birks's understanding of the category was that it is something in the nature of a category of modality.

However, Birks's whole project, the theory of unjust enrichment as described above, requires that there be a true justificatory category of unjust enrichment. Only such a category can play the role in analogical reasoning that is required of it. There is a deep-seated conflict between Birks's aim of reorganising the common law by analogical reasoning to recognise a category of unjust enrichment, and his insistence on trying to formulate the category of unjust enrichment without reference to any underlying principle or type of justification. The latter aspect of his thinking reflects the classic error of formalism or mechanical jurisprudence,[106] that unsettled law and controversial cases can be resolved purely by conceptual analysis, including the formulation of the law using the correct normative types or modalities by way of Hohfeldian analysis. Normally this sort of approach is thought to be completely inimical to the judicial development of the law by analogical reasoning, certainly in the dramatic way required by the theory of unjust enrichment.

---

[102] Ibid, 9–10.

[103] It seems that if there is a good justifying reason for the claim it will necessarily satisfy this condition.

[104] Birks extends this to 'five stage framework' that it is unnecessary to discuss here: above n 50, at 34.

[105] Birks excludes some such claims but the exclusions seem to be quite ad hoc; see ibid 22–24.

[106] Above p 4.

In my view, unjust enrichments, meaning benefits whose receipt generates a claim, form neither a justificatory category nor a category of modality. They do not form a justificatory category because there is nothing in the nature of a principle of unjust enrichment that could account for such a category. Neither do unjust enrichment claims in the above sense form a category by modality. They are all primary liability claims, but there are other primary right liability claims that are not unjust enrichment claims. As I have argued earlier, enrichment, or the receipt of a benefit, is simply an event or circumstance that can be relevant to a claim in different ways in different situations by virtue of different general principles, in the same way as 'reliance' or 'loss', and so a claim arising from a benefit can be a claim in property law or contract law or another justificatory category.

The Role of Property in Birks's Scheme

According to Birks, it makes no sense to refer to claims based on property or in the category of property.[107] This is understandable in the light of his understanding of property law: he regards it as the law of *in rem* rights in the Hohfeldian sense, that is to say, rights good against an indefinite class of people, to be contrasted with *in personam* rights that are good against one or a limited number of others.[108] In this sense, as discussed in chapter 3, property law is a category of modality, not a justificatory category,[109] and there are no property-based claims in the sense that there are contractual or tortious claims. In his understanding of property law, Birks thus follows Hohfeld, and like Hohfeld he marginalises property law as a result.[110] As pointed out in chapter 3, although this concept of *in rem* rights is useful and important, it is not helpful to equate it with the law of property. The law of property is a justificatory category based on the private property principle, and this is why it is indeed right to say that there are property-based claims.

In fact, Birks does not express his objection to the idea of property-based claims in this way. His objection is that a claim arises from a causative event and, whereas an unjust enrichment is an event (meaning the provision or receipt of a benefit rather than the reme-

---

[107] Birks, above n 50, ch 2.

[108] Birks, ibid. Cf LD Smith, *The Law of Tracing* (Oxford, Clarendon Press, OUP, 1997).

[109] Above p 92.

[110] Birks uses 'events' as the element of classification and Hohfeld 'rights' or 'relations'. Hohfeld's work does not have the internal conflict in Birks because he is not concerned with trying to reorganise the law through analogical reasoning.

dial legal relation following it), 'property is not an event'.[111] It is true that a claim arises from an event, though it is important to remember that a claim arises from an event by virtue of a primary relation. In the justificatory category of property, ownership of property is a primary relation, and by virtue of it there are the 'property events'—events that trigger property-based claims—of invalid transfers and unauthorised uses. To say that there cannot be claims in property because property is not an event is equivalent to saying that that there cannot be claims in tort or contract because a duty of care in tort is not an event and a subsisting contract is not an event, disregarding the events of a tort or a breach of contract that can occur by virtue of these primary relations.

CONCLUSION: THE FALLACY OF UNJUST ENRICHMENT

The theory of unjust enrichment depends on the assumption that there is a general principle that provides the basis for a justificatory category of unjust enrichment. Unfortunately for supporters of the theory, no plausible candidate for such a principle is to be found in the considerable academic literature. The theory has led to the recognition of a spurious justificatory category. Part of the reason for the development is the mistaken assumption that all claims for the remedy of restitution—used widely to mean the recovery of property, or payment for a benefit, or the removal of a benefit—must have a common basis, which is an example of the remedy-as-justification fallacy. Another factor that has hindered the examination of the basis of claims arising from the receipt of a benefit is the failure to recognise the primary liability relation from which such a claim arises. There are other plausible ways of explaining how claims can arise from the receipt of a benefit, including in property law and contract law. The theory of unjust enrichment is damaging to the proper understanding of benefit-based claims in these categories, and generally is a source of incoherence in private law.

---

[111] See P Birks, 'Property and Unjust Enrichment: Categorical Truths' [1997] *NZ Law Review* 623.

9

Constructive Trusts

The constructive trust differs from the express trust in arising 'by operation of law',[1] and not as a result of a deliberate act of a settlor intending to create a trust. The usual textbook account consists of a series of sub-headings dealing with different types of situation, and there is no generally accepted principle or formula that can unify the various cases and provide a guide for when a constructive trust should be awarded, though various theories have been proposed.[2] This controversy involves some of the problems discussed in earlier chapters, and some of the arguments of previous chapters can be brought to bear on it.

INVALID TRANSFERS OF PROPERTY

Where a fiduciary or trustee makes a transfer in breach of duty, the beneficiary or principal C, whose beneficial property has been transferred, has an equitable proprietary claim against the recipient D, if D is not a bona fide purchaser. C's equitable proprietary claim is a right of beneficial ownership of the property transferred or its traceable proceeds, and D has a legal or control title over the property.[3] The claim arises in accordance with the monist principle from C's primary right of ownership of the property transferred, by virtue of the invalidity of the transfer. Traditionally, the equitable proprietary claim has arisen only from a breach of trust or fiduciary duty, not from other types of invalid transfer; but in principle, it should arise from any invalid transfer, and transfers in breach of trust or fiduciary duty are

---

[1] It is 'constructive' in the sense that it is a 'deemed' trust rather than a true, express trust.
[2] See eg S Gardner, *An Introduction to the Law of Trusts* (Oxford, OUP, 2nd edn, 2003) 119.
[3] Above p 157.

simply the types of invalid transfer that have always been dealt with in equity.[4] Also, it is not the wrongful character of the breach of duty by the trustee or fiduciary that renders the transfer invalid and generates the claim, but the fact that the transfer was beyond his power.[5]

It is generally said that there is a constructive trust in this situation. This should be understood to refer to the separation of title arising from the invalid transfer, by which D has the legal or control title and C the beneficial ownership of the property. However, there are a couple of points of difficulty here. First, in some circumstances it appears that a proprietary claim arising from an invalid transfer has been described as a resulting trust rather than a constructive trust. 'Resulting trust' seems apt, since a resulting trust is generally understood as a trust in which the beneficial ownership is with the original owner of property transferred, the expression itself being derived from the Latin expression for 'jumping back'.[6] One might infer that this is an example of both a resulting trust and a constructive trust, but resulting and constructive trusts are usually regarded as mutually exclusive categories. I will persist with the expression 'constructive trust'—indeed, in my view, this is the standard case of a constructive trust—and come back to this issue below in a brief discussion of resulting trusts.

Secondly, sometimes it is said that in this type of situation there is no constructive trust until D becomes aware, or ought to be aware, that the transfer was invalid, which means, on the analysis suggested in chapter 7, that there is a constructive trust only once D has become subject to a duty in tort in respect of the property transferred or its surviving value, which is the basis of the claim for knowing receipt. Before this, although D is subject to an equitable proprietary claim, it is wrong, on this view, to say that there is a constructive trust.[7] This understanding is supported by the traditional idea that the trust depends on the 'conscience' of the defendant having been affected.[8] Similarly it is supported by the idea that there cannot be a trust without a trustee, and that a recipient cannot be described as a trustee if he has no duties in respect of the property.[9]

---

[4] Above p 157.

[5] Above p 157.

[6] 'Resalire'; P Birks, *An Introduction to the Law of Restitution* (Oxford, Clarendon Press, OUP, rev edn, 1989) 62.

[7] *Re Montagu* [1987] Ch 264, 285, per Megarry VC; *Westdeutsche Landesbank Girozentrale v Islington Borough Council* [1996] AC 669, 705, per Lord Browne-Wilkinson.

[8] *Westdeutsche*, ibid.

[9] *Re Montagu* [1987] Ch 264; *BCCI v Akindele* [2000] 3 WLR 1423.

This is a purely terminological dispute. An express trust has two dimensions, the property dimension and the contractual dimension, as explained in chapter 5. Following an invalid transfer, the equitable proprietary claim corresponds to the property dimension of the trust. Once the knowledge condition has been satisfied, the recipient becomes subject to a duty in tort in respect of the property. This is the tort dimension of the constructive trust. The duty in tort is analogous to but weaker than the duty arising in the contractual dimension of an express trust. The issue is whether 'constructive trust' is correctly used to refer to the property dimension on its own, or only to the combination of the property dimension and the tort dimension. There seems no good reason to confine the usage to the latter. For most purposes it is the property dimension of the trust that is important. But what is more important is the proper analysis of the trust and the constructive trust in terms of their separate dimensions in different justificatory categories.

The constructive trust, meaning the equitable proprietary claim, is a remedial relation. It arises from the primary right of ownership in accordance with the monist principle by virtue of an invalid transfer; thus it corrects an injustice, as defined by the primary relation. Unfortunately, as discussed in chapter 6, the description of the constructive trust as remedial is liable to be misunderstood to mean that no trust arises until the court makes a decision, in the exercise of a discretion, to impose one, which is the understanding behind what I described as the US remedial constructive trust. This approach is contrary to the monist principle and it was rejected in chapter 6.[10]

Liability in knowing receipt is often described as a liability 'as a constructive trustee'.[11] As argued in chapter 7, it is best understood as based on a breach of the duty in tort incurred by the recipient of an invalid transfer not to dispose of or consume the property received. This duty constitutes one dimension of the constructive trust, and in this sense the claim arises in connection with a constructive trust. But the knowing receipt claim is not itself the assertion of a constructive trust; it is not a proprietary claim. Strictly speaking, the claim is for compensation, though in the conventional form this is disguised in the form of a liability to account that combines the compensation claim with a claim for the surviving value of

---

[10] Above p 177.
[11] PH Pettit, *Equity and the Law of Trusts* (Oxford, OUP, 10th edn, 2006) 151; *Barnes v Addy* (1874) 9 Ch App 244.

an invalid transfer.[12] The claim for knowing or dishonest assistance is also traditionally understood in terms of constructive trusteeship, and it is also a wrong-based claim, not the assertion of a constructive trust or proprietary claim. It arises against an accessory of a trustee or fiduciary who makes a transfer of trust property in breach of duty.[13]

DISGORGEMENT

Disgorgement means the removal of a profit made through a wrong, by virtue of the principle that a wrongdoer should not profit from his wrongdoing.[14] Disgorgement is not strictly speaking a remedy, because its function is not to fulfil or satisfy a primary right of C's, but, like punishment, to promote the public interest in compliance with legal duties. Thus disgorgement should be distinguished from restitution, which is best used to refer to the reversal of a transfer from C to D in order to satisfy a primary right, for example an invalid transfer from C to D, as in the case of the equitable proprietary claim just considered. The expression 'disgorgement' is not a term of art in the law, but it is convenient to use it in this sense because there is no term in use that has exactly this meaning.

The closest thing to disgorgement at common law is punitive damages imposed on the ground of a profit motive, and this is controversial because of the 'procedural objection' discussed in chapter 2.[15] In equity, disgorgement is imposed by way of a constructive trust or account of profits in respect of wrongs traditionally dealt with in equity, including breach of fiduciary duty, breach of confidence, knowing assistance, and infringements of intellectual property. The principle that a wrongdoer should not be allowed to profit through his wrongdoing has been stated explicitly in this context.[16] In equity no concern seems to have been expressed over the procedural objection. In this respect there is a striking inconsistency with the common law. The reason for the approach in equity may be that the constructive trust and account of profits also operate as genuine remedies, as

---

[12] Above p 190.

[13] L Hoffmann, 'The Redundancy of Knowing Assistance' in P Birks, *The Frontiers of Liability* (Oxford, OUP, 1994) vol 1, 27; *Abou-Rahman v Abacha* [2006] EWCA Civ 1492.

[14] Above p 58.

[15] Above p 62.

[16] *Attorney-General for Hong Kong v Reid* [1994] 1 AC 324; *Attorney-General v Guardian Newspapers (no 2) (Spycatcher)* [1990] 1 AC 109.

in the case of the equitable proprietary claim and the claim for know-ing receipt, and in the case where a trustee or fiduciary is liable to account for receipts collected on behalf of the principal or benefi-ciary, and there is liable to be overlap between their role as genuine remedies and their role as disgorgement. This is also the reason why the expression 'disgorgement' cannot be simply equated with 'con-structive trust' or 'account of profits'.

One issue that has arisen in connection with disgorgement in equity is whether it should take effect by way of a constructive trust or an account of profits, ie as a proprietary claim or as a personal claim. A possible objection to the proprietary claim is that because disgorgement provides a windfall to C there is no reason why it should attract priority in D's bankruptcy.[17] Although it is also a wind-fall for D's creditors, possibly there is something to be said for using the windfall to mitigate the shortfall in the recovery for creditors rather than giving an out-and-out windfall to C,[18] especially since the creditors may have relied to some extent on the appearance of wealth created by the receipt.[19] The problem with effecting disgorgement by way of a personal claim is that the conventional measure of a per-sonal liability to account is the value of the benefit initially received by D, which excludes any consequential gains made by D by invest-ing it, whereas the measure of disgorgement should cover such con-sequential gains, since they are also benefits from the wrong. In the case of a proprietary claim, the tracing rules are applied to encompass consequential gains. This was the main reason why the proprietary claim was preferred in the leading modern case of *Attorney-General for Hong Kong v Reid*.[20] The limitation of the measure of the personal lia-bility to account to the value received, excluding any consequential gains, makes sense where, for example, D acts as C's agent to receive payments for him and to account to him for their value. But this does not of course provide any reason for excluding consequential gains in the case of disgorgement.[21]

---

[17] *Lister v Stubbs* (1890) 45 Ch D 1.

[18] One might want to go further and subordinate C's claim to the creditors' claims.

[19] Above p 175.

[20] [1994] 1 AC 324. According to Lord Templeman in *Reid*, at 336, the fiduciary has a duty to hand over the profit when he receives it, and this generates a proprietary claim according to the equitable maxim that equity regards as done what ought to be done. But this duty cannot in principle generate a proprietary claim, according to the monist prin-ciple.

[21] As suggested by Peter Birks: P Birks, *An Introduction to the Law of Restitution* (Clarendon Press, rev edn, 1989) 394.

In fact the problem here is that disgorgement is not a remedy in the strict sense at all, and it is not helpful to equate it with either a personal liability to account or a proprietary liability or constructive trust. It is not a remedial relation, but a non-remedial response, in the nature of confiscation, at C's instance and providing him with a windfall.[22]

Agreements to Take Property on Trust

An ordinary express trust arises from a valid transfer of property made for this purpose, which establishes the property dimension of the trust or separation of title, together with an agreement by the trustee to act as such, which establishes the contractual dimension of the trust (in the broad sense of contract discussed in chapter 5).[23] If the recipient of the transfer—the putative trustee—reneges on his agreement to act as trustee, there is still a valid express trust on the specified terms; either the recipient will be ordered to carry out the trust or he will be replaced by another trustee.[24]

A problem has arisen in connection with the formality requirement of evidence in writing for the creation of an express trust of land.[25] Say that C makes a transfer of land to D on trust, and D initially agrees to take on trust but then denies that he holds on trust, contending that the creation of the trust did not comply with the formality requirement. It appears that D still holds on trust.[26] This trust has sometimes been described as a constructive trust, because the formality requirement does not apply to constructive trusts, and this is taken to provide the explanation for why the trust exists notwithstanding the formality requirement.

---

[22] There are two sources of confusion with property that may have obscured the nature of disgorgement. First, it has been confused with the use claim in respect of the unauthorised use of property, under the head of 'restitution for wrongs': above p 235. And secondly, as just considered, it has been treated as a proprietary claim to catch consequential benefits through tracing.

[23] Above p 133.

[24] The recipient only takes beneficially if he is a bona fide purchaser. The contractual dimension of an express trust would go into suspense if there were an interregnum between trustees.

[25] S 52 Law of Property Act 1925.

[26] *Rochefoucauld v Boustead* [1897] 1 Ch 196; *Bannister v Bannister* [1948] 2 All ER 133.

But a trust cannot simply be labelled a constructive trust as a device to avoid the formality requirement; if there is no express trust, there must be some distinct basis for a constructive trust to arise instead. If the transfer was invalid,[27] there could be a constructive trust for the settlor C on the basis discussed above, but this is not how the position has been understood. If the trust arises by virtue of the transfer, exactly on the terms specified, it must be an express trust, not a constructive trust at all. This will be clear if the transfer was intended to create a trust for the benefit of a third party and the trust is enforced in favour of the third party. There is a question, of course, whether an express trust is really consistent with the statutory formality requirement. It is said that the statute cannot be used as an instrument of fraud and, if this is accepted as a principle of statutory construction, there can be no objection to the outcome.[28]

It is sometimes said that a constructive trust arises by virtue of D's unconsionability or fraud in invoking the formality requirement to deny the trust, having first agreed to take on trust. But if D acts unconscionably by trying to evade the trust, his unconscionability cannot explain why the trust binds him, since the trust necessarily precedes the unconscionability. Similarly, one might say that D acts unconscionably by reneging on his agreement to hold the property on trust, and the constructive trust arises as a remedy for this unconscionable conduct.[29] But again this cannot be the basis for a constructive trust. The implication is that no trust arises from the transfer itself, only from the agreement; but if no trust arose from the transfer to D, so that beneficial ownership passed to D, D's agreement to hold on trust would generate a trust only if it amounted to a declaration of himself as trustee. A simple breach of an agreement would not be capable, in accordance with the monist principle, of giving rise to a proprietary claim.[30] It could in principle account only for a personal claim for compensation. The better view is that if there is a trust it is an express trust arising to give effect to the intention behind the transfer.[31]

---

[27] eg, on the basis that there was a mistake concerning the legal effect of the transfer.

[28] Which appears to be the principle behind *Rochefoucauld v Boustead* [1897] 1 Ch 196.

[29] See eg B Macfarlane, 'Constructive Trusts Arising on a Receipt of Property *sub Conditione*' (2004) 120 *Law Quarterly Review* 667

[30] Above p 161.

[31] See eg Pettit, above n 11 at 96. The same arguments apply with respect to secret trusts in relation to the formality requirements for testamentary dispositions under the Wills Act 1837.

Protecting Contractual Rights against Third Parties

Sale Contracts

Where C has contracted to buy property from X, and the contract is specifically enforceable, X is said to hold the property on constructive trust. The basis for the constructive trust is the equitable maxim 'equity regards as done what ought to be done', by virtue of which it is said that beneficial ownership of the property passes to C, once X becomes subject to a duty to transfer title under the contract, ie from the time when he is liable to specific performance. The effect is that a contractual right is converted into a property right.[32]

Again, according to the monist principle there is no basis for a remedial property right to arise from a primary contractual right. Breach of the contract to transfer property should generate only a personal claim, for compensation or specific performance. Recognising a proprietary claim subverts the crucial distinction between an agreement and the transfer or grant of a property right. One consequence of recognising a property right in these circumstances is that C has a proprietary claim in X's bankruptcy if X goes bankrupt before transferring the property to C. There is surely no justification for this. Until X makes the transfer, the property should be available to X's creditors. This is the risk that C takes if he contracts to buy property but does not immediately take a transfer of it.[33]

A second consequence of recognising C to have beneficial ownership of the property is that he can recover the property from a third party D to whom X transfers the property in breach of the contract with C (unless D is a bona fide purchaser). Again it is difficult to justify such a claim on the basis of a property right of C's, but it may sometimes be justifiable for C to have a claim against D on the basis of D's complicity in X's breach of contract. If this is the true basis of the claim, it should in principle be, not a proprietary claim, but a personal claim for compensation, though it might often be appropriate for C's loss to be restored by way of an order of specific restitution,[34] and the distinction between a proprietary claim and a claim for specific restitution may not always be apparent.[35] On this approach,

---

[32] *Lysaght v Edwards* (1876) 2 Ch D 499; *Walsh v Lonsdale* (1882) 21 Ch D 9. This applies with respect to land but not all forms of property.

[33] For a possible justification, see S Gardner, above n 2, at 158.

[34] 'Specific restitution' is not really apt because the property is not being returned to C. The remedy of specific restitution has the advantage, as a form of compensatory remedy for a wrong, of avoiding the difficulties of quantifying the loss.

[35] Above p 163.

the link between C's claim for specific performance against X and C's claim against D is that if X is subject to specific performance he must have incurred a primary duty of performance of the contract (as opposed to a primary liability), so that it is wrongful for him to transfer to D,[36] and only then is it possible for D to be complicit in a wrong by X. Thus it seems doubtful whether there is really any basis for a constructive trust, in the sense of a proprietary claim, in this type of case.

Contractual Licences

An ostensibly similar type of case is where C has a contractual licence to use or reside in X's property, and X sells the property to a third party D. In this type of case, however, the contract is not intended to be the precursor to a transfer or grant of a property right to C. The contractual licence from X to allow C to use the property is the final arrangement intended. It is a contract governing the licence to use or reside in the property. There is no basis for saying that X has failed to carry out a duty to make a transfer or grant and that C should have a property right to give immediate effect to the duty that D has failed to perform. Thus the constructive trust doctrine that protects C's right to specific performance, based on the maxim that equity regards as done what ought to be done, cannot be invoked to protect C against D, a purchaser from X, in this situation.[37]

Nevertheless, in some cases of this sort the courts have held the third party D bound to respect C's contractual licence, by way of a constructive trust. It was suggested at one time that the contractual licence had itself acquired the status of a property right,[38] but now the position seems to be that the contractual licence is not itself a property right, but it will sometimes be protected by way of a constructive trust.[39] Again, however, it is more plausible to say that any claim against D can be satisfactorily explained without relying on C's having a property right. First, it may be explicable in terms of D's complicity in a wrong by X, as in the previous case, if the transfer to D puts X in breach of contract with C.

---

[36] Above p 48.

[37] C can enforce his right by injunction against X if the licence is irrevocable, but this does not mean that it is a property right, as pointed out in *National Provincial Bank v Ainsworth* [1965] AC 1175, 1253, per Lord Wilberforce.

[38] *DHN Food Distributors v Tower Hamlets* [1976] 1 WLR 852.

[39] *Ashburn Anstalt v Arnold* [1989] Ch 1.

Alternatively, sometimes D has given an undertaking to X to respect C's existing contractual right,[40] and then the true basis for C's claim may be that this contractual undertaking by D to X is enforceable by C, even though C was not party to it. On this basis, the supposed constructive trust is again merely a disguised way of effecting a personal claim against D,[41] which is here essentially a contractual claim, though not within the conventional law of contract. Such a claim may be in principle quite justifiable, though by allowing a claim based on agreement in equity while denying that such claim can arise as a matter of ordinary contract law it involves false differentiation.[42]

There is a further point to be made about this type of case. The idea of protecting a contractual licence as a property right by way of a constructive trust might suggest that the case law is beginning to replay the original transformation of the right of a beneficiary under an express trust from a personal contractual right into a property right.[43] This possibility draws attention to what may be an underlying problem in the contractual licences cases. In the development of the trust, it was clearly always the intention of the settlor that the beneficiary's right should be a property right. The problem originally was that there was no recognised property right of this sort—a beneficiary's property right under a trust—and as a result the right originally took the form of a mere personal right. Thus there was really a *numerus clausus* problem.[44] What was needed was the recognition of a new type of property right, to enable the settlor's intention to be realised, and this is what was eventually achieved when the trust in its modern form became established. In some of the contractual licence cases it may well have been that the grant of a property right, possibly something in the nature of a lease, though for a lifetime, would have been closer to the intention of the property owner X, and this intention was frustrated by the fact that the law does not recognise a property right of this sort.[45]

---

[40] *Lyus v Prowsa Developments* [1982] 2 All ER 953.

[41] See Gardner, above n 2, at 160–62.

[42] Macfarlane, above n 29, at 683–84, objects to the contractual analysis because of the problems of privity and uncertainty in contract law. He prefers a principle based on D's agreement in relation to property from which he benefits. But this also appears to be a particular application of the contractual principle, though outside the conventional law of contract.

[43] Above p 135.

[44] Above p 86.

[45] eg, *Binion v Evans* [1972] Ch 359. In the case of a specifically enforceable contract to transfer a property right considered above, the effect of the traditional doctrine is that making a contract amounts to the grant, or at least a conditional grant, of a property right in the form of beneficial ownership. It seems doubtful whether simply by making the

There are various complicated issues concerning the consequences of agreements involving property, as the discussion above shows. But the most important point is that in accordance with the monist principle the failure to perform an agreement should not in principle generate a proprietary claim. Thus the supposed examples of a constructive trust arising from an agreement, or from unconscionability or equitable fraud in the form of reneging on an agreement, are not best understood as true cases of a constructive trust. They are better regarded as personal claims, sometimes for specific restitution, or they may be disguised express trusts.

CONSTRUCTIVE TRUSTS OF MATRIMONIAL PROPERTY

In recent times much of the attention directed at constructive trusts has concerned the case of a married or cohabiting couple who are in dispute over the ownership of the matrimonial or quasi-matrimonial home. The basic rule of English law is set out in *Lloyds Bank v Rossett*[46]: there is a 'common intention constructive trust' if there was an 'agreement or common intention' between the two parties M and W that W should acquire a share of the property that would otherwise belong wholly to M, and W has acted to her detriment in reliance on the agreement or common intention.[47]

It is not entirely clear what is behind this rule. The doctrine might be taken to be essentially contractual, concerned with the principle that agreements should be carried out, though extended to agreements that might not be enforceable in the ordinary law of contract. Then this case might be thought to be related to the supposed agreement-based constructive trusts above, where reneging on an agreement is characterised as unconscionability or fraud in equity. But this principle cannot provide a satisfactory explanation of the doctrine, because in accordance with the monist principle an agreement cannot generate a proprietary claim.[48]

---

agreement the property owner intends to grant a property right in the form of beneficial ownership, but he may have an intention to grant a more limited property right having the effect only of securing the right to contractual performance vis-à-vis third parties.

[46] [1991] 1 AC 107.

[47] I will assume for convenience that the woman W acquires an interest in property that would otherwise be owned by the man M.

[48] Unless there is also an actual declaration of trust. In some cases the problem may be that there is an actual declaration that is unenforceable for lack of writing but this is not the usual problem addressed by the doctrine.

What then is the basis of the doctrine? It is relevant to point out a significant feature of the agreement. The agreement is not, it would appear, about what the parties will do—it is not an agreement to make a transfer or grant of a share of the property—but an agreement about what the legal position is, or what the parties can assume it is, in particular an agreement about the ownership of the property.[49] In my view, the basis for the doctrine is the principle that if W acts to her detriment in reliance on a reasonable assumption that she has a property right, she can be protected by the acquisition, by operation of law, of the property right. The doctrine is not an agreement-based or contractual doctrine, but a property law doctrine: it is an application of the principle discussed in chapter 3.[50] It is of the same sort as proprietary estoppel, bona fide purchase, adverse possession and prescription, which generate a property right in the absence of a valid transfer. Indeed it has often been suggested that the doctrine of the common intention constructive trust is essentially the same as the doctrine of proprietary estoppel.[51] In a typical proprietary estoppel case the property right in issue is a right in land, such as an easement, whereas in the case of the common intention constructive trust it is a beneficial share of property under a trust. Also, in the traditional proprietary estoppel cases there is said to be a representation rather than an agreement. On the suggested basis of the doctrine, what is relevant is not that there is an agreement as such, so that the principle that agreements are binding operates to generate a legal relation in contract, but that the circumstances justify W's reliance for the purposes of the property law principle.

In my view, this captures what is behind the *Rossett* approach. However, this principle cannot provide a satisfactory general basis for dealing with the allocation of the parties' wealth at the end of a matrimonial or quasi-matrimonial relationship. It seems fair to say that in such a relationship there is a mutual responsibility for support, and it is this that provides the moral basis for the right to maintenance and to a share of the wealth at the end of the relationship, and lies behind the modern statutory matrimonial jurisdiction to allocate property on divorce.[52] Outside the statutory jurisdiction, the common law continues to apply the narrower property law doctrine in

---

[49] Though this might be better described as an understanding than a common intention.
[50] Above p 87.
[51] *Oxley v Hiscock* [2004] 3 All ER 703.
[52] Matrimonial Causes Act 1973, s 24.

Rossett,[53] which sometimes appears inadequate because it cannot take account of considerations relevant to the broader approach.[54]

The broader approach is not based on a property law principle and it should not generate proprietary claims in the house, though the wealth of the parties will of course be relevant to the measure of the claim. It should generate personal claims against the other party, for continuing maintenance or a lump sum payment. This is indeed the effect of the statutory matrimonial jurisdiction. Through his famous 'new model constructive trust', Lord Denning sought to establish a discretion to divide the parties' property between them according to what was fair and just in the light of all the circumstances.[55] This must presumably be based on something in the nature of the broader approach based on a mutual responsibility for support; the problem was that it was understood and operated as a property law doctrine that generated property rights.[56]

WHAT IS A CONSTRUCTIVE TRUST?

Types of Constructive Trust

To summarise the discussion above, there are a number of distinct types of case that have been treated as examples of a constructive trust. There are, first, what are in my view the genuine cases of constructive trust, involving a proprietary claim or property dimension of a trust. There are two such cases. The first is where C has a proprietary claim against D as a result of an invalid transfer of property from C to D. As argued above, this should arise whenever there is an invalid transfer, but conventionally it arises only where the invalid transfer arises from a breach of trust or fiduciary duty. The second is where C acts in reliance on the assumption that he is entitled to a share of beneficial ownership under a trust. This is the doctrine of the

---

[53] Where the parties are not married, and where the issue arises of W's share as against a third party.

[54] Under the common intention constructive trust doctrine it is not enough to have an understanding that the property is intended to be the family home, because this is not an understanding about ownership: *Lloyds Bank v Rossett* [1991] 1 AC 107, 130, per Lord Bridge. Sometimes, conversely, the doctrine appears to be applied more broadly than can be easily reconciled with the underlying principle. See Gardner, above n 2, at 165.

[55] *Hussey v Palmer* [1972] 1 WLR 1338.

[56] Below p 257. The way to allow for a discretion to allocate the parties' wealth between them that also prevails over third party interests is through a system of common or family property.

common intention constructive trust. It is a variant of proprietary estoppel, which is itself one of a number of related doctrines that generate a property right from reliance on the assumption of a property right in different types of situation.[57]

These two cases of constructive trust fall in the justificatory category of property, and are ultimately based on the private property principle explained in chapter 3. In the first type of case, C is the original owner who recovers property invalidly transferred. In second type of case, C acquires a property right despite the absence of a valid transfer or grant from the pre-existing owner.

The other supposed cases are not best understood as constructive trusts. These are:

(i)   Where D breaches a duty not to dispose of or consume property invalidly transferred to him or a duty not to assist a trustee or fiduciary in making a transfer in breach of trust or fiduciary duty (knowing receipt and knowing assistance). These claims are essentially claims for compensation for a wrong.

(ii) Where C has a claim for disgorgement of profits made by D through wrongdoing. This is not best understood as a proprietary claim, or a claim or remedy in the ordinary sense at all. It is a non-remedial, quasi-punitive response, in the nature of punishment or confiscation.

(iii) Where an express trust is described as a constructive trust, for example because it appears to avoid a formalities problem.

(iv) Where C has a personal contractual right against X to the transfer or grant of a property right and a constructive trust is invoked to bind a third party D to whom the property has been transferred by X in breach of contract with C. The basis of C's claim is best understood as D's complicity in X's breach of contract, and accordingly the claim against D should be a personal claim for specific restitution rather than a constructive trust.

(v)   Where C has a personal contractual right against X in respect of X's property, for example a licence to use or reside on X's land, and X transfers the property to D, who undertakes to respect C's contractual right. If C has a claim against D it is justifiable on the basis that C is entitled to enforce the contractual undertaking given to X, and again the claim is a personal claim against D, not a constructive trust.

---

[57] Above p 87.

Some Theories of the Constructive Trust

There have been various attempts to formulate a general definition of a constructive trust, or a formula that will determine when a constructive trust will arise.[58] The tacit assumption behind such attempts is that there is a justificatory category of constructive trusts,[59] based on a general underlying principle. But no such exercise can succeed if it is meant to account not just for the genuine cases, but for all of the above cases, including the spurious ones. The problem is that there is a tendency to think of the constructive trust as a freestanding remedy,[60] in the nature of a remedy of the recovery of property, around which a body of law has developed to determine when it is available. This involves, first, the dualist fallacy[61]; and also it involves the remedy-as-justification fallacy, because the body of law is taken to form something in the nature of a justificatory category based on a general underlying principle.[62] In fact, these various cases encompass not only different justificatory categories, but various different types of remedy, including the proprietary claim or share of beneficial ownership or other property right, and also compensation, specific restitution and disgorgement. Nevertheless it is instructive to consider some of the possibilities that have been suggested for a general principle of the constructive trust.

A General Instrument to Achieve Fairness and Justice

The constructive trust is said to arise 'by operation of law' to remedy an injustice. This is unexceptionable if it means not injustice in the abstract, but the particular injustice defined by a primary relation. (This is true of any remedial relation.) But there is a tendency to think that the role of the constructive trust is to remedy injustice in the abstract, as a freestanding remedy. It has long been said to be a flexible or adaptable device, and Lord Denning developed this idea into the 'new model constructive trust' mentioned above, according to which a constructive trust should be imposed whenever it is fair and just to do so. Lord Denning used this idea largely in cases now dealt with in terms of the common intention constructive trust,[63] but also in connection

---

[58] Above n 2.
[59] Or sub-category.
[60] Above p 56.
[61] Above p 40.
[62] Cf above pp 122, 178.
[63] *Hussey v Palmer* [1972] 1 WLR 1338.

with the protection of a contractual licence against third parties.[64] But there is no discernible principle here at all, in the sense of a certain general basis for a claim. Thus this approach cannot bring unity or coherence to the law of constructive trusts, or provide a general basis for it.

This approach is sometimes understood to involve a remedial discretionary jurisdiction to reallocate subsisting property rights. This is also how the US remedial constructive trust is understood. But, as discussed earlier,[65] it is an example of the dualist fallacy to say that there are well-defined primary property rights, but the remedial property rights arising to protect them are a matter of discretion. The real implication is that the primary rights are completely indeterminate, and it was on this ground that the new model constructive trust was virulently opposed and then discredited.[66]

Constructive Trusts and Unjust Enrichment

Sometimes it is argued that the rationale of the constructive trust is to reverse unjust enrichment, so that one can say that the constructive trust is based on the principle of unjust enrichment.[67] It is true of most of the cases of constructive trust identified above (genuine and spurious), that D has received a benefit and the response is to remove a benefit or some part of a benefit that would otherwise remain with him.[68] But, as discussed in chapter 8, there is no plausible principle of unjust enrichment, and unjust enrichment is not a justificatory category. Thus this approach is also incapable of providing a unifying analysis of the constructive trust. It can provide no basis for saying when a constructive trust arises or why, and it also fails to distinguish between the different remedies and responses distinguished above. These are the same errors that the theory of unjust enrichment itself makes, as discussed in chapter 8.

Constructive Trusts and Unconscionability

It is sometimes said that unconsionability is the concept behind the constructive trust.[69] Originally this comes from the idea of the

---

[64] *Binion v Evans* [1972] Ch 359.

[65] Above p 178.

[66] *Cowcher v Cowcher* [1972] 1 All ER 943; *Burns v Burns* [1984] Ch 317.

[67] eg, DWM Waters, *The Constructive Trust* (London, Athlone Press, 1964); A Burrows, 'Proprietary Restitution: Unmasking Unjust Enrichment' (2001) 117 *Law Quarterly Review* 412, 417; EL Sherwin, 'Constructive Trusts in Bankruptcy' [1989] *University of Illinois Law Review* 297, 301; see also G Elias, *Explaining Constructive Trusts* (Oxford, Clarendon Press, OUP, 1990).

[68] Although, other than in the case of disgorgement, the basis of the claim is to restore a loss or otherwise protect an interest of C's.

[69] eg, *Paragon Finance v DB Thakerar* [1999] 1 All ER 400.

conscience of the court: as it was famously put in connection with the constructive trust, the constructive trust 'is the formula through which the conscience of equity finds expression'.[70] This reflects the idea considered above of the constructive trust as a general instrument to do justice. Nowadays it seems more common for 'unconscionability' to refer to some sort of culpable wrongdoing by the defendant (though this approach is completely opposed to the unjust enrichment theory of constructive trusts just mentioned, since unjust enrichment claims must be claims arising from a benefit, by virtue of a primary liability relation, rather than from a wrong).

Complicity in wrongdoing and reneging on a contract might be described as cases of unconscionability, as might a wrong giving rise to disgorgement. Liability in knowing receipt has been said to be based on unconscionability.[71] The claim arising from an invalid transfer has been said to be based on unconscionability,[72] but the true basis is simply the invalidity of the transfer. Claims under a constructive trust of matrimonial or quasi-matrimonial property have sometimes been described as based on unconscionability,[73] as have proprietary estoppel claims,[74] though again this is inappropriate for a claim understood as suggested above to arise from reliance on the existence or expectation of a property right.

In fact, where the claim is said to be based on unconscionability, it seems that the unconscionability is often understood to be the failure to provide a remedy to satisfy the claim, not any acts of D that generated the claim in the first place. Thus it says nothing about the reason why the constructive trust arises. This is a variant of the remedy-as-justification fallacy. Moreover, as pointed out in chapter 4,[75] referring to 'unconscionability' does not disclose any general principle that might provide guidance about when a claim might arise. Thus it cannot provide a satisfactory basis for the constructive trust. In addition, under the monist principle a proprietary claim cannot arise from a wrong.

Resulting and Constructive Trusts

A resulting trust is commonly defined as a trust in which the beneficiary under the trust was also the transferor or settlor whose transfer gave rise to the trust. This is certainly a characteristic feature of result-

---

[70] *Beatty v Guggenheim Exploration* (1919) 225 NY 380, 386, per Cardozo J.
[71] Above p 200.
[72] Above p 243.
[73] In Australia: see *Baumgartner v Baumgartner* (1897) 164 CLR 137.
[74] *Taylor Fashions v Liverpool Victoria Trustees* [1981] 1 All ER 897.
[75] Above p 118.

ing trusts, and it reflects the etymological origin of the expression,[76] but it is not helpful to treat it as definitive. As I pointed out above, one problem is that this feature is shared by what I have said is a standard case of the constructive trust, the constructive trust arising from an invalid transfer. In fact it becomes clear from considering the traditional examples of the resulting trust that there is more to the resulting trust than simply the fact that the beneficiary was also the settlor or transferor; and conversely it is also clear that the proprietary claim arising from an invalid transfer is not properly understood as a resulting trust, though it shares this feature with resulting trusts.

It is generally accepted that there are two categories of resulting trust.[77] First, where C makes a transfer to D without stating that he intends D to have the beneficial ownership of the property, there is a presumption, subject to evidence to the contrary, that C intends to retain beneficial ownership for himself, and accordingly D has only the legal title. This is the 'presumed' resulting trust. By extension, where two people buy property together and put it in the name of one or other or both, the presumption is that it is held on trust for the two of them in the proportions in which they supplied the purchase money, each being presumed to have intended to retain the share of the beneficial ownership derived from his or her own contribution to the purchase price. Secondly, where C creates a trust and transfers the trust property to D as trustee, but fails to provide for the allocation of some or all of the beneficial ownership of the property, this part of it will be held on trust for C, again subject to evidence of a contrary intention. This is said to be an 'automatic' resulting trust, on the basis that the unallocated part of the beneficial ownership remains automatically with C because it has not been disposed of.

What then is a resulting trust? Where there is a valid transfer of C's property, in principle it is the intention of C (or his agent), that determines the effect of the transfer. The resulting trust arises from a transfer that is valid but incompletely specified. The transfer is valid—it was not unauthorised or vitiated—but there is some doubt about what was intended, because C did not express an intention concerning the beneficial ownership or some part of it. The fact that the transfer is not fully specified does not justify treating it as invalid, any more than it would be right to hold a contract void because it fails to provide for every possible contingency; the court is bound to apply a default rule that applies, in the absence of and subject to evidence of

---

[76] Above n 6.

[77] *Re Vandervell's Trusts (no 2)* [1974] 1 All ER 47; *Westdeutsche Landesbank* [1996] AC 669.

actual intention, to the unallocated part of the beneficial ownership. The obvious default rule is in favour of C. This is likely to have been C's intention if he gave any thought to the point, and it is the prudent rule to apply because C can now dispose of this part of the beneficial ownership as he chooses. It is difficult to see what other default rule is possible. It is natural to express this default rule in the form of a presumed intention because intention is determinative if it is known, and sometimes the presumed intention will correspond to an actual though unexpressed intention. This approach makes sense for both categories of resulting trust. Possibly in the case of a presumed resulting trust there is likely to have been an actual though unexpressed intention, and in the case of an automatic resulting trust no relevant intention at all, but this is not necessarily the case.[78]

By contrast, neither of the two genuine types of constructive trust identified above arises from a valid transfer. One might say in brief that a constructive trust arises from an invalid transfer; more precisely, a constructive trust arises from an invalid transfer (the equitable proprietary claim), or from reliance on the assumption of a property right, in the absence of a valid transfer or grant (the common intention constructive trust or proprietary estoppel).[79]

Although the distinction between resulting and constructive trusts is clear in principle, it may become blurred in practice. First, take the case of the common intention constructive trust. Where property is acquired by two parties in a matrimonial or quasi-matrimonial relationship, on the suggested approach the shares of beneficial ownership arising purely by virtue of financial contributions to the initial purchase price are a matter for the resulting trust doctrine, but it is a matter for the constructive trust doctrine to determine whether one party is entitled to a greater share as a result of reasonable reliance on an understanding of a different allocation. In practice it appears that the common intention constructive trust doctrine has drawn on both of these approaches without maintaining a distinction between them, and in this context the courts have denied that there is any significance to the distinction between resulting and constructive trusts.[80]

---

[78] See P Jaffey, *The Nature and Scope of Restitution* (Oxford, Hart Publishing, 2000) 353–55. Cf RB Grantham and CEF Rickett 'Resulting Trusts—a Rather Limited Doctrine' in FD Rose (ed), *Restitution and Insolvency* (Oxford, Mansfield Press, 2000).

[79] Also, whereas a resulting trust is, like an express trust, a primary relation and does not in itself constitute a claim, a constructive trust constitutes a remedial relation or claim that has to be satisfied by a transfer or grant.

[80] As stated in *Lloyds Bank v Rosset* [1991] 1 AC 107. The distinction was thought to be important in *Re Densham* [1975] 3 All ER 726.

Secondly, where there is an invalid transfer because C's trustee or fiduciary has made a transfer in breach of duty, giving rise to an equitable proprietary claim, the trust is conventionally described as a constructive trust.[81] But it appears that where a proprietary claim has arisen from other types of invalid transfer, the proprietary claim has sometimes been described as a resulting trust.[82] A different understanding of the resulting trust, suggested by Birks and Chambers,[83] has been influential in this type of case. On their approach, a resulting trust arises where there was an 'absence of intention' to transfer. This expression is apt to cover both invalid transfers made with a vitiated intention, or without authority, and also valid transfers where the intention was incomplete or incompletely expressed. The consequence is to eliminate the distinction between constructive and resulting trusts arising from transfers, and at the same time to conceal the distinction between valid and invalid transfers. It appears that the origin of this approach lies in the theory of unjust enrichment and its remedial orientation, which pays insufficient attention to the justificatory basis for claims. No one concerned with the justification for claims would be tempted to adopt an approach that disregards the distinction between valid and invalid transfers.[84]

---

[81] Possibly the reason why it is not described as a resulting trust goes back to its origin in the idea that the liability of the recipient is based on his complicity in the breach of duty by the trustee.

[82] eg, a transfer on a void trust is said to give rise to a resulting trust, and this might be understood as an invalid transfer, though it is more often thought of as an automatic resulting trust: *Re Gillingham Bus Disaster Fund* [1958] Ch 300. Similarly a proprietary claim arising from an ultra vires transfer has been described as a resulting trust: *Sinclair v Brougham* [1914] AC 398. In *Chase Manhatten v Israel-British Bank* [1981] Ch 105, a proprietary claim arising from a mistaken transfer was described as a constructive trust.

[83] R Chambers, *Resulting Trusts* (Oxford, Clarendon Press, OUP, 1997); P Birks 'Restitution and Resulting Trusts' in SR Goldstein (ed), *Equity: Contemporary Legal Developments* (Faculty of Law, Hebrew University of Jerusalem, 1992) 335. Cf the 'proprietary inertia' theory in Gardner, above n 2, at 132.

[84] The same issue arises in connection with failure of consideration, above p 222.

INDEX